Jeremy Harmer
and Richard Rossner

MORE
THAN
WORDS

vocabulary for upper intermediate to advanced students

BOOK 2

 LONGMAN

Contents of Book 1

Contents

Acknowledgements

To Sue Maingay, who got **More than Words** started, many thanks. Adam Gadsby took the project over at a difficult time and deserves our gratitude, as does Lizzie Warren. To Alison Steadman, who has edited the two books, especial thanks. Thank you also to our reporters Sue Maingay, Pat Lodge and Fran Barnard. And as before, to Anita and Annick this book is affectionately dedicated.

Jeremy Harmer
Richard Rossner   Cambridge. July 1992

We are grateful to the following for permission to reproduce copyright material;

Cambridge University Press for an adapted extract from *Encyclopedia of Language* edited by David Crystal (1987); Hamish Hamilton Ltd & Alfred A Knopf, Inc for an adapted extract from *A Year In Provence* by Peter Mayle (1989), copyright (c) Peter Mayle, 1989; the author's agent for the poem 'Song for a Beautiful Girl Petrol-Pump Attendant on the Motorway" by Adrian Henri from *Collected Poems* (Allison & Busby, 1986); the author's agent for the poem 'One Flesh' by Elizabeth Jennings from *Collected Poems* (Carcanet Press Ltd); King's College, Cambridge & The Society of Authors Ltd as literary representatives of the E M Forster Estate for an adapted extract from *A Passage to India* by E M Forster; John Murray (Publishers) Ltd for an adapted extract from *India File* by Trevor Fishlock (1983); The Observer Ltd for the article 'Crime: The Facts, The Figures, The Fears' by David Rose from *The Observer Magazine* 17.2.91; The Observer Ltd, on behalf of *New Internationalist* magazine, for the article 'Occupation: Housewife' from *New Internationalist* March 1988 & extracts from the article 'How Green are You?' from *New Internationalist* January 1990; Pink Floyd Music Publishers Ltd for an extract from the lyrics of the song 'Another Brick in the Wall (Part II)' by Roger Waters, (c) 1979 Roger Waters, Pink Floyd Music Publishers Ltd; The Scotsman Publications Ltd for the adapted article 'Nuclear fusion breakthrough promises cheap, safe power' by Tom Knight from *The Scotsman* newspaper 11.11.91; Sidgwick & Jackson Ltd for an adapted extract from *Is That It?* by Bob Geldof (1986)

Thanks are due to the following for permission to reproduce photographs on the pages indicated:

Ace Photo Agency/Kevin Phillips p.44 (b),/Terry Sims p.44 (e),/ Jerome Yeats p.44 (h) (i),/ P Shirreff Thomas p.44 (f),/ Rolf Richardson p.44 (g),/ Paul Thompson p.46,/ Bo Cederwall p.50 (a),/ Mike Bluestone p.50 (g),/ Nawrocki Stock Photo p.50 (f), p.111 (e),/ Tony Price p.100 (a),/ Vibert-Stokes p.100 (b) (e), p.111 (f),/ Anthony Price p.100 (g),/ Richard Walker p.100 (h),/ Bill Bachmann p.111 (c),/ Geoff Johnson p.144,/ Roger Adams: pp.41h, 44 (a) (c) (d), 50 (h), 111 (a) (b), 143 (bottom right); J Allan Cash Ltd: pp.16, 71 (top, bottom left and bottom), 94 (1) (2) (4) (5) (8), 121 (3), 124 (b) (c) (d), 126 (a) (c) (d) (e) (f), 131, 139 (1) (2) (3) (7), 198 (power station, oil pollution and forest); Barnaby's Picture Library: pp.139 (8), 143 (top left, bottom right), 198 (Candian car and waterpump); BFI Stills, Posters and Designs/ © 1984 Cannon Screen Entertainment Ltd.

All rights reserved p.93; British Airways: p.41 (g); Camera Press, London: p.10/ Jungkwan Chi p.71 (top right),/ Conan Doyle p.71 (bottom right),/ Christopher Simon Sykes p.119; Greg Evans Photo Library: p.110 (f); Mary Evans Picture Library: pp.118, 160, 191 (a) (d) (e) (f); Format Photographers Ltd/ Brenda Prince p.41 (c),/ Jenny Matthews p.42,/ Joanne O'Brien p.50 (d); Sally and Richard Greenhill: pp.41 (a) (f), 50 (e), 126 (b), 129, 133, 196; Mansell Collection: p.191 (a) (c); Photofusion: pp.41 (d), 143 (top right); The Photographers Library: pp.100 (c), 111 (d), 122 (2) (6); Retna Pictures/ M. Putland p.86 (4); Science Photo Library/ Andy Clarke p.122 (1),/ Sinclair Stammers p.122 (4),/ John Hesel Tine p.122 (5),/ Hank Morgan p.203; Syndication International: pp.71 (top left), 86 (1) (2) (3) (5); Telefocus, a British Telecom photograph: p.41 (b); John Walmsley: pp.41 (a), 50 (b) (c); Zefa: pp.48, 66, 94 (3) (6) (7), 98, 124 (a), 139 (4) (5) (6) (9), 157, 166, 185, 198 (solar panels and satellite).

The illustration on p.31 is reproduced from *Where the Wild Things Are*, written and illustrated by Maurice Sendak. Published by The Bodley Head in London and HarperCollins Junior Books in New York.

Addison Wesley Longman Limited
Edinburgh Gate, Harlow,
Essex CM20 2JE, England
and Associated companies throughout the world

First published 1992
Third impresion 1996

Set in 11/13pt Futura Medium

Designed and produced by
The Pen and Ink Book Company Ltd.
Huntingdon, Cambridgeshire

Illustrated by Rowan Barnes-Murphy,Maureen and Gordon Gray, Martin Salisbury and Pen and Ink.

Printed in China
PPC/03

British Library Cataloguing-in-Publication Data
Harmer, Jeremy
  More than words - Book 2
  I. Title II. Rossner, R.
  428.1

ISBN 0-582-09202-7

Introduction for students and teachers

The aims of **More than Words Book 2** are:

a to make students aware of the vocabulary associated with certain defined topic areas (e.g. the media, politics, housework, transport, etc) and to provide material to help students memorize and practise these words.

b to provide material which will provoke and stimulate, thus engaging the students in the task of understanding more about the vocabulary of English.

c to make students more aware of words and to train them with skills which will help them to deal with new words in English.

d to provide material which can be used to develop general language skills in an integrated way and to promote other types of language study.

THE ORGANIZATION OF **MORE THAN WORDS**

More than Words Book 1 is divided into two parts which look at issues related to how words work and provide sixteen topic units on 'Human beings'.*

More than Words Book 2 is also divided into two sections in the following way:

Part A: Developing Your Vocabulary
6 units dealing with the resources which students can use to help them develop their own vocabulary: two units deal with dictionary use, and there is a unit on how to remember new words. Other units deal with wordbuilding, bridging vocabulary gaps and using words creatively.

Part B: Human Beings and the World We Live in
25 units looking at topic areas concerned with the world that human beings live in. We look at the vocabulary associated with families, communication, politics, homes, town and cities, education, crime, the environment, the animal kingdom, etc.

DICTIONARIES AND DICTIONARY USE

One of the most useful tools for studying vocabulary at this level is the monolingual dictionary. This is why we have devoted two units of Part A to training people how to use one.

A good dictionary will provide lots of information about the

*See page iv for a complete list of contents from **More than Words Book 1**.

words which students are looking up. But they should be careful not to use it all the time, or it will tend to get in the way of spontaneous communication. In **More than Words Book 2** we indicate where we think dictionary use may be appropriate by using this symbol: 📖

WHAT IS VOCABULARY?

To know a word fully we need to be aware of many things, for example:

a we need to know what a word (e.g. *shop*) means.

b we need to know how it is connected to other words which mean similar things (e.g. *buy, sell, bargain, discount, loan, hire-purchase*, etc).

c we need to know what other meanings it can have, e.g. *shoplifting, window shopping, to shop around, to set up shop* etc.

d we need to know how the word changes depending on its grammar (e.g. he was *shopping*, he *shopped*).

e we need to know what grammar the word uses, (e.g. when *shop* is a verb it cannot take an object unless it changes its meaning and becomes an informal word for telling tales about someone).

f perhaps, most importantly, we need to know what kind of situations the word is used in and who might use it.

In **More than Words Book 2** we try to ensure that students have a chance to know words in this way. Texts show the contexts words are used in, and exercises explore the various aspects of the words.

CHOOSING A UNIT

More than Words Book 2 is designed to be used in a number of different ways. Teachers and students can go through the units in sequence; they can pick and choose units which particularly interest them or which they need; they can do Part A and then some or all of Part B; or they can use units from Part B and then refer to individual units from Part A when appropriate (or for a change of focus).

WHAT THE UNITS CONTAIN

PART A

1 Units in Part A usually start with a language question, problem or explanation.

2 In Part A we frequently use texts to enlarge on topics or to provide training material for the area of study (e.g. using a dictionary, bridging vocabulary gaps, etc).

3 Exercises in Part A are designed to train students in the skills necessary to develop their own vocabulary. They include:

matching exercises

filling in blanks

filling in charts

activation exercises designed to allow students to use the words or concepts they have been looking at

PART B   Units in Part B always follow a set pattern (though with many variations). There are three parts to this pattern:

ENGAGE

STUDY

ACTIVATE

1   Engagement activities

These are activities designed to engage the interest and involvement of the students in both the topic and the words. Engagement activities usually consist of one of the following:

a A text: Students are asked to read a text and then react to it in some way. It may provoke discussion or a task. The purpose of the text is to arouse the students' interest as well as to introduce the words and concepts which are to be studied later. It is also there to provide a focus for general integrated skill work.

b A discussion/interaction: For example, students complete a questionnaire in pairs. It contains words and concepts to be used in the unit. Students discuss their opinions or compare information about a topic. These exercises provide an opportunity for students to consider topics in the light of their own experience.

c A word task: Students do a straightforward matching activity to remind themselves of the topic area and to give them information for a discussion/interaction.

Almost all of these engagement activities are designed for use in pairs or groups. Students should be encouraged to participate as fully as possible.

2   Study activities

There are many kinds of study activities which are designed to explore in more detail the words which the topic has introduced.

Some of these activities are:

a Completing charts: Students are frequently asked to complete charts with the correct part of speech or vocabulary item.

b Fill-ins: Students are frequently asked to fill in the blanks in sentences or paragraphs using words that they have been studying.

c Matching: Students are asked to match one set of things with another set of things (e.g. words and pictures, synonyms, antonyms, etc).

d Discussing words: Students are asked to discuss words and make decisions about them with the help of their own knowledge and their monolingual dictionaries.

e Searching for word meaning: Students are often asked to choose between two different meanings or two different words.

f Choosing between different words: Students are often asked to choose between two different meanings or two different words.

3   *Activate activities*

The Activate sections in each unit are designed to provoke the use of words which have been studied in the unit. There are many different kinds of such activities. Here are some examples:

a Headlines: Students are asked to explain headlines and write the stories which accompany them.

b Writing tasks: Students are asked to write descriptions, dialogues, advertisements, etc.

c Telling stories: Students are asked to use the words they have been studying in either oral or written stories.

d Commenting: Students are asked to comment on pictures and/or situations.

e Role-play: Students role-play a situation which invites the use of words they have been studying.

4   *Word Check*

A special feature of **More Than Words Book 2** is the set of Word Check activities at the end of each unit in Part B.

After the final list of Focus Words and Focus Phrases in each unit there is a set of four short exercises which the students have to do, referring only to the focus lists. These Word Check activities give both teacher and students a chance to see how well they have absorbed the meaning, use, and form of the words they have been studying in that unit.

5   How the pieces interact with each other

All the units in Part B start with an engagement activity and end with an activate activity. In between these two, the three types of activity in the unit (engage – study – activate) usually occur more than once. In other words students may do an engagement activity and then do some study exercises. Then they do a quick activate activity before doing some more study work. Or they may do an engagement activity, some study work and then do another engagement activity which will lead them onto a different track. This diagram shows some of the possible patterns.

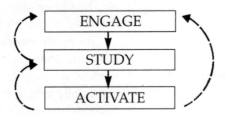

HOW TO USE THE MATERIAL

The material in **More than Words Book 2** is designed for use in two distinct situations, classwork and self study. How can it be used?

CLASSWORK

Almost all the exercises in **More than Words Book 2** can be done by students working in pairs or groups. Indeed we believe that such interactions are a vital part of creating a healthy and cooperative class atmosphere. It is then the teacher's role to guide, advise and inform the students.

In small classes, however, the use of pairs and groups becomes rather artificial and in such cases there is no reason why the teacher and the students should not go through the material together.

It should be remembered that one of the teacher's main responsibilities is the ability to encourage the students to connect their own life experiences with the topic: in that way, lessons will not only be about learning language, but also about the topics themselves and how they affect us all.

Some of the study exercises are clearly useful for students working on their own, either in class or as homework. In such cases it is advisable to try to do the exercises before referring to the key.

In general we believe that involvement in the material is the most important way to start the process of vocabulary learning and it will be a combination of the students' enthusiasm and desire to learn, and the teacher's encouragement of those attitudes, which will make **More than Words Book 2** successful in the classroom.

SELF STUDY

While many of the activities in **More than Words Book 2** work well with groups of students, we have also tried to think carefully about students working on their own.

The most obvious way of helping such students is to provide an answer key, which can be found on page 206. Students on their own can thus do some of the exercises and then check with the key.

The progression of the exercises associated with reading tasks, etc, has been designed so that students working on their own are still able to complete the tasks.

Obviously the more interactive exercises will lose something if they are done alone. Nevertheless, questionnaires, for example, are still well worth reading through and thinking about, especially where they contain words which are to be studied.

Students working on their own should not forget Part A, which provides training issues in vocabulary learning and vocabulary techniques, speaking directly to the user.

CONCLUSIONS

More than Words Book 2, like its predecessor, is about vocabulary and how it works. It is about the words associated with certain topics. It is about language and how it is used.

Getting involved with words is what learning a language is all about. We believe that when students are engaged with topics they learn words which they can keep for themselves – which they can then 'own'. We hope that **More than Words Book 2** will help many students to own many many words.

Jeremy Harmer
Richard Rossner

PART *A* DEVELOPING YOUR VOCABULARY

1 | *Using dictionaries: definitions*

One of the things an English-English dictionary does is to give you definitions of words – to tell you what they mean. How can we find those meanings? What happens when a word has more than one meaning? What does a dictionary tell you about how words are used?

Note: In this book 'dictionary' means a monolingual dictionary especially designed for learners of English. All the examples used in this book are taken from the *Longman Dictionary of Contemporary English: New edition – 1987*, but other English monolingual dictionaries can be used.

FINDING THE RIGHT WORDS

The first thing you have to do when you want to use a dictionary is to find the word you're looking for. In dictionaries (as in indexes) items are arranged alphabetically.

1 Put the numbers 1 to 12 against the words to show their order in a dictionary.

explanatory —	together —
sticky —	teaspoon —
island —	admittance —
admitted —	expletive —
furniture —	explain —
pineapple —	scorpion —

ACTIVATE

2 Use at least four of the words from exercise 1 to make a story.

*Some entries in dictionaries, however, are made up of compound words – a 'word' made up of two parts like **bus driver**, **kind-hearted**, etc. They occur alphabetically in an English dictionary, too.*

3 Put the numbers 1 to 16 against these words to show their order in a dictionary.

jumper —	nestle —
sportsmanlike —	sports —
place —	jumpsuit —
elemental —	negative —
sportsmanship —	jumping-off place —
elementary particle —	rampage —
sports car —	elementary school —
elements —	ramrod —

*It is important to know what the base form of a word is, so that you can look it up in the dictionary. For example, if you see the word **worrying** you should look for it under **worry** – the base form.*

4 Read these reviews of a book called *The Songlines* by Bruce Chatwin. What is the base form of the words which are underlined?

THE POETRY of Chatwin's remarkable pages flitters quietly about, steering a course, as it were, between William Blake and Dr Johnson . . . a masterpiece.
(John Bayley, *London Review of Books*).

A BOOK of remarkable richness, scope and originality.
(*Patrick Leigh Fermor, Spectator*).

ON COMPLETING *The Songlines* one thinks – as one does not often think when reading contemporary British authors – of the word 'enormous'.
(Nicholas Shakespeare, *London Daily News.*)

DEFINITIONS

In order to use a dictionary you need to be able to read definitions – the explanations of a word's meaning.

5 Match the words in the box with their definitions.

> break (up) with   whinge   warmth   shuffle
> drag   thongs

a   to move along with great effort, having contact with the ground

b   the state of having kind, friendly feelings

c   to complain, esp. continually and in an annoying way

d   a kind of sandal, held on by the toes and made of rubber

e   to end a friendship or connection with somebody

f   to walk by dragging one's feet slowly along

6 Read this extract from *The Songlines* without referring to a dictionary, and then answer the questions.

a   How many people are there in the extract and what are their names?

b   In pairs decide what you think 'this other Bruce' looks like (colour of his hair, height, clothes, etc). Describe him to the rest of the class. Does everyone have the same description?

The Songlines

Back at the motel, I was half asleep when there was a knock on my door.
'Bru?'
'Yes.'
'It's Bru.'
'I know.'
'Oh!'
This other Bruce had sat next to me on the bus from Katherine. He was travelling down from Darwin, where he had just broken up with his wife. He had a big pot belly and was not very bright.
At Tenant Creek, he had said, 'You and me could be mates, Bru. I could teach you to drive a dozer.' Another time, with greater warmth, he said, 'You're not a whingeing Pom, Bru.'
Now, long after midnight, he was outside my door calling,
'Bru?'
'What is it?'
'Want to come out and get pissed?'
'No.'
'Oh!'
'We could find some sheilas,' he said.
'That a fact?' I said. 'This time of night?'
'You're right, Bru.'
'Go to bed,' I said.
'Well, goo'night, Bru.'
'Goodnight!'
'Bru?'
'What do you want now?'
'Nothing,' he said and shuffled off, dragging his rubber thongs *shlip* . . . *shlip* along the corridor.

CHOOSING THE RIGHT ENTRY

A single word can have a number of meanings and it is important to choose the right one. You will often be helped to do this by the examples given.

7 Look at these dictionary entries for *bright* and *mate*. What is the number of the entry in each case which matches the use of the words in the text above?

3)   4

bright / braɪt/ *adj* **1** giving out or throwing back light very strongly; full of light; shining: *bright sunlight* | *The weather forecast said it would be mostly cloudy with a few bright intervals.* | *She longed for the* **bright lights** (= interesting and exciting activity) *of the big city.* | (fig.) *one of the brightest moments in our country's history* | (fig.) *It's rather a dull film – the only bright spots are the dancing scenes.* **2** (of a colour) strong, clear, and easily seen: *bright red* **3** full of life; cheerful; happy: *Her face was bright with happiness.* | *bright eyes* **4** clever; quick at learning: *a bright child/idea* | *She should do well – she's very bright.* – see CLEVER (USAGE) **5** showing hope or signs of future success: *You have a bright future ahead of you!* | *The long-term prospects for this industry are beginning to look brighter.* – see also **look on the bright side (of things)** (LOOK¹) – ~ly *adv*: *shining/smiling brightly* – – **ness** *n* [U]

4

mate¹ / meɪt/ *n* **1** (often in comb.) a friend, or person one works with: *Her mates/workmates/schoolmates waited for her by the gate.* | *He's a mate of mine.* – see also RUNNING MATE **2** one of a male-female pair, usu. of animals: *The male hunts for food while his mate guards the nest.* **3** (not in the navy) a ship's officer next in rank below the captain: *the first mate* **4** *BrE & AustrE infml* (a friendly way of addressing a man, used esp. by working men): *"What time is it, mate?"* – see also MATEY; see LANGUAGE NOTE: Addressing People **5** someone who works with and helps the stated kind of skilled workman: *a builder's/plumber's mate*

DEALING WITH UNFAMILIAR WORDS

We often come across words we do not understand. One way of resolving this is to use a dictionary. Sometimes, however, we do not have the dictionary, or the dictionary does not have the word. But we can still make a good guess at what the word means.

8 a Without looking at a dictionary say what parts of speech these words from the text are.

| dozer | pom | sheilas | shlip |

b Now complete these sentences from the text by putting as many words in the blanks as possible to replace the original words (provided that they make sense).
  i I could teach you to drive a __c____
  ii You're not a whingeing _____, Bru.
  iii 'We could find some _____', he said
  iv He shuffled off · · · dragging his rubber thongs _____ · · · _____ along the corridor

c Compare your words with a partner or in groups. Decide on the word that is most likely in each case, and compare your words with the meanings of the original words. Were you close?

STYLE AND REGISTER

When you look up a word it is important to know when you can use it. For example, the word **berk** *(meaning a fool) is a slang word. We can say 'You should have told me it was a formal party, I felt a right berk in my jeans.' But if you wanted to be more formal you might use the expression 'I felt rather foolish.'*

9 Look at the following dictionary entries. Fill in the boxes with the letter corresponding to the appropriate term. Explanations of some of the terms are given. You may have to use some of the words more than once.

a 'forbidden' word
b definition
c derogatory (showing dislike or lack of respect)
d English spoken in America
e English spoken in Australia
f English spoken in Britain
g informal
h typical expressions
i slang (very informal language that often includes new and not very polite words. Used by groups. Not usually found in serious speech or writing)

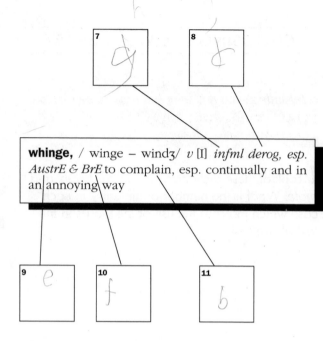

whinge, / winge – windʒ/ *v* [I] *infml derog, esp. AustrE & BrE* to complain, esp. continually and in an annoying way

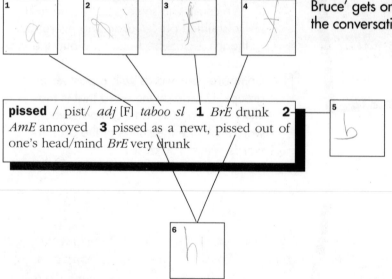

pissed / pist/ *adj* [F] *taboo sl* **1** *BrE* drunk **2** *AmE* annoyed **3** pissed as a newt, pissed out of one's head/mind *BrE* very drunk

10   You are on an overland bus. There is an empty seat next to you. At one stop 'this other Bruce' gets on the bus and sits next to you. Write the conversation he has with you.

Using dictionaries: technical information

Apart from information about the meaning of words and indications about when and where to use them, English-English dictionaries also contain a great deal of technical information about pronunciation and grammar, about word collocation and parts of speech.

CALL MY BLUFF

1 Follow the instructions:

1 Divide into two teams. Team A looks at Box A, Team B looks at Box B. Look up the definitions of the words in your box.

   Do not look at the other team's box.

BOX A	BOX B
smirk janissary	smooch scalene
languid laparoscopy	stertorous pique

2 Write out the definition you find in the dictionary.
3 Invent two more definitions which look like real definitions.
4 Representatives from each team read out the true and false definitions and make example sentences. The other team has to guess which is the true definition.

COLLOCATION

Dictionaries can often tell you what words frequently go together with other words. The information often comes from the example sentences in the dictionary.

2 Use a dictionary to match the verbs on the left with the phrases on the right. You can use the verbs more than once.

1 clear	a	_____ a difference
2 kill	b	_____ a crime
3 commit	c	_____ air
4 expel	d	_____ the bubble
5 do	e	_____ the washing up
6 have	f	_____ a laugh
7 preach	g	_____ an excuse
8 burst	h	_____ the table
9 make	i	_____ a sermon
10 give	j	_____ a lecture
	k	_____ plans
	l	_____ an accusation
	m	_____ time
	n	_____ the air

PRONUNCIATION AND SPELLING

3 Look at the following dictionary entries. Fill in the boxes with the letter corresponding to the appropriate term.

a alternative spelling
b pronunciation (including stress)
c other words derived from the main word
d stress (shows which part of the word is stressed)

```
┌─1─────────┐              ┌─2─────────┐
│           │              │           │
└───────────┘              └───────────┘
```

judg·ment, judgement / ˈdʒʌdʒmənt/ *n* **1** [U] the ability to make decisions that are based on careful consideration of facts, principles, etc.: *a man of sound/weak judgment* | *Her decision seems to show a lack of political judgment.* | **an error of judgment** | *I can't decide for you; you'll have to use your own judgment.* | *He did the right thing, but* **more by luck than judgment**. **2** [C] an opinion: *to form a judgment* | *In my judgment, we should accept the employer's offer.* | *I let him go,* **against my better judgment**. (= although I knew it was probably a mistake) **3** [C;U (on)] an official decision given by a judge or a court of law: *He* **passed** (= gave) **judgment** *on the guilty man.* | *an impartial judgment* **on 4 sit in judgment** to take the responsibility of judging (a person or their behaviour), esp. in order to find fault: *You have no right to sit in judgment on her; you'd probably have done exactly the same thing if you'd been in her position.* – see also VALUE JUDGMENT

3

de·ci·sive / dɪˈsaɪsɪv/ *adj* **1** showing determination and firmness; RESOLUTE: *You'll have to be more decisive if you want to do well in business.* **2** leading to a clear result; putting an end to doubt: *They won the war after a decisive battle.* **3** unquestionable: *a decisive advantage* – opposite **indecisive** – ~ ly *adv* – ~ ness *n* [U]

4

1

col·lapse¹ kəˈlæps/ *v* **1** [I] to fall down or inwards suddenly as a result of pressure or loss of strength or support: *The bridge collapsed under the weight of the train.* **2** [I] to fall helpless or unconscious: *He collapsed at the end of the long race.* | (fig.) *The children* **collapsed with laughter** *when their father fell in the river.*

2

fraught / frɔːt/ *adj* **1** [F+**with**] full of something unpleasant: *The expedition through the jungle was fraught with difficulties and danger.* **2** *infml* troubled by anxieties; very TENSE

3

fur·ni·ture / ˈfɜːnɪtʃəʳ‖ ˈfɜːr-/ *n* [U] large or quite large movable articles such as beds, chairs, and tables, that are placed in a house, room, or other area, in order to make it convenient, comfortable, and/or pleasant as a space for living in: *This old French table is a very valuable piece of furniture.* | *garden furniture*

4

grease² / griːs, griːz/ *v* [T] **1** to put grease on: *Grease the dish with butter before pouring in the egg mixture.* | *Ask the mechanic to grease the axle.* **2 grease someone's palm** *infml* to give money to someone in a secret or dishonest way in order to persuade them to do something

6

5

look into sthg. *phr v* [T] to examine the meaning or causes of; INVESTIGATE: *The police have received the complaint, and they're looking into it.* | *a report looking into the causes of unemployment*

4 Use a dictionary to correct the spelling of these words, if necessary.

a prettyness
b responsable
c nudity
d fetus

e heaviness
f completeley
g sterilise
h movment

5 Use a dictionary to underline the part(s) of the following words which are stressed.

a import (**v**)
b topical
c topicality
d export (**n**)

e progress (**n**)
f progression
g prohibition
h professionalism

GRAMMATICAL INFORMATION

Apart from telling you about a word's meaning, its spelling and pronunciation, a dictionary has a mass of useful information about grammar.

6 Look at the dictionary entries in the next column. Fill in the boxes with the letter corresponding to the appropriate term on the left. Explanations of some of the terms are given.

a can take an object
b cannot take an object
c uncountable noun (you can't count it or pluralize it)
d phrasal verb
e position of direct object
f followed by a particular preposition or adverb

7 Use a dictionary to say what the mistake is in each of the following sentences. Can you correct the mistakes?

a They collapsed the building with dynamite.
b Acid rain is harmful at trees.
c The informations I have received will be very useful.
d She is looking her keys for.
e He graduated to the University of East Anglia.
f The mechanic greased.
g The mournfulnesses of the symphony made me sad.
h She is different of her brother.
i She found a way to get the problem around.
j She gave to me the keys.

One of the difficulties with phrasal and prepositional verbs is knowing where to put the direct object. Sometimes it comes only after the complete verb, e.g. **Pick on somebody your own size**. Sometimes it can come before or after the adverb or preposition, e.g. **Hand in your papers, Hand your papers in** (note that a pronoun can only come before the preposition or adverb, e.g. **Hand them in**, not *Hand in them*). Finally, sometimes a phrasal verb can have two objects, e.g. **Put the accident down to inexperience**. Your dictionary should tell you which kind of phrasal verb you are looking at.

8 Make sentences using the following phrasal or prepositional verbs. Use a dictionary to check the grammar.

a	pick up	**e**	run away with
b	look after	**f**	try on
c	look up	**g**	live down
d	give up	**h**	live up to

Understanding and remembering new words

How can we deal with new vocabulary when we meet it in speech or writing? How can we use our knowledge about how vocabulary works to help us understand new words?

1 While you read the following article, look for the answer to the following questions.

a Is the writer white or black, male or female? How can you tell?

b The writer describes two 'kinds of miracle'. What are they?

STEVE BIKO was a black leader in South Africa who opposed apartheid, the system which made all blacks second-class citizens and deprived them of their rights. He died while in prison nearly twenty years ago. This is an account of his funeral, published in a South African newspaper at that time.

A KIND OF MIRACLE

Take a crowd of twenty thousand blacks at the funeral of a well-loved leader who has died while in the custody of white security police; add to their anger more anger at the callousness of police minister Kruger for saying such a death leaves him cold; add more anger over police prevention of tens of thousands of other mourners from attending the funeral; and add fresh anger whipped up by emotional speeches against white oppression.

Add to this multitude of angry, grieving blacks a small group of whites intermingled in this huge, volatile crowd, and in this land of racial tension it requires only one stumble, one jostle, one tactless remark to touch off a tragic explosion of retribution.

Yet no incident of the sort took place at the funeral of Steve Biko this week. Through five hours of speeches by spokesmen of all those allegedly anti-white organizations, not one white present was made to feel unwelcome or under direct threat by the emotional multitude.

Not that we few whites were free from fear. Far from it. It was the most frightening five hours of my life. My wife and I were in the middle of the standing crowd and knew many moments of apprehension as the rhetoric was aimed at white viciousness, white cruelty, white exploitation, white

Steve Biko

privilege, and white murder of black martyrs.

One is very conscious of one's whiteness on such occasions.

I think what motivated many whites who attended, apart from the natural motives of condolence, was an act of faith with the country South Africa could become with apartheid removed and people judged simply as individuals. That certainly was a point made in many of the speeches.

Admittedly it was a minor theme to the major theme of black activism, yet consistent throughout was the message that the end envisaged was a nonracial, non-ethnic society.

That no whites in that crowd were menaced or hurt is a kind of miracle.

Yet if you look at the record, black South Africans are noticeably not racist by inclination. To the extent that one can generalize, they seem not as readily disposed to racial bigotry as so many whites seem to be.

Which, in the circumstances, is also a kind of miracle.

Donald Woods
South African Dispatches

2 Find a word in the text which describes <u>your</u> feelings about the text. If you cannot find one in the text, choose your own.

There may be many words that you don't understand in a piece of writing. To look up the meaning of all of them would take a long time, and your chances of learning a large number would not necessarily be good. A better idea, perhaps, is to choose a limited number of words and deal with them.

3 a Write down the five words from the extract that you most want to know the meaning of.
b In pairs or groups compare your lists and agree on a joint list of five words.
c Look up the words in a dictionary. What do they mean?

When you know the meanings of new words are there any ways of remembering them? One way seems to be to group them together – into groups of words with similar meanings.

4 Which of these words is used most often in the text?

anger   viciousness   fear   callousness
cruelty   apprehension   exploitation
murder

a What effect is created by using the word in this way?
b What do you think the writer's mood is?

5 Put the nouns from exercise 4 into the correct columns in the table.

State of mind	Behaviour

It is important to discover not only the meaning of unfamiliar words but also their grammar.

6 a In the following extracts from the text which of the two-word verbs are phrasal verbs?

   i . . . fresh anger *whipped up* by emotional speeches . . .
   ii . . . one tactless remark to *touch off* a tragic explosion . . .
   iii . . . no incident of the sort *took place* . . .
   iv Yet if you *look at* the record . . .

b Are the meanings of the two-word verbs different from the original verbs *whip, touch, take,* and *look*?

Using a dictionary, say what can follow the verbs.

7 Look at this sentence from the text on page 10.

'. . . black South Africans are noticeably not *racist* by inclination.'

a What does *racist* mean?
b Who suffers from *racism*?
c Can you give both extreme and mild examples of how racism operates?

d In a British court case a black defendant recently objected to the use of the term *blackmail*. He said it was an example of racist language. Do you agree?

MAKING YOUR OWN WORDBOOK

One of the ways of learning and remembering more vocabulary is to keep your own wordbook where you put the words that you think are especially important. Obviously you must decide what words to put in and what to say about them. Should you translate them, give definitions, give grammatical information? The decision is yours.

8 Look at this page from Maria's wordbook. (Maria is a Spanish speaker.)

hammock (n)	hamaca. A bed made from string. You can hang it up. He fell out of his hammock because of a bad dream.
happily (adv)	felizmente. In a happy way. She smiled happily as she put down the phone.
hut (n)	choza. A small building, made of wood or mud. Julia lived in a hut at the edge of the jungle until she won the lottery. Then she bought a house.

a How has Maria arranged the words? How else could you arrange the words?

b How has she shown what the words mean? How else could you record the meaning?

c What grammatical information has she put in? Would you add any more? Would you put less?

9 How would you write the entries for your personal wordbook:

a for your five words (see exercise 3)?

b for these nouns (see exercise 4)?
anger   viciousness   fear   callousness
cruelty   apprehension   exploitation
murder

c for these verbs (see exercise 6)?
whip up   touch off   take place   look at

10 Here are some ways that students have of remembering new words. Do you use any of them? Do you have any other ways of trying to commit new words to memory?

a Practising by making sentences in your own mind using the new word(s).

b Practising by writing out sentences with the new word(s).

c Learning lists of words (say ten new words a night).

d Labelling things in your own house with English words (using sticky labels).

e Thinking of an image for a new word (e.g. a picture or a colour) to help you remember the word by remembering the image.

Word formation and compound words

SUFFIXES, PREFIXES AND ROOT WORDS

*Many words in English are built from more than one part: a root, a beginning, an ending, two different words, and so on. For example, the word **impossibility** is based on the root **possible**. At the beginning, there is im-, meaning 'not', and at the end -ity, one of the endings used to form abstract nouns.*

1 Which of the words below:

a have a root and a beginning (prefix)?
b have a root and an ending (suffix)?
c has a root and both a prefix and a suffix?
d is made out of two different words?

(Use a dictionary if you are not sure of the meaning.)

> darkness   postwar   fishtank   realignment
> unfriendly   makeshift   tonsilitis   laptop
> televise   stepmother

*The difference between a prefix or suffix and a root word is that prefixes and suffixes cannot stand alone. For example, **re-** and **-ology** cannot be used by themselves (although they have some meaning). However, in **fishtank**, both **fish** and **tank** can be used separately. In addition, many two-word words appear in two parts e.g. **bank manager**.*

2 Read the following passage and complete the table with the underlined words from the passage.

The <u>rosewood walking-stick</u> had belonged to Jemima's <u>great-grandmother.</u> The <u>white-haired</u> old lady had lived in the <u>granny flat</u> over the <u>workshop</u> at the back of the <u>semi-detached house</u> where Jemima and her <u>stepbrother</u> spent the early years of their <u>childhood</u>. 'Great-gran', as they <u>nicknamed</u> her, who must have been in her <u>mid-nineties</u> by then, had used the walking-stick to make her way, <u>spider-like</u>, from her <u>bedroom</u> to the <u>kitchenette</u>, where she drank <u>endless</u> cups of tea from a cracked <u>teapot</u>. Jemima would sit with her, listening <u>wide-eyed</u> to the <u>hair-raising</u> stories she told of her <u>girlhood</u>. Jemima remembered that Great-gran had been the <u>second eldest</u> in a family of eight children, living in a <u>coalmining</u> valley in South Wales. She had never been to school. By the time she was twelve, she was a <u>chambermaid</u> in the house of a very wealthy <u>landowner</u>. She worked a <u>fourteen-hour</u> day, making beds, scrubbing floors and cleaning <u>saucepans</u>; not a life for the <u>faint-hearted</u>.

Two words*	One word with a prefix	One word with a suffix
rosewood	semi-detached	kitchenette
(* Note: some have a suffix as well)		

3 Choose two of the following roots. How many other words can you make from them by adding prefixes and suffixes? You may have to change the spelling of the root word slightly before adding the affixes.

Example:
Real: unreal, reality, unreality, really, realism, realistic

a use
b care
c safe
d touch
e responsible
f reason

(See Part A, Unit 8 of Book 1 for more on prefixes and suffixes)

4 The compound words below have been selected from the passage on the previous page. With a partner, decide which compound word from the box on the right is most similar *in form* to each of them.

a granny flat
b second eldest
c walking-stick
d coalmining
e hair-raising
f chambermaid
g fourteen-hour
h workshop
i wide-eyed

redfaced   ten-week
knitting needle
playroom   cowshed
blood-curdling
fourth fastest
rice-growing
shop assistant

ACTIVATE

5 Use any five of the words from the box in a story, beginning:

'Once upon a time, there was a poor farmer who had a very clever young daughter . . .'

Then tell it to a neighbour.

*Many speakers of English invent their own words by combining prefixes or suffixes with roots, or by combining two separate words. For example, the suffix **-ish**, as in **smallish**, means 'quite' or 'rather'. In informal English people combine it with almost any other (short) adjective, although the resulting words may not appear in the dictionary. It can also be fun to try to make new compound words from two other words.*

6 Make common compound words to describe people by combining words in box A with words in box B.

Box A
baby   girl   frog
big   bank   van
tax   tennis

Box B
robber   friend
sitter   head
player   driver
man   payer

7 Now make some new funny compound words by combining the words in different ways.

8 What compound word would you use to describe each of the following?

Example:
a pool which people can swim in: a swimming pool

a a container or small 'tray' which you can put cigarette or cigar ash in
b cleaning and other work that has to be done in the house
c a test done on someone's blood
d the action of dreaming during the day (while awake)
e a room which is dark so that you can develop photographs in it
f a book which has a cover or 'back' made of paper

9 What adjective would you use to describe the following?

a someone who works hard
b someone who has a 'narrow mind', who has many prejudices
c something which has been made by hand
d something to eat which is made at home
e steps or measures taken to cut costs

ACTIVATE

10 Use compound words from the exercises above, or similar ones, in new headlines to replace those opposite.

*Many compound words are made by combining a noun with a verb participle, e.g. **heart-broken** (**heart** + past participle of **break**), **cost-cutting** (**cost** + present participle of **cut**). In both these cases the result is a new adjective. However, the **-ing** participle is also used to form nouns.*

JAPANESE WORK HARDER THAN EUROPEANS, SURVEY SHOWS

PEDESTRIAN WHO WAS DREAMING CAUSES TEN VEHICLE PILE-UP

BREAD MADE AT HOME healthier than supermarket loaves, doctors say

Tests made on drivers' breath shows one in five DRINK TOO MUCH

11 a What do you think of these sports involving
animals? Grade them from 1 to 5
according to how cruel you think they are,
and how much enjoyment they give to
people. Then compare your answers with a
neighbour's and discuss the differences.

Sport	Cruelty	Enjoyment
bull-fighting		
fox-hunting		
salmon-fishing		
cock-fighting		
horse-racing		

b Would you ban any of these sports? Why?

As you will have noticed in the above
exercises, compound words can be nouns,
adjectives or verbs. Words can be combined in
various ways;

object + verb (**e.g. fox-hunting**)
adverb + verb (**e.g. day-dreaming**)
purpose + noun (**e.g. knitting needle**)
two nouns (**e.g. boyfriend**)

12   Find two other compound words that fit into
each of the categories above.

Bridging vocabulary gaps

When we learn a foreign language, one of the
main difficulties we have is to remember
enough words to say what we want to say.
However much new vocabulary we learn,
there still seem to be many gaps, both in our
own vocabulary and in our understanding of
other people's vocabulary.

1 Look at these pictures. Do you recognise the
objects or people in them?

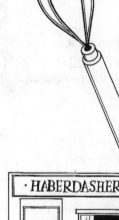

Complete one of the following phrases for each
object, place and person.

Example:
A person who collects rubbish from outside your
house

a a place where you can . . .
b a person who . . .
c an instrument for . . .
d a shop where you can . . .
e a utensil for . . .

We can often bridge the gaps in our
vocabulary by using general words like
thing, instrument, person, place, shop,
etc, and a relative clause beginning with
which, who, where, etc, or a prepositional
phrase beginning with **for, with, like,** etc.
Expressions like **kind of, sort of, type of,**
etc, are also useful: e.g. **She's the kind of
doctor who looks after young children.
It's a type of green vegetable.**

ACTIVATE

2 Divide into two teams. Each team prepares definitions like those in exercise 1 for six unfamiliar words using a dictionary if necessary. Members of each team take it in turns to test the other team.

Example:

Team A:	What's the word for a person who looks after the health of animals?
Team B:	Ermmm . . . a veterinary, a vet.
Team A:	Right.

3 Look at the picture sequences opposite. Tell one of the stories to a partner <u>without using a dictionary</u>. Mention all the objects in the pictures.

ACTIVATE

4 Think of a technical process which you know about (e.g. making a batik, developing a film, etc). <u>Without using a dictionary</u>, describe the process to a partner.

> *It can also be hard to understand someone who is using vocabulary that you don't know. If they are speaking on TV or radio, or are acting in a film, all we can do is try to work out the meaning from the context (see Book 1, Part A – Unit 1), as we do when we are reading something which contains unfamiliar vocabulary. If we are speaking to someone face to face, then it is possible – and not at all impolite – to ask them to clarify the meaning of unfamiliar words.*

5 The contributions of one of the speakers in the following dialogue between two friends, one of whom isn't English, is only half-complete. Put Isabella's contributions (in the box below) back into the dialogue.

SARAH: . . . There I was, merrily driving along this country lane when suddenly a tractor pulled out in front of me. I swerved, and . . .

ISABELLA: You what?

SARAH: Swerved . . . you know, I pulled the steering wheel over to one side to avoid this twit . . .

ISABELLA:

SARAH: (*laughing*) No, of course not – a 'twit' is an idiot, a stupid person.

ISABELLA:

SARAH: No. I just missed the back of the spreader . . . that's a machine for spreading manure . . .

ISABELLA:

SARAH: . . . natural fertiliser – animal droppings, but I ran into a ditch, which is a sort of channel used for draining. The car somersaulted . . .

ISABELLA:

SARAH: Sorry . . . the car turned over . . .

ISABELLA:

SARAH: Yes, and I ended up driving through the hedge . . .

ISABELLA:

SARAH: No, the hedge – the line of bushes between the road and the fields. Where was I?

ISABELLA:

SARAH: Fine . . . and I found myself in the middle of the field he'd just spread with manure . . .

ISABELLA:

SARAH: No I was in the car, in the middle of the field. Of course, the car was a write-off.

ISABELLA:

SARAH: Yes, a complete write-off.

---

a Oh, right . . . Did you hit him?
b Write-off . . . Does that mean the car was destroyed, that you couldn't drive it any more?
c Oh, my God, did it really?
d I'm sorry, could you explain what that means
e Driving through the 'hedge' – is that the correct pronunciation?
f Oh, no (*laughing*)! You mean, you fell out of the car? Were you hurt?
g The edge? The edge of what?
h 'Manure'?
i Is a 'twit' a kind of tractor?

6 Which of these pictures form part of the story, and which are not part of it?

a

b

c

d

e

7 List the relevant expressions from the dialogue in the boxes below. Then add some other expressions for a more formal conversation between two people who don't know each other well.

Ways of asking for help with vocabulary	Ways of giving help with vocabulary
Informal:	
More informal:	

ACTIVATE

8 With a partner, choose one of the following topics.

a a do-it-yourself repair that went wrong
b a wedding that went wrong
c a concert or circus performance that went wrong

With the help of a dictionary, list any technical or special words that you need. Then invent another 'story' dialogue between an English speaker and someone who doesn't speak English very well.

Using words creatively and inventing new words

People who write novels and poems exploit the creative features of language to achieve specific effects in their descriptions or narratives, and to get the reader to react emotionally to the text.

1 a Imagine a very cold day in a big city. You are in a street, not in a heated building. List five words or phrases in English that you might use to describe the atmosphere vividly.

b Now imagine a very hot day in the same place, and list five other words or phrases that come to mind.

Compare your lists with those prepared by two other people. Are the lists similar or different?

2 Discuss the following question with a partner:

If you had to choose between spending time in such a city in very hot weather or in very cold weather, which would you prefer? Why?

3 Read the following description from a detective novel about police work in the imaginary 87th precinct (police district) of a large American city, very similar to New York, where the author of the passage once worked with the police.

4 In the passage, 'July' and 'Heat' are depicted as rather frightening and striking women. What are the following depicted as?
- the air
- the surface of the street
- the sky
- the buildings

5 Use a dictionary to find which of the following words:

a refer to colour
b relate to stickiness
c relate to proud, ostentatious behaviour
d have to do with clothing
e describe a kind of light

> strut bitch bleached rhinestone slash
> flaunt saffron viscous gum dizzying
> dungarees shimmer

July.
Heat.
In the city, they are synonymous, they are identical, they mean one and the same thing. In the 87th Precinct, they strut the streets with a vengeance, these twin bitches who wear their bleached blond hair and their bright red lipstick slashes, who sway on glittering rhinestone slippers, who flaunt their saffron silk. Heat and July, they are identical twins who were born to make you suffer.

The air is tangible. You can reach out and touch it. It is sticky and clinging. You can wrap it around you like a viscous overcoat. The asphalt in the gutters has turned to gum, and your heels clutch at it when you try to navigate the streets. The pavements glow with a flat off-white brilliance, contrasting with the running black of the gutter, creating an alternating pattern of shade and light that is dizzying. The sun sits low on a still sky, a sky as pale as faded dungarees. There is only a hint of blue in this sky for it has been washed out by the intensity of the sun, and there is a shimmer over everything, the shimmer of heat ready to explode in rain.

The buildings bear the heat with the solemnity of Orthodox Jews in long, black frock coats. They have known this heat. Some of them have withstood it for close to a century, and so their suffering is a silent one. They face the heat with the intolerant blankness of stoics.

Scrawled onto the pavement in white chalk are the words: JESUS VIENE. PREPARENSE POR NUESTRA REDENCION!

The buildings crowd the sidewalks and prepare neither for their redemption nor their perdition. There is not much sky on this street.

Ed McBain *See Them Die*

Does it capture the atmosphere you were thinking of in exercises 1 and 2? If so, how?

6 Choose four phrases from the passage which you consider exemplify good creative use of language. Then compare your selections with a neighbour's.

Inventing new words, borrowing words from one topic (e.g. computing) and using them for another (e.g. politics), and the other possibilities mentioned below are some of the ways in which writers of literature, journalism and advertising achieve new and fresh effects, often with great success
See also Part A, Unit 4 of Book 1 for more on metaphor.

Here are some things that writers of literature do with language:

1 compare things which are not usually considered similar.
2 describe things using words normally used to describe something quite different.
3 refer to abstract things as if they were concrete objects.
4 use words which are not normally nouns as nouns, or not normally adjectives as adjectives, etc.
5 invent totally new words.
6 use metaphors: describe things by referring to them as something else.

7 How do you feel about the different images in this text? Which do you find: effective? exaggerated? offensive? inappropriate? Why? Does this extract make you want to read any more of the book?

8 With a partner, match the excerpts below with points 1 to 6 above. Don't worry if you don't understand them completely – they are small parts of much longer poems.

a
> She was a butterfly

b
> The authentic! It rolls
> Just out of reach, beyond
> Running feet and
> Stretching fingers
>   *(Denise Levertov)*

c
> The heavens are blue
> But the sun is murderous
>   *(Grace Nichols)*

d
> *anyone lived in a pretty how town*
> *(with up so floating many bells down)*
> *spring summer autumn winter*
> *he sang his didn't he danced his did*
>   **(ee cummins)**

e
> The trees are coming into leaf
> Like something almost being said
>   *(Philip Larkin)*

f
> *And as in uffish thought he stood,*
> *The Jabberwock, with eyes of flame,*
> *Came whiffling through the tolgey wood*
> *And burbled as it came.*

One of the fantastic things about human language is that it changes according to the needs of those who use it. As technological and other progress happens, language develops so that we can talk or write about it. In addition, new words come into the language – and old ones go out – rather in the same way that fashions in clothing change.

9 a Think of some new words and expressions in your own language. How did they come into use?

b Look at these quotations from a dictionary of new words. Identify which word or expression is new, and, with a partner try to work out the meaning of it. Then check the definitions (from the same dictionary) in the key.

i │ THE BOOKFAIRIES are only interested in a very small range of books. Most bookfairs consist of dealers selling to dealers . . . Bookfairies only wish to buy the best edition mint in the dustwrapper, signed by the author . . .
Guardian 14.1.89

ii │ The new Secretary of State for Energy yesterday surprised the energy conservation lobby by backing the idea of a carbon tax to limit the burning of fossil fuels by developed countries.
Independent 20.9.89

iii │ MR Coleman's own political views – which have flip-flopped over the years as much as Mr Wilder's and are now generally conservative – are almost irrelevant.
Economist 28.10.89

iv │ IT IS in the double no-go area of green belt and conservation area. In truth, this is rurbania, that uneasy edge-of-city mix of flooded gravel pits, M25 motorway, stockbrokers' houses and fragments of old villages.
Sunday Times 25.3.90

c Do you think these words and expressions will last? Why/why not?

ACTIVATE

10 Read a newspaper or magazine this week (in your own language). Try to find at least three words or expressions (not names) which you <u>wouldn't</u> expect to find in any dictionary.

While reading or listening to English or any other language, it is often good to try to identify and remember the words and phrases that are used in a particularly effective or new way, where the language is being stretched beyond its normal everyday use.

11 Discuss the following statements with a partner. Which do you disagree with? Why? What other statements would you add?

a There should be an 'academy' or similar organization for each language to decide which new words are acceptable and which are not.

b Dictionaries should contain more rules about what is 'good' in a language and what is not acceptable.

c People should be free to use what language they want, in the same way as they choose the clothes they wear.

d Children at school should be encouraged to explore the possibilities of language and to be creative with it.

PART B HUMAN BEINGS AND THE WORLD WE LIVE IN

1 | *Families*

1 Note down answers to the following questions about marriage in your country.

a At what age do most women get married? And men?
b How do most people meet their future husbands/wives?
  i through the family
  ii at parties, discos, clubs, etc.
  iii at work or college, etc.
c Do parents have to approve the choice of partner?
d Do parents ever choose the partner for their sons/daughters?
e Do people get engaged? If so, how long do engagements last?
f How long do weddings last?
g Are there any interesting features of marriage in your country?

Compare your answers with those of a neighbour (if possible, someone from a different culture). Are there many differences between your answers?

2 Read the passage to find out why and how one of the partners was replaced at this wedding. What is the attitude of the writer to this story? How do you know what his attitude is?

There was a story in the morning newspaper about a drunken bridegroom. He and his friends had been drinking before the ceremony and arrived in an excited condition. The bride's family were furious, and its senior male representatives went to their counterparts in the bridegroom's family to protest. The unfortunate bridegroom was sacked on the spot. But both sides needed to save family honour. Fortunately, there were several young single men at the wedding and a likely bachelor on the bridegroom's side was selected. His income, family background and prospects – and, we can assume, his horoscope, too – were quickly checked by the bride's family. He fitted the bill and was, moreover, sober. The marriage went ahead with the replacement bridegroom. One can only guess at the feelings of the bride.

adapted from *India File* by Trevor Fishlock

MEANING IN CONTEXT

3 Find words or phrases in the passage which mean:

a a woman who is about to be, is being or has just been married
b a man who is about to be, is being or has just been, married
c equivalents
d dismissed
e future expectations
f was suitable

4 How do you think the following people felt?

a the bride
b the original bridegroom (when he became sober)
c the new bridegroom

Discuss your answers with a partner.

USING A
DICTIONARY

DEFINITIONS

5 Use a dictionary to help you answer the following questions.

a What differences in meaning and use are there between these
words?
  i *wedding* and *marriage*
  ii *bride* and *wife*; *bridegroom* and *husband*
  iii *to marry, to get married,* and *to be married*
  iv *bachelor, single, unmarried* and *unattached*
b What do the words below mean?

bridesmaid	*best man*	*reception*	*honeymoon*

c Which of the following words can be used with *wedding* to form
a compound noun like *wedding ceremony*?

dress	*church*	*present*	*family*	*guests*

ACTIVATE

6 Can you explain these headlines from local papers in Britain?

a
BRIDESMAID ELOPES WITH GROOM IN CHAUFFERED LIMO

b
HANDSOME VICAR LEFT STANDING AT ALTAR

c
'FOR RICHER, FOR POORER' SAYS MILLIONAIRE BRIDEGROOM

d
BEST MAN WEDS BRIDE IN LAST MINUTE SWITCH

f
COFFINS AS TABLES AT UNDERTAKER'S 'TILL DEATH DO US PART' RECEPTION

e
Honeymoon couple not married, says real husband

Choose one of the headlines and write a short news report to go
with it.

7 Read the following advertisments. What kind of people do you think these are? Who do you find more sympathetic? Why? Do you feel sorry for either of them?

PERSONAL

Good-looking and vivacious widow aged 40, wanting companionship and a lasting relationship, wishes to hear from a fun-loving but mature bachelor or widower. He should share an interest in modern art and tennis, and be a considerate non-smoker. Reply Box Z 351.

Unattached male divorcee, 55, with custody of three teenage children, wants friendship with a single woman who has no family responsibilities and a willingness to travel far. Reply Box Z 542

MEANING

SENSE RELATIONS

8 Some of the words in the following list are from the ads above. Decide which refer to females (F), which to males (M) and which to both (FM). Then complete the sentences below.

> widow   bachelor   spinster   lover   fiancée   spouse
> mistress   fiancé   divorcee   widower

a A woman's _____ is the man who is engaged to be married to her.
b _____ are people who have been married but have divorced and are now single.
c A _____ is a woman whose husband has died. A man whose wife has died is called a _____.
d _____ is a formal term for 'husband or wife'.
e Someone's _____ is a person other than their wife with whom they have a sexual relationship.
f A _____ is a rather old-fashioned and derogatory word for an unmarried woman over forty.

ACTIVATE

9 Imagine that you wish to reply to one of the advertisements in exercise 7. Write a short letter explaining your own (imaginary or real!) situation and suggesting a next step.

OR: Using two of the words from exercise 8, write an advertisement for yourself to attract the type of partner you would like to have. DON'T put your name on it, but do give it a code or box number. Put it on the class noticeboard and wait for replies!

MEANING

RELATED MEANINGS

10 Discuss with a partner where these family relations should be put on the grid opposite. Which do you consider to be close to you, and which more distant? Which are normally older, and which younger? Do you both agree? If not, why not?

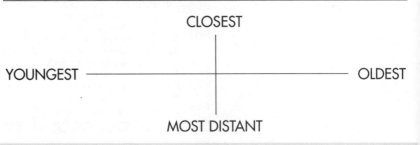

son   niece   mother-in-law   stepdaughter   cousin
second cousin   great uncle   ex-husband   grand-daughter
twin sister   grandparents   half-brother   mother
sister-in-law   great-grandmother   wife   aunt   sister   father
brother   daughter   nephew   mother   husband

CLOSEST

YOUNGEST ——————————————————— OLDEST

MOST DISTANT

WORD FORMATION

PARTS OF SPEECH, PREFIXES AND SUFFIXES

11 Use a dictionary to help you answer these questions if necessary.

QUIZ

1 Which two of these words can be used as a verb?

father   son   sister   mother   uncle

What does each mean?

2 Which three of these words can take the suffix *-less* to form an adjective meaning 'without'?

father   son   mother   brother   child

3 Which of the following:
a is someone who your parents are looking after as if he were a member of the family?
b is related to you through your own or your sister's marriage?
c is the child of your stepfather or stepmother but not of your natural mother or father?
d is the natural child of one of your own natural parents?

brother-in-law   half-brother   stepbrother   foster brother

4 Which of the word-parts in the box can be used with each of the relations below?

-in-law   step-   half-   foster-

a sister   **d** father   **g** parents   **j** grandchild
b mother   **e** son   **h** children
c cousin   **f** uncle   **i** daughter

5 a Which of these words and expressions means 'a child whose parents have both died'?

only child   orphan   unique child   lonely child

b What do the others mean?

ACTIVATE

12 Draw your own family tree. Describe it to a partner.

13 The pictures below are from a children's book called *Where the Wild Things Are*. The artist, Maurice Sendak, has said that he based his characters on his aunts, uncles and other relations, when he was a child.

Ask a partner the following questions:

a Who are your favourite and least favourite relatives?
b Which of your relatives do you find:
   i the most interesting?
   ii the funniest?
   iii the most unpleasant?
   iv the kindest?
   v the meanest, etc.?
c Do you *take after* any of your relatives? Which?

FOCUS WORDS
FAMILIES

aunt	grandson	spinster
bachelor	great uncle	stepbrother
best man	great-grandmother	stepchildren
bride	half-brother	stepdaughter
bridegroom	half-sister	stepfather
bridesmaid	honeymoon	stepmother
brother-in-law	lover	stepsister
cousin	marriage	stepson
divorcee	marry/get married	uncle
ex-husband	mistress	unmarried
father-in-law	mother-in-law	wedding
fiancé	nephew	wedding dress
fiancée	niece	wedding guests
foster-	only child	wedding present
grandchildren	orphan	widow
granddaughter	reception	widower
grandfather	second cousin	wife
grandmother	single	
grandparents	sister-in-law	

FOCUS PHRASES

only child
take after

WORD CHECK

Refer to Focus Words and Focus Phrases only.

1 Which four family members are missing from the list because they are so well known?

2 How many of the family words can be used to include both male and female members of the family?

3 Choose family members from the list. In pairs have conversations like this:

A: How many aunts do you have?

B: Three altogether.

A: How are they related to you?

B: One is my mother's sister, another is the wife of one of my mother's brothers, and the other is my father's sister.

4 Write a short paragraph about a real or imaginary wedding. Use as many of the relevant words as possible.

1 a Read the following letters written to an 'agony' column in a British newspaper. Which of the two people do you think has the bigger problem? Has anyone you know ever been in a similar situation . . .

Dear Samantha . . .

I'm torn in two – I'm 23 with a three-year-old daughter, Hannah, and I live with my boyfriend, Mike, who is Hannah's father. I was very happy until a year ago. But then things seemed to change: although I'm fond of Mike and admire him a lot, I have no desire to hug and kiss him, or to make love. Three months ago I met David, and we fell madly in love. Everything is fine – except for the fact that David has got a new job in Australia. He wants me and Hannah to go out there with him in two months' time. I know David is the right man for me, but my daughter would be thousands of miles away from her father, who absolutely adores her. I don't want to hurt either of them, but I must if I want to follow David. Can you offer me any advice in this tricky situation?

Dear Samantha . . .

You've got to help me. I'm in a dreadful dilemma. I'm mad about my wife, and we've got two adorable children. But I can't stand my wife's parents. And now that her father has retired because of illness, my wife, who is an only child, feels she must ask them to come to live with us because they can't afford to pay their rent. I hate my mother-in-law because she's always interfering in the way we run the house and bring up the children. Also, she's a racist, and I think she secretly despises me for being black. As for my father-in-law, I really detest him because he used to punish my wife severely when she was a child. I loathe violence, and I'm afraid of what he might do to our children. I've talked to my wife about this, but she can see no alternative. What should we do?

b With a partner, discuss what advice you would give to the writers of these letters if you were Samantha. Are there any questions you would want to ask the writers?

MEANING IN
CONTEXT

MEANING IN CONTEXT

2 How many different words meaning 'like' can you find in the first letter?

How many different words for 'dislike' can you find in the second letter?

MEANING

RELATED AND UNRELATED MEANINGS

3 Match the beginnings of the numbered sentences below with the endings on the right. Write the complete sentences out using appropriate punctuation.

1 She's always *flirting* with other men

2 He *adores* his wife

3 They became *acquainted*

4 They have terrible *rows*

5 He was really *attracted* to her

6 I don't think his *love* for her will last very long;

7 I don't think she's trying to *seduce* him;

8 It's surprising that they go on *living together*

9 They're quite *close* to each other, really

10 She really *fancies* him

a but they've never actually hit each other.

b so he asked her out to dinner.

c it's just *infatuation*, really.

d and she's very *fond of* him.

e but she's too shy to ask him out.

f although they *quarrel* quite often.

g when they no longer *respect* each other.

h it's just that she's a very *affectionate* person.

i so he often gets *jealous*.

j at a mutual friend's birthday party.

WORD FORMATION

PARTS OF SPEECH

4 Put the words in *italics* from exercise 3 into the table. Then, using a dictionary, add as many missing words as possible. An example has been given to help you.

Verbs	Adjectives	Nouns
adore	adoring, adorable	adoration

WORD GRAMMAR

PHRASAL VERBS

ACTIVATE

5 In the following, put the words in the correct order.

a Martin and I/and/met at a party/each other/for/immediately /fell

b You/that pretty waitress/saw/chatting/on Friday night/at Bilbo's Restaurant/I/up

c 'get/you/with/how/ on/do/Bill'? 'Very well.'

d 'How's Mary?' 'I don't know. and/up/she/broken/have/I

e Darling, I can't bear you to be angry with me. make/can/up/it/we ? Can we let bygones be bygones?

6 Put the following pictures in the right order (the first one is in the right place). Tell the story of Tina and Brad's relationship using words from exercises 1–5.

BRAD: Hi! I haven't seen you here before. Can I get you a drink?

TINA: No, I think I'd rather just dance . . . You dance pretty well . . .

BRAD: Listen, Tina. I'm sorry about the other night. Can we *make a fresh _____*?

TINA: Oh, Brad. I've *missed you* so much . . .

BRAD: I've behaved like a fool. Can we *let _____ be bygones*?

TINA: Oh, Brad . . .

BRAD: Who was that on the phone?

TINA: Oh, it was only Dave.

BRAD: What, your _____ *flame* again? *Can't he take a _____?*

TINA: He was just asking if we wanted to . . .

BRAD: I'm sick of this. Why don't you go out with your precious Dave tonight? I'm leaving!

TINA: But Brad . . .!

VICAR: Do you, Tina Leonora Smith, take Bradley Desmond Brown to be your lawful wedded husband, for richer, for poorer, in sickness and in health, from this time forward, till death do you part?

TINA: I do . . .

TINA: Kiss me, Brad. Tell me that you'll never leave me.

BRAD: How can I leave you? I loved you *from the moment I _____ eyes on you.*

TINA: Me too. *Love at first _____,* don't they say?

BRAD: Who's that guy you were talking to? He *couldn't _____ his eyes off you.*

TINA: Oh that was Dave. Would you believe it, I used to be *crazy _____ him!*

BRAD: Well, he still seems to fancy you.

TINA: Don't be so jealous, Brad. He's just immature . . . and a bit _____ *sick* still, maybe.

WORD USE

METAPHOR AND IDIOM

📖 **7** Use a dictionary to complete the expressions in italic in the dialogue. Match the expressions with their definitions below.

a very much in love with
b forget about the past
c felt unhappy because you weren't there
d a previous girlfriend/boyfriend
e from the first time I saw you

MEANING

RELATED MEANINGS

8 Match these words with the definitions below.

> friend   colleague   partner   ally   companion
> comrade   acquaintance   lover   enemy   accomplice

Someone who:

a is associated with you in business or plays sport with you.
b helps you in war or confrontation.
c you know only superficially.
d you disagree with violently and dislike.
e keeps you company.
f you have a sexual relationship with.
g is a member of the same political or military group as you.
h you like a lot and have things in common with.
i works in the same place as you.
j helps you in illegal or criminal activities.

WORD FORMATION

NOUNS

9 The words above are nouns referring to people. Other nouns referring to the *relationship* can be formed from some of them by using the suffix *-ship*. Which ones?

10 Read this incomplete poem once and answer the questions.

a What picture do you have of the people described in it?
b How old do you think they are?
c Do they have a close relationship now?
d What sort of relationship have they had previously?
e What are their feelings at the moment described here?

One Flesh

Lying apart now, each in a separate bed,
He with a book, keeping the light on late,
She like a girl dreaming of childhood,
All men elsewhere – it is as if they wait
Some new event: the book he holds unread,
Her eyes fixed on the shadows overhead,

Tossed up like flotsam from a former passion,
How cool they lie. They hardly ever touch,
Or if they do it is like a confession
Of having little feeling – or too much.
Chastity faces them, a destination
For which their whole lives were a preparation.

Strangely apart, yet strangely close together,
Silence between them like a thread to hold
And not wind in. And time itself's a feather
Touching them gently . . .

USING A DICTIONARY
DEFINITIONS

11 Use a dictionary (if necessary) to answer these questions.

a *Flotsam* is a kind of rubbish. Where would you expect to find it *tossed up*, and where could it come from? Why do you think this couple is compared with flotsam?

b *Chastity* is considered by many people to be a virtue. For whom is it obligatory to be *chaste*? Why do you think chastity faces this couple?

c Where would you expect to find *thread*? Why do you think these two people don't *wind in* the thread of the silence between them?

12 Here are the last two and a half lines of the poem. Do these lines make you want to change any of your answers from exercise 10?

> . . . Do they know they're old,
> These two who are my father and my mother
> Whose fire from which I came has now grown cold?
>
> *Elizabeth Jennings*

MEANING IN CONTEXT

13 With a partner, decide which of these statements you think best describes the relationship between the two people in the poem.

a They are very fond of each other but don't love each other any more.

b They love each other deeply but feel no need to share physical love.

c They are too preoccupied with growing old to be able to love each other as they used to.

d As they have grown older, they have got so accustomed to each other that they are bored.

If you don't agree with any of these statements, write another that you and your partner do agree with.

ACTIVATE

14 The sentences below are the beginnings or ends of paragraphs on the back covers of (imaginary) romantic novels. Choose two of them and complete the paragraph. Then use expressions from exercise 6 to prepare and act out a dramatic scene from the novel.

a

ETERNALLY YOURS . . .

Susanna was taken completely by surprise when she accidentally opened a letter to her husband that began 'Darling' and ended 'Eternally yours.' . . .

b

ESCAPE TO MY ARMS

. . . Racing barefoot through the forest with the dogs getting closer and closer, Diana fell straight into the arms of a tall, dark stranger.

c

HEART TO HEART

Roger's illness meant either an early death or an early transplant. Given the choice, he didn't hesitate, but he had never met a heart surgeon quite like April Davies before . . .

d

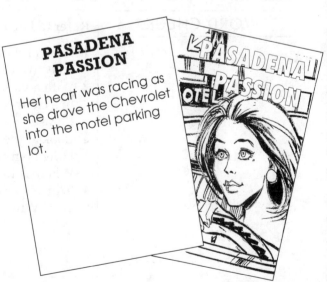

PASADENA PASSION

Her heart was racing as she drove the Chevrolet into the motel parking lot.

FOCUS WORDS
RELATIONSHIPS

accomplice	desire	lover
acquainted	despise	make up
acquaintance	dreadful	miss (someone)
admire	enemy	mistreat
admiration	fancy	partner
adorable	fanciable	partnership
adoration	flirt	quarrel (n)
adore	flirtation	quarrel (with) (v)
affection	flirtatious	quarrelsome
affectionate	fondness	respect (n)
alliance	friend	respect (v)
ally	friendship	respectful
alternative	hug	row (n)
colleague	infatuated	row with (v)
companion	infatuation	seduce
companionship	jealous	seductive
comrade	jealousy	seduction
comradeship	kiss	

FOCUS PHRASES

be close to	let bygones be bygones
be fond of	love at first sight
be torn in two	live with
break up with	make a fresh start
can't/couldn't take (your) eyes off	make love (with)
chat up	old flame
from the moment (I) set eyes on	take a hint

WORD CHECK

Refer to Focus Words and Focus Phrases only.

1 Look at the <u>adjectives</u> in the list. How many different adjective endings are used?
2 With a partner write a short dialogue between two people in a close relationship. Use at least three of the Focus Phrases.
3 Look at the Focus Words with <u>three</u> or more syllables. How many of them have the stress on the <u>second</u> syllable? Where is the stress in the others?
4 Which six words and phrases from the list do you like best? Why? Which six will be most useful to you? Why?

Communication and language

1 Look at these photographs with a partner. What kind of communication is taking place in each? What 'messages' do you think are being sent and received?

a

b

In which photographs:
a is the communication two-way?
b is one of the participants in a position of power?
c is language being used?
d is speech being used?

c

d

2 Which of the following kinds of communication have you been involved in during the last 24 hours?

a getting or giving information
b asking for something/telling someone to do something
c agreeing or refusing to do something
d apologising
e expressing thanks
f expressing sympathy
g expressing pleasure
h showing affection
i showing anger
j another kind of communication – which?

Did you do any of these: in writing; on the phone; using an automatic machine; or using signs or signals?

e

f

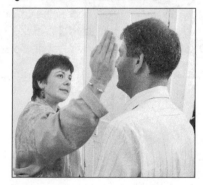

g

h

3 Read the following quickly. What kind of relationship does Diane have with her parents, to judge from the communication she has with them in this story?

Diane had *argued* for a long time with her parents about her hairstyle. She had *begged* her mother to let her get rid of her straight brown hair. But her mother, who thought it very attractive as it was, *insisted* that she should wait. A long *argument* had followed in which Diane had *screamed abuse* at her mother, and her mother had *shouted insults* at Diane.

Diane had then tried to *persuade* her father, who *implied* that she was too much under the influence of her friends. In the end he had *forbidden* her to speak about it again. Diane had *pointed out* that she was over fifteen and *mentioned* that a friend had offered to do her hair for her. Her father had *emphasized* the fact that she would not legally be an adult until she was eighteen, and *stressed* that, until then, she would have to live by his rules. He had then *ordered* her to *apologize* to her mother. But Diane had *repeated* her determination to 'be her own person', and *accused* her father of being a dictator. She had then stormed out of the house and stayed with a friend for three days.

When Diane phoned home three days later, her mother wept with relief. She *pleaded* with Diane to come home. That evening, Diane's father apologized, *explaining* that he was under a lot of pressure at work. Diane then *suggested* that they should compromise and *asked* her parents to allow her to do what she wanted with her hair after her sixteenth birthday, which, as it happened was only a fortnight away. Her parents readily *agreed*.

Diane came out of the hairdressers' into the brilliant sunshine. She felt good: finally she had the hairstyle that she'd wanted for nearly a year. The sides of her head were shaved and the hair in the middle of her head had been cut, dyed black and orange and arranged in an impressive vertical brush. She couldn't wait to get home to show her parents . . .

MEANING IN CONTEXT

4 With a partner, complete the following dialogue using the information in the story above.

DIANE: Dad, why won't you let me have the hairstyle I want? I mean, it won't make any difference to you . . .

FATHER: Your friends have too much influence over you, young lady!

DIANE: That's not true . . . please, Dad . . .

FATHER: (*interrupting*) _____ .

DIANE: I'm over fifteen. And, anyway, _____ _____ .

FATHER: Until you're eighteen, _____ _____

Now, go and apologize to your mother!

DIANE: _____ .

Now act out the dialogue which took place after Diane's three days away from home.

MEANING

CONNOTATION

5 Complete the table with the verbs of communication (in *italics*) from Diane's story.

Persuasive or weak communication	Angry or forceful communication	Neutral communication
	argued	suggested

WORD GRAMMAR

VERB COMPLEMENTATION

6 Which of the verbs in exercise 5 can be followed by the following patterns?

a *to* + infinitive
b *that* + clause
c both *to* and *that*

WORD FORMATION

NOUNS AND VERBS

7 Using a dictionary if necessary, make nouns based on as many as possible of the verbs in exercise 5.

ACTIVATE

8 Describe a real argument that you have overheard (or had), OR an imaginary argument between a husband and a wife, using words from exercise 5.

MEANING

RELATED AND UNRELATED MEANINGS

9 Look at these pictures of different communications devices. Match them with the words in the box.

> cordless phone
> answering machine
> fax machine   cardphone
> entryphone   telex machine
> mobile phone   satellite TV
> radio-pager

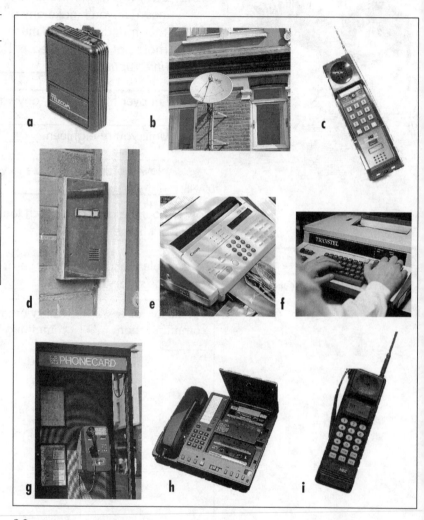

10 Complete each sentence with a device from exercise 9 and a verb from the box below.

> make   talk   send   leave   page   watch   phone   receive

Example:
With _____, _____ the person who has just rung your doorbell without opening the door.

With <u>an entryphone,</u> <u>you can talk to</u> the person who has just rung your doorbell without opening the door.

a With _____ , _____ a phonecall using a special card instead of money.

b With _____ people who phone you _____ messages for you when you aren't at home.

c With _____ , _____ documents instantaneously through the telephone network.

d With _____ in your pocket, people can _____ you and ask you to contact them soon.

e With _____ , _____ TV programmes that are being transmitted through space from another country.

f With _____ , _____ people from your car, the train, etc.

g With _____ , _____ short messages to someone on the other side of the world instanteously.

h With _____ , _____ a phonecall at home without moving from where you happen to be: the garden, the bathroom or your comfortable chair.

WORD USE

COLLOCATION

11 Which of these words are used together? Tick the correct boxes.

	a message	a phonecall	a telex	a person	a phonecard	a fax
make						
use						
contact						
phone						
get/receive						
send						
page						
leave						

ACTIVATE

12 Write a story beginning with the following sentence:

If it hadn't been for his mobile phone, Gerry would never have . . . . In the story, mention as many different means of communication as possible.

WORD USE

METAPHOR AND IDIOM

13 Work with a partner to try to guess what the expressions *in italics* mean. Check your answers in a dictionary if necessary.

a No, I'm afraid we're talking *at cross purposes*; I was talking about my boss, not my girlfriend.

b I'm sorry, we *got our wires crossed*; I thought I said 8.30, not 8 o'clock.

c I know I said you were mean, but I *take it all back*. The present is lovely!

d Sheila, you've got the *wrong end of the stick*: I'm not trying to end our relationship at all.

e What the bank manager said about my overdraft didn't *make any sense* at all.

f I said Mary had stopped bothering about her appearance, but I suppose I'll have to *eat my words*: she looks great.

g I'm going to *give* that Dave *a piece of my mind* when I see him. How dare he say such things about my children!

h That lecture wasn't very clear, was it? I *couldn't make head or tail of it*.

FOCUS WORDS

agree	disagree	page
agreement	disagreement	persuade
answering machine	entryphone	persuasion
apologize	fax machine	phonecard
apology	forbid	phonecall
argue	forgive	propose
argument	forgiveness	proposal
beg	imply	radio-pager
blame (*n*)	implication	receive
blame for (*v*)	inform	repeat
cardphone	information	repetition
complain	insist	request (*n*)
complaint	insistence	request (*v*)
contact	mention (*n*)	satellite TV
contradict	mention (*v*)	send
contradiction	message	suggest
cordless phone	mobile phone	suggestion
demand (*n*)	offer (*n*)	telex
demand (*v*)	offer (*v*)	underline
deny	order (*n*)	warn
denial	order (*v*)	warning

FOCUS PHRASES

can't make head or tail of
not make sense
eat your words
get your wires crossed
get the wrong end of the stick

give someone a piece of your
   mind
leave a message
take it all back

WORD CHECK

Refer to Focus Words and Focus Phrases only.

1 Look at the words for communications devices. Have you used any of them recently? Where? Which others have you seen being used? Where?
2 Look at the nouns for ways of communicating and compare them with the verbs. How many different noun endings are exemplified? How many of the nouns are the same as the verbs?
3 How many words can you find with this stress pattern: ■▮?
4 Tell a story about a misunderstanding, using at least two of the Focus Phrases.

4 | *Speaking and writing*

1 a In your experience, which of the following do people do in speech, which in writing, and which in both? Tick the boxes.

b Compare your answers with a partner. Then tell him/her about people you know who habitually do one or more of these things when talking or writing.

People	Speech	Writing	Both
repeat themselves			
more often choose long words			
are careful not to make mistakes			
sometimes go off the point			
don't finish their sentences			
organize their ideas quite carefully			
sometimes get quite emotional			
may choose colloquial or slang words			
sometimes find it hard to make themselves clear			
may get quite emotional			
use shortened forms			

2 Read the following text. Is your experience of conversation similar to the writer's?

CONVERSATION

There is a great deal of ritual in conversation, especially at the beginning and end, and when topics change. For example, people cannot simply leave a conversation at any point, unless they wish to be considered socially inept or ill-mannered. They have to choose their moment (such as the moment when a topic changes) or find a special reason for leaving. Routines for ending a conversation are particularly complex, and co-operation is crucial if it is not to end abruptly or in embarrassed silence. The people involved may prepare for their departure a long way in advance, such as by looking at their watches or by giving a verbal early warning. A widespread convention is for visitors to say they must leave some time before they actually intend to depart, and for the hosts to ignore the remark. The second time leaving is mentioned then permits both parties to act.

The topic of the conversation is also important. In general, it should be one with which everyone feels at ease: 'safe' topics between strangers in English situations usually include the weather, pets, children, and the local context (e.g. while waiting in a room or a queue); 'unsafe' topics include religious and political beliefs and problems of health. There are some arbitrary divisions: asking what someone does for a living is generally safe; asking how much they earn is not. Cultural variations can cause problems: commenting about the cost of furniture or the taste of a meal may be acceptable in one society but not in another.

adapted from D. Crystal *Encyclopedia of Language*

3 Complete these sentences about the passage, using your own words as far as possible.

a In Britain, if you leave a conversation without waiting for an

appropriate moment, _____.

b There may be an embarrassed silence if _____.

c If you look at your watch some time before you need to leave,

you _____.

d When talking to strangers in Britain, you will be unlikely to give

offence if _____.

e If you ask a British person you don't know about their religious

or political beliefs, he or she may _____.

4 In your country, what are the safe and unsafe topics of conversation for people who don't know each other well? What are the favourite topics of conversation? List some topics that are definitely unsafe!

WORD GRAMMAR

VERB COMPLEMENTATION

5 Choose the correct verbs in the following passage:

The doctor (**1** told/said) Mr Martin that he was overweight. She (**2** told/said) him to join Weightwatchers or (**3** speak/tell) to a dietician. Mr Martin (**4** said/told) that, as he didn't (**5** speak/talk) English very well, he would prefer the doctor to (**6** say/tell) the dietician about his problems. He (**7** said/told) he would go on a diet anyway, and would (**8** say/tell) his family that they should eat fewer fatty foods and potatoes. But he was (**9** saying/telling) a lie; he liked food too much, and mealtimes were the only times he could (**10** talk/speak) about the things that interested him with his family and friends.

6 Complete the following sentences with *say, tell, speak* or *talk*.

a _____ can be immediately followed by a personal object.
b _____ can be immediately followed by direct speech, or *that*.
c _____ can be immediately followed by the name of a language.
d _____ can be immediately followed by *to* + the name of a person.
e _____ can be immediately followed by *a lie, the truth, a story*.

MEANING

RELATED MEANINGS

7 The words in the box are all descriptions of kinds of communication. Match them with the speakers below.

> conversation   gossip   lecture   argument   interrogation
> debate   chat   heart-to-heart

a 'Did you hear what happened to Dan Smith last night? . .'

b 'For the last time, will you tell us what you were doing on the evening of the 13 May?

c 'This morning we're going to look at the second law of thermo-dynamics'.

d 'We had a lovely time in Wales during our holiday . . .'

e 'Now, Mary, why don't you tell me why you've been feeling so unhappy lately?'

f 'I would like to set out the arguments in favour of the resolution before the meeting.'

g '. . . surely you would agree that quality of life is more important than a high salary?'

h 'You damaged my car!' 'Oh no, I didn't.' 'Oh yes, you did!'

WORD FORMATION

NOUNS AND VERBS

8 Use verbs relating to the nouns in exercise 7 to describe each picture?

Example:

a He was gossiping about Dan Smith.

b _____

c _____

d _____

e _____

f _____

g _____

h _____

MEANING

SENSE RELATIONS

9a Look at these different ways of speaking, and complete the table, using a dictionary if necessary.

	chatter	whisper	shout	mutter	babble	mumble	moan
loudly							
normally							
in a low voice							
with no voice, just breathing							
slowly							
quickly							
too quickly							
cheerfully							
complaining							

b Which of the verbs above cannot fit into the following sentence?

'I'm very hungry,' she _____.

WORD USE

10 Choose an appropriate verb to replace *said* in each of the following.

a 'John, come over to this side of the road! I want to talk to you,' said Jane.

b As they entered the house later that night, Mike said 'Shh! I think my parents are asleep.'

c 'I'm sorry I'm late,' said Mary in a low voice. 'The trains were delayed again.'

d George was very excited to hear that he had passed his exam. He said 'I passed, I passed! . . . can't believe it.'

e 'Oh, not fish and chips again! I'm fed up with eating the same food,' Sarah said.

ACTIVATE

11 Using one of the speeches in exercise 7 as a beginning, tell a short story. Use at least four words from exercises 7 to 9.

12 a Each of the following is the beginning of a kind of written communication. How many of them can you name?

1
```
To:       Managing Director
From:     Sales Manager
Subject:  Forecast of Sales for 1992
```

3

I wandered lonely as a cloud,
That floats on high o'er vales and hills,
When all at once I saw a crowd,
A host of golden daffodils . . .

2
```
                  26, The Avenue
                  Harrow

                  5 March 1992

Dear Mr Harris,

With reference to your
advertisement in the
Evening Globe, I would
like to apply for the
post of sales assistant
. . .
```

5
```
Invoice to:
          SMITH & JONES Ltd

Quantity    Description
1 Cleaning and            £750
  painting two rooms
```

7
```
This is the last will
and testament of . . . .
```

6
```
MEETING OF THE ADMINISTRATION
         SUB-COMMITTEE

     Thursday 6 July 11 a.m.

              AGENDA

1 Matters arising from last
  meeting
2 Organization of the offices
3 Punctuality
```

8
November
Friday 12 A lovely morning. Went to the top of Cliff Hill with the dog and saw three swans flying south.

4
Jane,
Just gone down to the shop to buy some milk.
Mark

b Which of these kinds of writing do you do? Which others?

MEANING

RELATED WORDS

13 Complete the table for the different kinds of writing

	Purpose	Who writes it?	Who reads it?
essay			
diary			
novel			
catalogue			
summons			
biography			
curriculum vitae			
invoice/bill			
receipt			
poem			
love letter			
directory			

14 Complete the following sentences using nouns from exercises 12 and 13 and verbs from the box below. Use each verb and noun only *once*.

look up	*write down*	*pay*	*scribble*	*read*	*prepare*	
receive	*issue*	*send*	*consult*	*reply to*	*type*	*write*

a As she was _____ the last chapter of the latest _____ by her favourite writer, Margery fell asleep.

b The policeman didn't know the number of the fire brigade and had to _____ (*it*) in the telephone _____.

c Yesterday David _____ a _____ to appear in Court on a charge of drunken driving.

d The Finance Department still haven't _____ the _____ they received for the repair work which was done last year.

e As she was going to be late, Ann _____ a _____ for her husband and put it under the windscreen wiper of his car.

f I tried to _____ what she was saying but she was talking too fast.

g 'When I was _____ the _____ for this meeting, I omitted one or two items which I think should be added now,' said the Secretary.

ACTIVATE

15 The following dialogue takes place in the office of the Director of a pharmaceutical laboratory. Read it and then prepare a short written account of the conversation from the point of view of each speaker. Write them in two different forms, e.g. a memo from Jane to the Managing Director, and a letter from Jim to his union.
Jim Read is a laboratory technician. He has just been off sick for three days. Jane Wilson is Director of the laboratory and his boss.

JIM: Mrs Wilson, can I have a word with you?
JANE: Certainly, Jim. Come into the office. I'm glad to see you back.
JIM: Yes, I'm feeling a bit better today. But I wanted to ask you if anything could be done about smoking.
JANE: Smoking? What do you mean?
JIM: Well, the doctor says I've got a weak chest and may be allergic to tobacco smoke. But the staff common-room is a smoking area. It's always full of smoke, and there's nowhere else to go during the coffee breaks.
JANE: I'm not sure we can do anything about that. As you know, we can't let people smoke inside the laboratories. It's too dangerous.
JIM: Yes, but why should non-smokers like me have to suffer?
JANE: Well, a majority of the staff seem to be smokers. I'm a smoker myself.
JIM: I don't think it's right, that's all. Can't the common-room be divided into two sections?
JANE: I'm sure that would be very expensive. Look, let me have a think about it. I'll talk to the Managing Director and see if anything can be done . . .

16 Write the written communication which you would most like to receive from someone. It may be someone you know or someone you don't know.

FOCUS WORDS

agenda	gossip	receive
application	heart-to-heart	remark
argue	interrogate	reply to
argument	interrogation	report
babble	invoice	say
bill	issue	scribble
biography	lecture	shout
catalogue	letter	silence
chat	look up	silent
chatter	love letter	speak
comment	memo	story
consult	minutes	summons
conversation	moan	talk
conversational	mumble	tell
curriculum vitae	mutter	thesis
debate	note	type
diary	novel	whisper
directory	poem	will
essay	prepare	

WORD CHECK

Refer to Focus Words only.

1 How many different types of written text are mentioned in the list? Which of them do you most enjoy reading? Which do you least enjoy reading? Why?

2 Many of the verbs of speaking have two syllables. Which of them have the stress on the *first* syllable? Which have the stress on the *second*?

3 Which of the *verbs* of speaking and writing cannot also be used as a noun?

4 With a partner, prepare a short dialogue between a manager and an administrator in which at least five forms of communication are mentioned.

1 Read these mini-dialogues. Which speaker do you agree with most?

A

I hate watching TV. It's such a waste of time, and most of the programmes are quite boring.

Really? I love TV. I watch quite a lot for relaxation – and I've learnt a lot from TV too.

David and Sarah

B

I don't buy a newspaper every day, but I like to read one whenever something important has happened: it's better than TV or the radio.

I never buy them. You can't believe half of what you read; a lot of it just reflects the political beliefs of the owners.

Mr Davies and Mrs Clark

C

Do you think Jimmy should be watching that programme at his age? So much violence can't be good for adult viewers, let alone youngsters.

Oh I don't know. Even kids can tell the difference between TV and real life.

Mrs Davies and her daughter-in-law

2 What is your opinion of the media? Put the words from the box in the appropriate place on the lines below. Then compare your opinions with a partner's.

radio	television	newspapers	magazines

least informative 1 _____ 2 _____ 3 _____ 4 _____ most informative

least interesting 1 _____ 2 _____ 3 _____ 4 _____ most interesting

most harmful 1 _____ 2 _____ 3 _____ 4 _____ least harmful

MEANING

RELATED AND UNRELATED MEANINGS

📖 **3** These words all have to do with the media. Put them in the appropriate box, using a dictionary if necessary.

> *publish   broadcast   edit
> article   live (adj)
> record (v)   censor
> programme   headline
> advertise   report (v)
> column*

TV and radio	Newspapers and magazines (The press)	Both

WORD FORMATION

PARTS OF SPEECH

📖 **4** Use the right form of the words from exercise 3 in these sentences.

a My friend is a _____. She works for the BBC, which stands for British _____ Corporation. *broadcast*

b Many Sunday newspapers these days are just full of _____. *advertise*

c The assassination attempt wasn't _____ in the press until two days later. *report*

d These days there are very few _____ broadcasts on TV. They usually _____ them and show them much later. *live, record*

e There is quite a lot of _____ of the media in some countries, especially during times of conflict. *censor*

f The _____ of this student magazine is a friend of ours. *edit*

g This _____ in the *Chronicle* writes very well, doesn't she? I enjoy reading what she has to say every Saturday. *column*

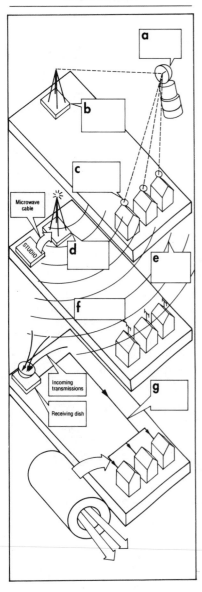

5 Read the following passage. Then use the information in it to number the·diagram below and to label it with the words in italics.

As a result of technological progress, many people in the world already have, or will soon have, access to many more TV channels than in the past.

As you can see from the illustrations, there are now three ways in which TV programmes can reach your home, compared with the one way which existed until a few years ago:

1 Most of the TV channels in the world operate in the traditional way: national public or commercial *TV stations* use *transmitters* to send UHF (ultra-high frequency) *signals* round the country. The *aerials* on our roofs receive these signals and pass them to our TV sets. Simple, and very similar to the way radio broadcasts work.

2 Some international TVchannels use satellites in space. Programmes are transmitted up to the *satellite*, which then re-transmits them to a wide geographical area. If you have a special *satellite dish aerial* on your roof, you can receive these signals – though usually you have to pay for a signal-decoder. In this way, people can watch TV programmes transmitted on the other side of the hemisphere.

3 In many countries, and especially in the US, there is a third system which transmits programmes from studios or from satellites through a cable system. You pay a subscription for each channel that you receive, and the signals are transmitted to your home through underground *fibre-optic cables*. The advantage is that there is much less interference, and, if you want to, you can pay to receive many, many channels.

6 Answer these questions.

a How many hours per week do you watch TV?
b If you have a TV at home, how many different channels can you receive?
c Have you ever watched a satellite TV channel? What did you think of it?
d What's your favourite TV programme? Why?

7 a Tick (✓) any statements that you agree with, and put a cross (✗) against any that you disagree with.

If there are more TV channels available:

1 _____ the quality of programmes is likely to improve.
2 _____ there will probably be fewer differences between channels, because they will all imitate the most popular one.
3 _____ it will be good to be able to specialize and watch the sport channel or the news channel.
4 _____ it will be much harder to choose what to watch, and people will keep switching from channel to channel.
5 _____ there will be less money for making educational or special-interest programmes; most money will be spent buying ready-made programmes or serials.
6 _____ there will be more commercials as more TV companies try to make money from advertising.

b Discuss your opinions with a partner. Do you agree with him/her?

MEANING

RELATED MEANINGS

8 Match these kinds of TV and radio programme with the descriptions. Which kind of programme do you like best?

soap opera	**a**	30 minutes of topical reporting from around the world.
quiz game	**b**	More drama and emotion as deserted Julia seeks revenge on her lover . . .
documentary	**c**	Your host, Dan Woods, meets actress Meryl Streep, author Chris Hughes, and singer Angelo.
news	**d**	More questions to test the memory as four semi-finalists chase the Trivia Prize.
chat show	**e**	Laughs galore as Johnny gets into trouble decorating Jenny's flat.
sitcom (situation comedy)	**f**	Fascinating programme about the blue whale, which is threatened with extinction.

WORD USE

COLLOCATION

9 What kinds of TV or radio programme are:

a presented? **d** starred in?
b read?   **e** chaired?
c hosted?

10 Which words go together? Tick the boxes.

	newspaper	magazine	section	supplement
daily				
evening				
Sunday				
fashion				
local				
business				
tabloid				

MEANING

CONNOTATION

11 Complete the table. What are the differences between these items in the list?

Item	Writer
report column forecast letters page editorial review horoscope crossword	 readers astrologer compiler

WORD FORMATION

NOUNS

12 A *journalist* is a general term for someone who writes for a newspaper or magazine. Who writes the following items?

13 Which of the items in exercise 11 does each item come from?

a **OUTLOOK FOR TUESDAY: more rain in the South, sunny in the west.**

b McKellan's portrayal of *Richard III* was memorable.

c Elections were held in Angola yesterday. A high turnout was reported.

d THE GOVERNMENT should think very hard before it raises interest rates again.

e I CANNOT agree with the view expressed in your editorial (9 February) that our railway system needs more subsidies from the Government.

f Take care that your fiery temper does not lead you to say anything you might regret.

📖 **14** Here are several other items you may find in newspapers or magazines. What would each of them consist of?

obituaries	small ads	share prices	announcements
results service	strip cartoons	pin-ups	programme listing

ACTIVATE

15 Work with a partner to suggest the contents, layout and design of your ideal newspaper. How many pages would it have, what would it contain, what wouldn't it contain, how much space would be given to what, etc?

16 What would you do in each of the following dilemmas?

a You are reporting on a war which your country is involved in. Military censors control your movements and check everything you write in case the information you give is helpful to the enemy. But you believe that people should know what horrific things are going on . . .

b Your editor has told you to get an interview by whatever means with a filmstar whose son was recently killed in a road accident. You unexpectedly recognize her sitting in a church . . .

c You receive a letter from someone who claims to have had an affair with the president, suggesting a meeting – and a payment of $5,000 if a story is published . . .

WORD USE

IDIOM AND METAPHOR

17 Explain the following headlines. Which reflect problems that exist in your country?

a CHRONICLE PHOTOGRAPHER ACCUSED OF INVASION OF PRIVACY

b MURDERER'S WIFE SELLS STORY TO PAPER FOR £25,000

c Right-wing bias dominates popular press, says PM

d Clarion editor on libel charge as industrialist sues

e 'My life's in ruins after newspaper allegations' says singer

FOCUS WORDS

advertise
advertisement
aerial
article
astrologer
broadcast (n)
broadcast (v)
broadcaster
censor (n)
censor (v)
censorship
chair (v)
chat show
column
columnist
commercial
crossword
crossword compiler
daily
documentary
edit
editor
editorial
fibre-optic cable

forecast (n)
forecast (v)
forecaster
headline
horoscope
host (n)
host (v)
listing
live
news
obituary
pin-up
present
presenter
programme
publish
publication
quiz game
record (v)
report (n)
report (v)
reporter
review (n)
review (v)

reviewer
satellite
satellite dish
section
share prices
signal (n)
sitcom
situation comedy
small ads
soap opera
star (n)
star (v)
strip cartoon
supplement
transmit
transmitter
TV set
TV station
weekly

WORD CHECK

Refer to Focus Words only.

1 Which words in the list do you find most similar to the corresponding words in your own language? Which seem to be similar but are in fact different in meaning and/or use?

2 How many different items from the list can be found in newspapers or magazines?

3 Using a dictionary if necessary, try to explain the origin of two of the following words: *broadcast   crossword documentary   pin-up   soap opera*

4 Several of the words in the list are jobs in the media world. Which of these jobs would you prefer to have? Why?

6 | *Politics*

1 Complete the following questionnaire in groups.

THE POLITICIAN QUESTIONNAIRE

1 Tell the others about a politician (living or dead) who you admire.

2 Think of three adjectives to describe politicians who you admire.

   a _____

   b _____

   c _____

3 Think of three adjectives to describe politicians who you don't admire.

   a _____

   b _____

   c _____

4 Would you like to be a politician? Why? Why not? Discuss your answer with a partner.

5 What are the arguments for and against a political career? Record the arguments in the table below.

For	Against

USING DICTIONARIES

DEFINITIONS

2 Match these words with their dictionary definitions.

a democracy
b totalitarianism
c monarchy
d dictatorship
e oligarchy
f tyranny
g police state

1 | government by a small group of people, often for their own interests

2 | government by the people or the elected representatives of the people

3 | *derog* a country in which most activities of the citizens are controlled by (secret) political police

4 | a political system in which every citizen is subject to the power of the state, which exercises complete control

5 | a system ruled by someone with complete power, especially if that power was gained by force

6 | the system of rule by a king or queen

7 | the use of power cruelly and/or unjustly to rule a person or country

Can you give examples from history or current affairs of any of these types of government?

MEANING

CONNOTATION

3 Decide where these words should go in the diagram. The first one has been done for you.

> anarchist   capitalist
> communist   conservative
> fascist   liberal   nationalist
> socialist   social democrat

state control

extremist ———————————————— moderate

X *anarchist*   individual responsibility

a Is it difficult to decide where to put the words? Why? Why not?
b Where would you put yourself?

WORD FORMATION
PARTS OF SPEECH

4 a Complete the chart with words from exercises 2 and 3 where possible.

Noun (concept)	Noun (person)	Adjective
democracy	democrat	democratic

b Now use the right form of the words in these sentences.
   i We should always fight to maintain our (democracy) _____ institutions.
   ii I hate (extremist) _____ in any form. It never solves anything. I am all for (moderate) _____.
   iii The spectre of (totalitarianism) _____ rule hangs over this troubled country.
   iv For someone who is supposed to be a (radical) _____ you seem to have a very (conservative) _____ way of thinking.
   v What we need in this country is (socialist) _____. We don't need a (monarchy) _____ sitting on a throne telling us what to do.

ACTIVATE

5 a Choose one of the characters on the right and argue in favour of their political point of view. Convince your neighbours.

b Write a political slogan which each person could use on posters telling the people how 'good' they are.

1 Jo Nichol
Anarchist

2 Gloria II
Monarch

3 Mark Tango
Fascist

4 Sal Rodd
Socialist

5 Paco Pendi
Dictator

WORD USE

METAPHOR

6 Explain what each of the speakers is talking about.

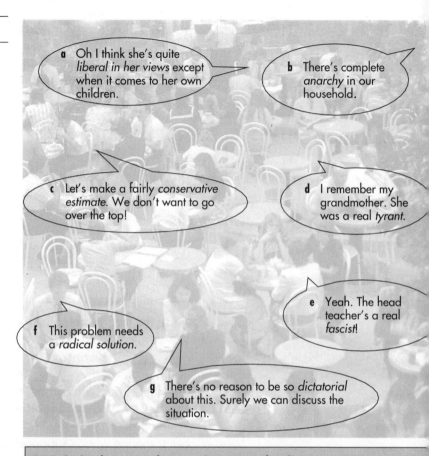

a Oh I think she's quite *liberal in her views* except when it comes to her own children.

b There's complete *anarchy* in our household.

c Let's make a fairly *conservative estimate*. We don't want to go over the top!

d I remember my grandmother. She was a real *tyrant*.

e Yeah. The head teacher's a real *fascist*!

f This problem needs a *radical solution*.

g There's no reason to be so *dictatorial* about this. Surely we can discuss the situation.

7 a Does your country have similar types of politician? How are they different?

b Politicians often have to resign. What reasons might there be for this?

In Britain there are three main types of politician.	
Councillors	They are elected locally to represent the different areas in the region.
Members of Parliament	MPs are elected to form the national government. There is one representative from each of the 635 different areas – or constituencies – of the country. The party with the biggest majority forms the government. The other parties are 'in opposition'; they try to persuade the government to act differently, on many occasions.
Members of the House of Lords	The House of Lords is an unelected body: the members are either created by the government or inherit their title.

WORD USE

COLLOCATION

8 Match the verbs with their complements. Tick the boxes.

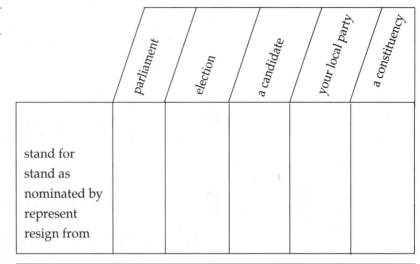

	parliament	election	a candidate	your local party	a constituency
stand for					
stand as					
nominated by					
represent					
resign from					

MEANING

9 a Look at the chart on the right and check the meaning of the words in italics.

b Fill in the blanks in the chart with the following words.

selected   nominated
election   stand for
represent   councillor
cabinet   candidate
opposition

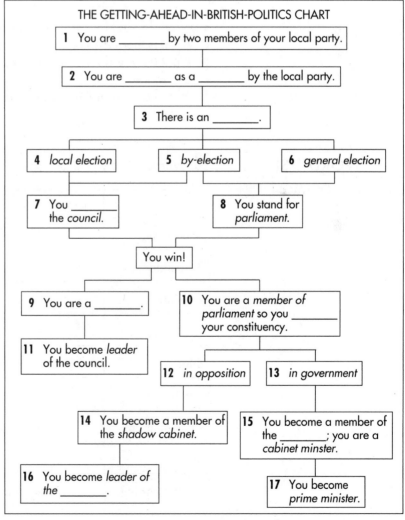

THE GETTING-AHEAD-IN-BRITISH-POLITICS CHART

1 You are _____ by two members of your local party.

2 You are _____ as a _____ by the local party.

3 There is an _____ .

4 *local election* **5** *by-election* **6** *general election*

7 You _____ the *council*.

8 You stand for *parliament*.

You win!

9 You are a _____ .

10 You are a *member of parliament* so you _____ your constituency.

11 You become *leader* of the council.

12 *in opposition* **13** *in government*

14 You become a member of the *shadow cabinet*.

15 You become a member of the _____; you are a *cabinet minster*.

16 You become *leader of* the _____ .

17 You become *prime minister*.

ACTIVATE

10 Look at the chart again. How is the system in your country different? What similarities are there?

11 Can you tell the political story of your country or another country you know over the last few years?

MEANING

RELATED MEANINGS

12 Use the phrases in the box to answer the questions.

> *vote in favour of/against   a tied vote   a casting vote   a vote of (no) confidence   abstain*

a What do you do if you don't agree with a motion or a bill?
b What is there if someone wants to bring down the government?
c What do you do if you don't want to agree and you don't want to disagree?
d What happens if the Yes and No votes are equal?

WORD USE

COLLOCATION

13 Which of the words go together? Tick the boxes.

	victory	defeat	majority
sensational			
landslide			
crushing			
humiliating			
slim			
small			
unassailable			
large			
overwhelming			

14 a Use words from exercises 12 and 13 to fill in the blanks in the text.

The Downfall of Chairman George

George was very confident. He thought that he had an a)_____ majority on the committee and so he was not worried when Jack resigned. But to his horror Maureen Washington stood for election and, with her radical politics, won a b)_____ victory, completely defeating her main rival. As soon as she arrived on the committee she began to cause trouble; votes on this, votes on that. Whatever George advised them to vote in favour of, she c)_____. And as the weeks went by others began to support her. Finally, some weeks later, at the end of a long discussion, there was a d)_____ vote with half the members voting one way and half voting the other. Of course George saved it by using his e)_____, but it was the beginning of the end. Ten days later Maureen tabled a vote of f)_____ and in the wake of his g)_____ defeat George had no alternative but to resign. He felt bitter and betrayed and went off to live in his luxury villa in Santa Lucia. But the rest of us felt saved.

b Can you invent a scenario to fit the facts in this story? What was the committee for? Why did the narrator feel relieved when George resigned?

ACTIVATE

15 Explain the stories behind these headlines.

e **Police state allegations denied**

a GOVERNMENT MAJORITY WINS THE DAY

f FROM COUNCILLOR TO CABINET MINISTER IN JUST FIVE YEARS

b ELECTION HUMILIATION FOR DISGRACED MINISTER

c Shadow Minister alleges sell-out by Party Leader

COUNCILLOR'S LANDSLIDE VICTORY STUNS RULING GROUP

FOCUS WORDS

abstain	landslide	sensational
anarchist	liberal	slim
cabinet	majority	social democrat
candidate	Member of	socialist
capitalist	Parliament	stand as (a
casting vote	moderate	candidate)
communist	monarchy	stand for
conservative	MP	(parliament)
constituency	nationalist	state (*n*)
councillor	nominate	tied vote
crushing	oligarchy	totalitarianism
defeat	opposition	tyranny
democracy	overwhelming	tyrant
dictatorship	parliament	unassailable
election	(political) party	victory
extremist	police state	vote (*v*) (in favour
fascist	politician	of/against)
House of Commons	represent (a	vote (*n*)
House of Lords	constituency)	vote of (no)
humiliating	resign	confidence

FOCUS PHRASES

be dictatorial about
complete anarchy
conservative estimate
liberal/conservative/radical in your views

WORD CHECK

Refer to Focus Words and Focus Phrases only.

1 Find all the nouns which refer to:
  a people (e.g. *anarchist*)
  b political institutions (e.g. *The House of Lords*)
  c abstract concepts (e.g. *democracy*)
2 Choose two or three of the Focus Phrases and use them to describe people or families that you know or know of.
3 How many nouns can you find with this stress pattern: ■ ■■ ?
4 Is it possible to construct a sentence which includes all the verbs in the Focus Words?

Peace, war and international relations

MEANING

1 Where do they work?
Using a dictionary put the following people in as many places in the table as possible.

	consulate	embassy	ministry	official residence (e.g. The White House)	Palace	Parliament	United Nations
ambassador							
consul							
diplomat							
emperor							
foreign minister							
foreign secretary (Britain)							
secretary of state (USA)							
secretary general							
head of state							
king							
president							
prime minister							
queen							

2 Give an example (either from the past or the present) of each of the following.

> border   empire   continent   country   state   region
> hemisphere   community   province

3 Fill in the blanks with words from exercises 1 and 2. The first letter of the missing word is given to help you in some cases.

Emeria today recalled its a)_____ from Darda 'for consultation' after a b)_____ incident in which Dardan troops crossed into Northern Emeria. Carlo Fredricks, Emeria's c)_____ _____, on a visit to the United Nations, said that unless Dardan soldiers stopped the incursions into his country's territory the government of d) P_____ _____ Bandrikarta would have to think seriously about retaliation.

e) P_____ Sylvia Ngobole of Darda, speaking from the f)_____ in Fallo, her g)_____'s capital, blamed members of the Emerian armed forces for the incidents, saying they had provoked the Dardan troops. She warned Emeria that any use of force would be met by equal force from her own soldiers. As tension mounts in the h)_____ Maria Richardson, Secretary General of the United Nations, has invited both sides to bilateral talks at the UN headquarters.

WORD FORMATION
AFFIXES

4 *Bilateral* means 'two-sided'. What words would you use for the following?

a a decision you take on your own, whether or not other people agree (e.g. _____ action, _____ disarmament)

b something done with three groups (e.g. _____ talks, _____ arms agreement)

c something done with a lot of groups (e.g. _____ disarmament, _____ talks, _____ peace-keeping force)

What other words can you think of which start with the same prefixes?

ACTIVATE

5 Describe either a country other than your own or an international event from the recent past using as many of the words from exercises 1 to 3 as possible.

6 Read the two descriptions. Which country would you prefer to live in? Why?

DARDA exports beans and rice and imports just about everything else. There is a serious trade imbalance between it and its partners (including Emeria). Darda has asked for foreign aid to help it deal with the current food shortage.

Amnesty International has detailed widespread abuse of human rights, including imprisonment without trial. There are allegations of torture.

The Emerian government has asked the United Nations to impose economic sanctions on its neighbour because of its human rights record and because of the problems at the border.

EMERIA enjoys good relations with its trading partners, but it has no oil and has to depend on other countries for its supply. Recently it has asked the World Bank for a loan of $250 million to help it rebuild its industrial capacity.

There are many so-called political prisoners in Emeria and the death penalty exists for many crimes (including subversion against the state). But there is no real evidence of torture or imprisonment without trial.

A faction in the country (the Emerian People's Liberation Army) has recently taken three Western journalists as hostages in their campaign for independence for the northern province of Kasmul.

MEANING

7 Find words or phrases in the text which mean the following.

a help (often money) from other countries

b suggestions that people have been physically harmed to get information from them

c people who are kept prisoner so that they can be exchanged for money or other things

d people in prison because of what they say or think

e sells things to other countries

f the conditions of freedom, safety, etc, which everybody should have

g the stopping of trade with a country because you don't like its policies

h buys things from other countries

i an unequal level between countries which sell to each other

8 Complete the following sentences with words from exercise 7.

a We are going to stop _____ oil now that we have discovered that we have our own oil fields.

b The government's first act was the release of all _____ _____ who had been arrested because they disagreed with the policies of the ex-president.

c After the invasion the world community imposed _____ _____ on the aggressive nation.

d We have managed to _____ coal to Darda even though they have coal themselves.

e They need _____ _____ if they are to survive the cold winter.

f The _____ _____ record of the last government was appalling. People were regularly imprisoned and tortured.

WORD USE

COLLOCATIONS

9 Which noun phrases go with which verb phrases, either as subjects or objects? Tick the correct boxes.

	a treaty	a cease-fire	war	talks	a country	diplomatic relations
break down						
invade						
declare						
break off						
sign						
restore						
agree to						

a Which one verb can't take an object?

b Write a paragraph placing the events from the table in a logical order. Begin with this sentence:

Diplomatic relations between the two countries were broken off a year ago.

ACTIVATE

10 Tell the story behind these newspaper headlines about the conflict between Emeria and Darda.

TRADE WAR LOOMS

b EMERIA ALLEGES HUMAN RIGHTS VIOLATIONS

c EMERIAN ENVOY WALKS OUT OF UN MEETING

TENSION MOUNTS ON EMERIAN BORDER

e NO SIGN OF AN END TO WAR IN DARDA

f EMERIAN ARMY 15 MILES INSIDE NEIGHBOURING DARDA

MEANING

RELATED MEANINGS

📖 **11** What is the difference between the following pairs of words? Put them in the correct sentences.

a a *rebellion* and a *riot*
b a *rebellion* and a *revolution*
c a *protest* and a *demonstration*

d a *civil war* and a *guerrilla war*
e a *revolution* and a *coup*
f a *battle* and a *war*
g *autonomy* and *independence*

1 _____ means having the right to run your own affairs in your own *part* of a country; _____ is the status of complete freedom from others' control.

2 A _____ is an uprising against any central authority; a _____ is the successful changing of a government (and the political direction of the country) by force.

3 A _____ is any peaceful act which shows extreme displeasure; a _____ usually involves a large number of people marching with banners to show (peacefully) their support or displeasure.

4 A _____ is an uprising or fight against any central authority: a _____ is an incident when a crowd gets wildly and violently out of control.

5 A _____ is the successful changing of a government (and the political direction of the country) by force; a _____ is the sudden seizing of power from the government by an unelected small (armed) group.

6 A _____ is a fight between the armed forces of two enemies; a _____ is a prolonged period of armed fighting between two countries.

7 A _____ is a war in which two opposing groups from the same country enter into conflict with each other; a _____ is when a (usually) small unofficial group carries out repeated small attacks on the government or the main official force.

WORD USE

CONNOTATION

📖**12** Give each of these words a score from 1 to 5, according to whether the speaker feels positive (1 to 2), neutral (3), or negative (4 to 5) about the person they are describing.

rebel ___   guerrilla ___

revolutionary ___   freedom fighter ___

terrorist ___

ACTIVATE

13 a Read the following information about an attack in Emeria.

> IN Emeria two men from the EPLA (Emerian People's Liberation Army) attacked a government army camp. They blew up an ammunition dump. Government troops counter-attacked and a gun battle developed. In the fighting a schoolhouse was set on fire causing the death of the teacher and three of the children. The attackers were killed after twenty-five minutes.
>
> The EPLA want independence for the province of Kasmul. They have launched a full scale rebellion against Prime Minister Brandrikarta, in spite of the fact that Emeria is still involved in a full-scale rebellion against Darda.

b In groups rewrite this story in one of the following ways using words from exercises 11 and 12 where appropriate:

i as an Emerian government report.
ii as an article from the EPLA paper.
iii as an article from a foreign newspaper (i.e. not an Emerian newspaper).

WORD USE

COLLOCATION

14 Read this text of a speech by Maria Richardson, Secretary General of the United Nations, about the conflict between Emeria and Darda. Complete the sentences below with words from the text.

> ❝ I believe that unless the two parties sit round a negotiating table there will be no chance of resolving this dispute. I know that tension is high but we have to pray that the cease-fire will hold, at least until peace negotiations can start.
>
> There are problems of disputed territory between Emeria and Darda, and I know that both sides have made statements that they will not surrender anything that they have won, but I have to say that unless there is some sign of compromise there will be many more funerals and much much more grief.
>
> Emeria and Darda need to be at peace. They need to enter into a new relationship with each other, and when they do that I am sure that the trade boycott against the two countries will be lifted. ❞

a I want to _____ this dispute agreeably.

b If the cease-fire _____ we can start preparing for peace _____.

c The _____ territory belongs to us. We will never _____ it.

d I'm sure that sanctions will be _____ now that the government has abandoned its repressive policies.

e If we can stop the fighting there is a chance that our country can _____ into a new relationship with yours.

ACTIVATE

15 In groups choose *either* Emeria *or* Darda (you must not look at the other delegation's information) and then look at the delegation information for your choice below. Using words and phrases from this unit write a short statement which you will make at the beginning of the peace negotiations. It should express your desire for peace and your position on the territorial dispute between your countries.

DARDAN DELEGATION

❑ You want peace because you simply can't afford the war, and it has had a disastrous effect on your bean and rice crops, so now you are not exporting anything. There is a threat of economic sanctions. Anyway the Emerians appear to be winning.

❑ You want to make sure that the Emerians admit their fault in invading your country. They must withdraw their troops right back behind their own borders.

❑ If they do this you will undertake not to provoke any more incidents at the border between your two countries. You might (if they agree to your other demands) agree to improve your human rights behaviour.

EMERIAN DELEGATION

❑ After Darda kept provoking you by attacking your border guards you launched a full-scale invasion. You are now twenty miles inside Dardan territory.

❑ You want to stop the war because it's unpopular, because of the problems with the EPLA at home, and because the World Bank is threatening to withdraw foreign aid if you don't.

❑ You are prepared to give up most of the land you gained in exchange for peace guarantees from Darda. But you do want to keep a two-mile strip (of that twenty miles) for your own security. And they must admit that they started it.

FOCUS WORDS

agree to	disputed	invade	riot
ambassador	embassy	invasion	sanctions
autonomy	emperor	king	secretary of
battle	empire	lift	state (USA)
bilateral	export (v)	ministry	secretary
border	foreign aid	multilateral	general
break down	foreign	official	sign
break off	minister	residence	state
cease-fire	foreign	palace	talks
civil-war	secretary	parliament	territory
community	(GB)	political	terrorist
consul	freedom	prisoner	torture
Consulate	fighter	president	trade
continent	guerrilla	prime minister	imbalance
country	(war)	protest (n)	treaty
coup	head of state	province	trilateral
declare (war)	hemisphere	queen	unilateral
demonstration	hold	rebel	United
diplomat	hostage	rebellion	Nations
diplomatic	human rights	region	war
relations	import (v)	restore	
dispute (settle	impose	revolution	
a dispute)	independence	revolutionary	

WORD CHECK

Refer to Focus Words only.

1 Which of the nouns (about things, not about people) refer to 'good' things?
   Which refer to 'bad' things? Which are neutral?
   Talk to someone else. Do they agree with your categorizations?
2 Construct sentences which include:
   a one noun (phrase) which describes a person.
   b one verb (phrase).
   c one noun (phrase) which describes a place.
3 Which of the words from the list do you find:
   a easiest to pronounce?
   b most difficult to pronounce?
4 Which words in the list:
   a are like words in your language and mean more or less the same thing?
   b are like words in your language, but mean something different?

8 | *Crime, the law and the police*

1 Guess the answers to these questions on the basis of what you know about crime and what you know or have heard about Britain.

a What percentage of all crime in Britain is against people?
b What age group in Britain are the most frequent victims of crime; the very young, the young or the very old?
c Which of the following countries have the highest crime rates? Put them in order.

> Britain   Canada   Finland   Germany   Holland   Northern
>   Ireland   Switzerland   United States

d What percentage of people commit crimes in Britain every year?

2 Read this text about crime in Britain. Does it match your conclusions from exercise 1? What are the differences?

The next twenty-four hours will see police in Britain record two murders, ten rapes, 50 sexual assaults, 50 assaults causing grievous bodily harm, 113 muggings and other robberies, 2,800 burglaries, and 1,200 car thefts. Yet these figures – part of an annual total of about five million recorded crimes – represent only the tip of an iceberg. And that is not all. Each of the three quarters of this year for which figures have already been published showed a rise of about 14 per cent on the same period 12 months before. This is a big disappointment for policymakers, because in the last two years the recorded crime rate actually fell.

The public's understanding of crime is not impressive, however. A recent survey found that two-thirds of the population believe that 50 per cent of crimes are violent offences against the person. The true figure is 6 per cent. Small wonder, perhaps, that a government committee claimed fear of crime to be as great a problem as crime itself.

The elderly, for example, fear crime the most, especially violent crime, although they are the least likely to become victims (The most dangerous age of all is under one year old with 28 homicide victims per million babies. People of 70 are far less likely to be murder victims than any adult group, with only eight victims per million. Only children aged 5-15 are safer.)

According to an international survey published last year, Britain's crime rate is lower than the European average and lower than that of Holland, Germany, Canada and Australia. About 18 per cent of Britons were victims of crime last year. In Canada 28 per cent had experienced a crime, in Holland 26 per cent and in Germany 22 per cent. At the other end of the scale Switzerland (15.6 per cent) and Finland (15.9 per cent) had low overall victim rates. But safest of all was Northern Ireland: there only 15 per cent of the population experienced a crime.

The US appeared to live up to its reputation for lawlessness overall, with 28.8 per cent of the population having been a victim of a crime. America's murder rate makes ours seem infinitesimal. Nearly twice as many murders (1,051) were committed in the city of New York in the first six months of last year as in England and Wales (627).

But nobody in Britain is complacent. A computer study of every person born in a certain month in 1953 revealed that by the age of 30, one in three men had been convicted of a crime. One in 16 had been in prison. One in eight born in 1953 who had been convicted of an offence had commited a crime of violence by the age of 20. For those born in 1963, this proportion had risen to one in five.

MEANING

> murder   rape
> sexual assault
> assault causing grievous
> bodily harm   mugging
> robbery   burglary   car theft
> homicide

3 a Put these words and phrases from the text in the correct box.

Crimes against people	Crimes involving things or property

b Add these crimes to the boxes.

| arson   blackmail   child abuse   embezzlement   kidnap |
| fraud   pickpocketing   shoplifting   stealing |

ACTIVATE

4 List the crimes in order of which should get the greatest punishment. For example, should all murderers be punished in the same way? What would make a difference to the punishment?

MEANING

SENSE RELATIONS

5 a Read the sentences and then complete the chart by ticking the objects that go with the verbs.

He *stole* her briefcase from her car.
We have a video of the accused *robbing* a bank.
I was *mugged* in broad daylight.
The *burglary* took place some time in the night.

	the bank	a house	a warehouse	a watch	an old lady	a car	the bank manager
steal							
rob							
break into							
burgle							
mug							

b Which of these words has the connotation of violence?

MEANING

SENSE RELATIONS

6 Complete the sentences with the correct form of the word in brackets.

a Nobody at the company realised that he had been (embezzle) _____ money until someone noticed some errors in the books.
b The (rape) _____ admitted that he had spoken to the woman but denied that he had (rape) _____ her.
c It is difficult to protect children from (abuse) _____ who are members of their own family.
d The (blackmail) _____ was caught when someone recognised her handwriting.
e Armed (robbery) _____ is increasingly common, with criminals using shotguns and other weapons.

f The (mug) _____ came up to her in the street and produced a knife.

g The (murder) _____ of women tend to be their husbands (48%) whereas only 10 per cent of men (murder) _____ by their wives.

h The (theft) _____ got into the gallery at night and took three Picassos.

i The (assault) _____ was vicious and the victim needed 56 stitches.

j The (arson) _____ who set fire to Anne Hathaway's cottage did it because he had had a row with his girlfriend.

MEANING IN CONTEXT

7 Read the extracts and find words or phrases which mean:

a people who saw the crime/something
b seized with the power of the law
c nasty and cruel
d search
e tested for the amount of alcohol
f less important and serious
g someone who is thought to have done it
h information that may help police discover something
i arrested for going too fast
j someone who breaks the law frequently
k signs, indications
l officials in the police force (list them in order of seniority)

BICYCLE COP SPEAKS OUT

The woman in charge of investigating bicycle thefts in the city has become impatient with the criminals who make her life difficult. 'This kind of petty crime is really annoying,' says Constable Merrington. 'It inconveniences a lot of people

MAN HELD IN PUB ROBBERY

The police have arrested a man in connection with the 'Three Horseshoes' pub robbery. 'There were a number of clues which led us to the suspect,' said Chief Inspector Locke, in charge of the operation. 'The man we have arrested is an habitual offender and we are confident that he is the man we were looking for.'

DOC STOPPED BY CITY POLICE

Mary Edwards, a surgeon at the City's biggest hospital, was booked for speeding and then breathalysed, a police spokesperson said last night.

POLICE BAFFLED IN HILLSIDE KILLING

The police still have no leads in their hunt for the killer of the young hitchhiker whose body was found three days ago at the foot of Sunbury Hill.
'We are appealing for witnesses to come forward,' said Superintendent Jones, 'this was a particularly brutal murder and

WORD USE

COLLOCATIONS

8 Match the adjectives in column A with the nouns in column B.

A	B
vicious	murder
brutal	criminal
cold-blooded	offender
common	crime
habitual	
petty	

ACTIVATE

9 Choose one of the following sentences and write a newspaper article about it using as many words as possible from exercises 1 to 8.

a 'Despite our familiarity with this kind of thing, we were sickened,' said a police spokesperson.

b He was banned from driving for two years and fined £1,000.

c The victim is recovering in hospital.

d They got away with £50,000 in used notes.

e The missing paintings were described by the director of the museum as 'priceless'.

WORD USE

METAPHOR AND IDIOM

10 Put the words from the box in the blanks.

murder   robbery   stole

a I could _____ a steak.

b He screamed *blue* _____ when I told him.

c Honestly, because he's so charming he can *get away with* _____

d *It was absolute* _____ trying to push the car.

e You must be joking! I'm not going to pay that much for it. It's *daylight* _____ .

f She _____ *the show*. The rest of us were virtually ignored.

What do the phrases in italics mean? Can you think of other contexts where they might be used?

MEANING

11 a Look at the chart on this page and check the meaning of the words in *italics*.

b Fill in the blanks in the chart with the following words.

fined   found   life   lose   probation   plead *reduced   sentence   win*

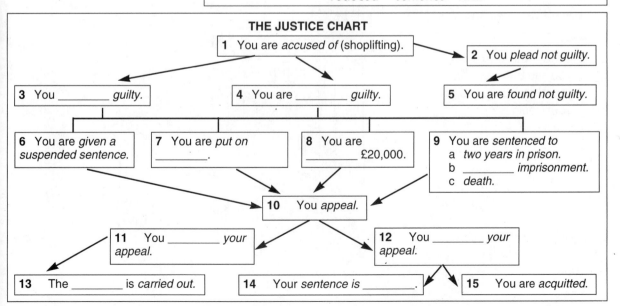

THE JUSTICE CHART

1 You are *accused of* (shoplifting).

2 You *plead not guilty.*

3 You _____ *guilty.*

4 You are _____ *guilty.*

5 You are *found not guilty.*

6 You are *given a suspended sentence.*

7 You are *put on* _____ .

8 You are _____ £20,000.

9 You are *sentenced to*
a *two years in prison.*
b _____ *imprisonment.*
c *death.*

10 You *appeal.*

11 You _____ *your appeal.*

12 You _____ *your appeal.*

13 The _____ is *carried out.*

14 Your *sentence is* _____ .

15 You are *acquitted.*

WORD GRAMMAR
VERB COMPLEMENTATION

12 Put the right preposition after each verb.

He

a confessed _____

b was accused _____

c was charged _____

d was convicted _____

e was found guilty _____ } shoplifting.

f was sentenced _____

g was booked _____

h was arrested _____

i was suspected _____

13 a Look at the picture of a trial in progress. Match the words with the numbers.

> judge   jury   the accused
> defending counsel   witness
> police officer   witness box

b What differences can you see between this courtroom and one in your country?

14 Complete these courtroom sentences with words from exercises 11 to 13.

a I am _____ you with attempted murder.
b Call the first _____.
c Members of the _____; how do you find the accused? _____ or not guilty.
d The _____ of this court is that you are guilty and I therefore _____ you to life imprisonment.
e I want to _____ against my sentence.

ACTIVATE

15 Read the following information and then role-play the trial according to the details given.

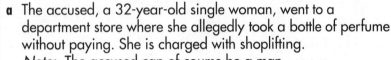

a The accused, a 32-year-old single woman, went to a department store where she allegedly took a bottle of perfume without paying. She is charged with shoplifting.
Note: The accused can of course be a man.

b Choose one of the roles below and then look at your role card. It is important that you do not look at anyone else's card.
○ the judge (see page 84)
○ the defending counsel (see page 84)
○ the prosecuting counsel (see page 84)
○ the accused (see page 84)
○ the store detective (see page 84)
○ the character witness (see page 84)
○ the jury (12 people): it is your job to listen to the evidence and decide whether the accused is guilty or not.

c The procedure at a trial is as follows:
1 The prosecuting counsel makes a speech saying why the accused is guilty.
2 The defence counsel makes a speech saying why the accused is innocent, or at least why the prosecution cannot prove the accused's guilt.
3 The prosecuting counsel puts his or her witness(es) in the witness stand and gets them to tell the court what they know.
4 The defending counsel tries to find fault with what the witness(es) has said.
5 The procedure is reversed: now the defending counsel puts a witness in the stand.
6 The defending counsel makes a closing speech to the jury saying why they should acquit the accused.
7 The prosecuting attorney makes a speech saying why the jury should find the accused guilty.
8 The jury make their decision.
9 The judge passes sentence or sets the accused free.

3

7

Store detective

❏ You saw the accused put a bottle of perfume into her bag. She then paid for some other goods before walking out into the street. When you stopped her outside the store she said "I didn't realise the store had detectives otherwise I would never have done it."

The Accused

❏ You were shopping in a department store. You bought a number of toilet articles and, without thinking, you put a bottle of perfume into your bag and forgot about it. After leaving the shop you were stopped by the store detective. You said to him, "I didn't realise that I had put the perfume in my bag. I would never have done it on purpose."

Barrister: defence counsel

❏ It is your job to try and pick holes in the witness's evidence. You will put your client in the witness box and try to get her to prove her innocence.

Barrister: prosecuting counsel

❏ It is your job to get your witness to give evidence that will convince the jury that the accused is guilty. You will also have a chance to pick holes in the evidence of the accused and the character witness. You might try to find out how and where the character witness met the accused.

Character witness

❏ You say that you have known the witness for long time and that she is a respected member of the community. You do not want the court to find out that you actually met the accused in a police station where you were being charged with being drunk and disorderly.

Judge

❏ It is you job to make sure the trail runs smoothly and fairly. Don't let things get out of hand. When all the evidence has been heard ask the jury to decide if the accused is guilty or not. If the accused is found guilty (and only if she is found guilty) you can tell the court that she has already been found guilty of three other shoplifting charges. This will help you to decide what kind of sentence to give her.

16 Write a report of the trial for your local newspaper.

FOCUS WORDS

accúse (v)	confess (v)	law	robbery
(the) accused	constable	lose (your	sentence (v)
appeal (n)	counsel	appeal)	sentence (n)
appeal (v)	crime	mug	sexual assault
arrest (v)	criminal	mugger	shoplifting
arson	death	mugging	steal
arsonist	sentence	murder (n)	stealing
blackmail	defending	murder (v)	store detective
blackmailer	counsel	murderer	superintendent
book (v)	embezzle	offender	suspect (n)
break into	embezzlement	pickpocketing	suspect (v)
breathalyse	fine (v)	plead	suspended
brutal	fraud	probation	theft
burglary	guilty	prosecuting	thief
burgle	habitual	counsel	vicious
charge (v)	homicide	rape	win (your
chief inspector	judge	rapist	appeal)
child abuse	jury	rob	witness
common	kidnap	robber	witness box

FOCUS PHRASES

be absolute murder	get away with murder
be daylight robbery	scream blue murder
cause grievous bodily harm	steal the show
I could murder a (steak)	

WORD CHECK

Refer to Focus Words and Focus Phrases only.

1 In groups, play the 'Crime Chain' where you speak in turns, e.g.

   A: I'm Sandro and I've never robbed a bank.

   B: Sandro's never robbed a bank. My name's Maria. I've never been charged with shoplifting.

   C: Sandro's never robbed a bank. Maria's never been charged with shoplifting. I'm Margherita . . .

   Don't use the same crime more than once in any one round. If someone can't think of a new crime or makes a mistake, they drop out and a new round starts.

2 Write a short paragraph (maximum four sentences) about a criminal trial. Use as many Focus Words as you possibly can!

3 Use at least two Focus Phrases to talk about people that you know or know about.

4 Which ten words on the list are going to be most useful to you, do you think?

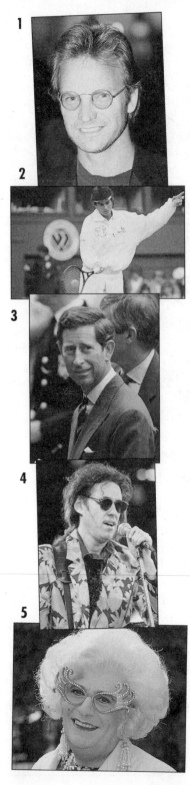

1 Read the text and complete the following tasks.

a Put these words in the blanks. Use them once unless otherwise indicated.

as   at   by   in (2)   off   on   out of   outside   through

b Decide which of these people wrote this passage.

As for the rest, I gradually switched A) _____. Arithmetic, algebra and geometry I did so well B) _____ that my total mark in three exams one year was three per cent. Maths could be made tolerable only C) _____ boring holes in the master's chalk with the point of a compass, then packing the hole with the heads of matches and filling the end with chalkdust so that the chalk would explode like a firework as he wrote his obscure theorems D) _____ the blackboard. German was memorable only for the odd little master who cycled to work and parked his bike E) _____ the classroom window. During the time it took him to walk along the outside of the building to the entrance and then back along the corridor to the classroom the trick was to haul his bike F) _____ the window, take it to pieces and then lay the bits on his desk. We did it once too often and he stormed G) _____ the classroom to fetch the Dean, but by the time the two masters returned it had been reassembled and put back through the window H) _____ its original parking place. History I could have enjoyed but they never told you any of the interesting stuff: that Napoleon was I) _____ agony the night before Waterloo and got no sleep because he had to lie on his stomach; or that Wellington had a reputation J) _____ a womanizer. Instead it was all: Battle of Austerlitz 1805, Battle of Waterloo 1815, Congress of Aix-la-Chapelle 1818. I picked up my schoolbag at night but it would never be opened until it returned to the classroom the next day.

c Find three things about the writer's schooldays that were different from your own experience.

2 Complete these tasks.

a Either explain the trick with the chalk, or the trick with the master's bike

b What is Waterloo, when was it and who took part?

c List three important dates that pupils in your country always learn.

USING DICTIONARIES

DEFINITIONS

3 a Using a dictionary, decide which of the words in the box can go in which sections of the chart. You can put words in more than one column.

> kindergarten   high school   college   playgroup
> nursery school   comprehensive   public school
> preparatory school   sixth form   reception class
> evening classes   polytechnic   technical college   university
> master   mistress   teacher   lecturer   professor   tutor
> head teacher   headmaster   headmistress   deputy head
> student   pupil   graduate   postgraduate   doctorate
> playground   classroom   lecture theatre

Pre-school Education (0–5)	
Primary Education (5–11)	
Secondary Education (11–16+)	
Further Education	
Higher Education	
Adult Education	

b Some of the words in the box refer to private education in Britain rather than state education. Which are they?

4 In Britain there are first degrees (where you are called a Bachelor of . . .), postgraduate degrees (where you are called a Master of . . . or Doctor of Philosophy) and medical degrees. What do you think the following letters mean?

a BSc   **d** MD   **g** MPhil
b BEd   **e** BA   **h** PhD
c MSc   **f** MA

5

> Recent reports have shown that in Britain some (but not all) private schools have better exam results than state schools, and girls sometimes do better academically at single-sex schools than at co-educational schools. For boys there is no difference.

On the basis of the above information and your own opinions, which square of the chart below would you choose for your child? Why?

	Private	State
Single-sex		
Co-educational		

ACTIVATE

6 Describe the education of some or all of the following people.

a yourself
b your mother or father
c a rock and/or movie star
d a famous historical figure from your country

Say what kind of educational establishment(s) you/they went to and how you/they got on there.

MEANING

7 a Read the conversation and put the children's names into the correct columns.

HEADTEACHER: How's your class getting on, Miss Keane?
MISS KEANE: Well, how can I put it? Samantha's a very *slow learner*, Tom's permanently *disruptive*, Jemma's *illiterate*, Sarah never *pays attention*, Jeffrey has *numeracy problems*, Sasha goes to the *special needs* teacher because she's too *brainy*, Dulal's *mind keeps wandering*, Stella is *conscientious* but seems to have *learning difficulties*, Bill's so *absent-minded* he forgets his own name, Mary's *dyslexic*, and the Mishram sisters (Penny and Jasmin) seem to have no concept of *discipline* at all. Otherwise the class is fine!

Behaviour problems	Learning problems

b Say in your own words what Miss Keane thinks the problem is with each pupil.

8 a Decide where the following words describing clever and not so clever people should go on the grid below.

> clever   bright   intelligent   brainy   a genius   brilliant
> gifted   thick   silly   idiotic   stupid   daft   dim   moronic
> absent-minded

very clever

X brainy

formal English ———————————————— informal English

very unintelligent

b Can you make the adjectives into nouns by adding appropriate suffixes?

9   Explain the pun in the following cartoon.

ACTIVATE

10 a How would your teachers have described you if they had wanted to be:

    i negative?
    ii positive?

  b Describe a fellow pupil from your early school years who had either behaviour or learning problems.

WORD USE

COLLOCATIONS

11 a Which verbs go with which nouns? Tick the boxes.

	test	exam	degree	distinction	school	university
cram for						
get						
get into						
get a place at						
expel from						
exclude from						
send down from						
take						
pass						
fail						
resit						

b What can you put between the verbs and the nouns? *The, a* or nothing?

12 Use expressions from exercise 11 to complete these exchanges.

a How well did you do in the test?
Oh, I'm afraid I _____ it. I'm going to have to do it again.
b You look happy!
Yes, I've just _____ Cambridge University.
c Why were you _____ university?
Because I cheated in the final exams.
d Have you got your exam results yet?
Yes, and I did better than I thought. I _____

WORD FORMATION
ADJECTIVES AND NOUNS

13 What do you call the following?

a an education at university
  a _____ education

b the room where the exam is held
  the _____ room

c a test of a new car
  a _____ run

d a tie from the school
  the _____ tie

e the team from the school
  the _____ team

f a situation in which you are tested emotionally
  a _____ situation

What does this tell you about adjectives and nouns?

ACTIVATE

14 a Which is the worst of these activites, in your opinion?
  i *playing truant*
  ii being the *teacher's pet*
  iii being *bullied*

b Now discuss the following:
  i What is the best memory you have from your schooldays?
  ii What is the worst?
  iii What subjects were you best at?
  iv What subjects were you worst at?

15 Is school a good experience or a bad experience according to these two passages? Do you agree with either or both of them.

In school we are taught that valuable learning is the result of attendance; that the value of learning increases with the amount of input; and, finally, that this value can be measured and documented by grades and certificates.

  In fact, learning is the human activity which least needs manipulation by others. Most learning is not the result of instruction. It is rather the result of unhampered participation in a meaningful setting.

Ivan Illich *Deschooling Society*

We don't need no education
We don't need no thought control
No dark sarcasm in the classroom
Teacher leave them kids alone
Hey teacher leave them kids alone.

Pink Floyd *Another Brick in the Wall*

FOCUS WORDS

absent-minded	education	difficulties	pupil
adult education	evening class	lecture	reception class
brainy	exam	lecturer	resit
bright	fail	lecture theatre	school
brilliant	first degree	master	secondary school
bully (v)	further education	mistress	silly
class	genius	moronic	single-sex school
classroom	get into (university)	numeracy	sixth form
clever	get a place at	nursery school	slow learner
co-educational	gifted	pass	special needs
college	graduate	pay attention	state school
comprehensive school	headmaster	play truant	student
daft	headmistress	playground	stupid
degree	head teacher	playgroup	teacher
distinction	higher education	polytechnic	teacher's pet
dim	high school	postgraduate	technical college
discipline	idiotic	preparatory school	test
disruptive	illiterate	primary school	thick
doctorate	intelligent	private school	tutor
dyslexic	kindergarten	professor	university
	learning	public school	

FOCUS PHRASES

be sent down from university   (his) mind keeps wandering

cram for an exam

WORD CHECK

Refer to Focus Words and Focus Phrases only.

1 How many adjectives can you find? Divide them into 'good' adjectives, 'bad' adjectives, and 'neutral' adjectives according to your own opinion. Show your list to someone else. Do they agree with your categorizations?

2 Use at least two of the Focus Phrases to describe an experience in your own education.

3 **a** Find all the nouns that refer to people who teach. Find all the nouns that describe where they might teach.

  b Have a balloon debate. All of the people who teach are in a balloon which is losing air and can only support the weight of one person. Discuss who should be thrown out of the balloon, and who should survive.

4 How many words can you find with these stress patterns:

  a ▪▪■▪ ?

USING DICTIONARIES 1 **a** What do the following words mean?

DEFINITIONS

> belief   Christian   creed   Hindus   holy   Islam   Muslims
> mosque   temple

b Use them to fill the blanks in the following passage.

He had always liked this xxxxx. It was gracious and the arrangement pleased him. A mosque by winning his approval let loose his imagination. The xxxxx of another Hindu, xxxxx or Greek, would have bored him and failed to awaken his sense of beauty. Here was xxxxx, his own country, more than a faith, more than a battle-cry, more, much more . . . Islam with an attitude towards life both exquisite and durable, where his body and his thoughts found their home.

His seat was the low wall that bounded the courtyard on the left. The ground fell away beneath him towards the city, visible as a blur of trees, and in the stillness he heard many small sounds. On the right, over in the club, the English community contributed an amateur orchestra. Elsewhere some xxxxx were drumming and others were bewailing a corpse. There were owls, the Punjab mail . . . and flowers smelt deliciously in the station master's garden. But the mosque – that alone signified, and he returned to it from the complex appeal of the night, and decked it with meanings the builder had never intended. As he did so one of the pillars on the mosque seemed to quiver. It swayed in the gloom and detached itself. xxxxx in ghosts ran in his blood, but he sat firm. Another pillar moved, a third, and then an English woman stepped out into the moonlight. Suddenly he was furiously angry and shouted: 'Madam! Madam! Madam!'

'Oh! Oh!' the woman gasped.

'Madam, this is a mosque, you have no right here at all; you should have taken off your shoes; this is a

xxxxx place for xxxxx .'

'I have taken them off.'

'You have?'

'I left them at the entrance.'

'Then I ask your pardon.'

Still startled, the woman moved out. He called after her, 'I am truly sorry for speaking.'

'Yes, I was right, was I not? If I remove my shoes, I am allowed?'

'Of course, but so few ladies take the trouble, especially if thinking no one is there to see.'

'That makes no difference. God is here.'

Victor Banerjee and Peggy Ashcroft in the film of A Passage to India

2 Answer these questions.

a What do you think the woman meant by saying, 'That makes no difference. God is here'?

b The woman had to take off her shoes to go into the mosque. Are there any other customs to do with dress or physical preparations in your religion?

c What adjectives would you use to describe your feelings when you are in a religious building in your country?

MEANING

3 a Can you match the words with the pictures?

> cathedral   church   shrine   temple   synagogue   chapel
> monastery   mosque

1 Place: _____

Religion: _____

2 Place: _____

Religion: _____

3 Place: _____

Religion: _____

4 Place: _____

Religion: _____

5 Place: _____

Religion: _____

6 Place: _____

Religion: _____

7 Place: _____

Religion: _____

8 Place: _____

Religion: _____

b Which of these religions are practised in the places in the pictures? There may be more than one answer.

> *Christianity   Hinduism   Islam   Judaism   Buddhism
> Shintoism*

4 a Do you know any other religions which are not included in the list on the previous page, or in the extract in exercise 1?
  b Do you know which of the religions believes in :
   i reincarnation?
   ii resurrection?
  c In which religious could you find these people?

pope	rabbi	imam	priest	monk	gurunun

  d What are the differences in status between these Christian officials?

archbishop	cardinal	vicar	minister	bishop	priest	pope

WORD USE

COLLOCATIONS

5 a Match the verbs in Box A with their complements in Box B.

A	B
sing	a sin
chant	in prayer
say	a hymn
kneel	a prayer
preach	a sermon
confess	the holy book
read from	

  b Which of the following are likely to perform the actions in A and B?
   i *the priest*
   ii *the choir*
   iii *the worshippers*

ACTIVATE

6 Describe a religious building that you know or have seen. What happens there? What is the sequence of events in a normal gathering there?

WORD USE

RELATED MEANINGS

7 Read these childrens' descriptions of Christianity and then answer the questions which follow.

> If you live a good life, and obey God's commandments you will go to heaven when you die, but if you sin and obey the devil you will go to hell. Heaven is full of angels, but hell is full of demons.

> If you've been bad but confess your sins and truly repent, your sins can be forgiven and you can still go to heaven.

> Saints are good people who performed miracles. (like raising people from the dead) But martyrs are even better. They died for their religious beliefs.

> Some christian people decide to live a completely religious life and go and live in monastries. These monks or nuns spend their time in prayer or helping the sick or poor. Some of them never speak!

> My dad's a missionary. He keeps going away and converting people.

> My mum says Britain is a secular society 'cos not many people go to church. But my teacher says we're a Christian country.

> I want to be a pilgrim so I can go on a long journey to visit a saint's shrine.

> I wish I was a prophet. Then I'd know who was going to win the match!

What is the difference between the following pairs of words?

a *heaven* and *hell* **e** an *angel* and a *demon*
b *repentance* and *forgiveness* **f** a *saint* and a *martyr*
c a *monk* and a *nun* **g** *secular* and *religious*
d a *pilgrim* and a *prophet* **h** a *missionary* and a *pilgrim*

WORD USE

METAPHOR AND IDIOM

8 Complete these sentences with words from exercise 6. Some words may be used more than once.

a She knew that she must decide whether she had the courage to be a _____ and die for her faith.

b I wouldn't like to be a _____, especially if I had to stay silent with all the other men.

c I watched all the _____ making their way to the shrine. They had been travelling for more than two weeks and they were very tired but very happy.

d If you want my _____ for the terrible things you have done you must realise your mistakes. Unless I can see genuine signs of _____ I will not have you back into this house.

e The problem with _____ societies is that they are only interested in material success, according to one priest.

f She stared at the paintings of _____ with their sharp teeth and cruel eyes. They made her feel frightened.

g If you live a good life you will definitely go to _____ according to a Christian friend of mine. But I fear that if I go anywhere it will be to _____.

ACTIVATE

9 Work in pairs. You are writing a book about religions of the world. Interview a representative of a religious faith. Ask the following questions:

a whether there is an after-life.
b what happens if you behave well.
c what happens if you behave badly.
d what kind of holy people are there.
e how strong the religion is today.

WORD FORMATION
NOUNS AND ADJECTIVES

10 What is the adjective from each of these nouns? How many different endings are there?

Noun	Adjective
heaven	heavenly
sin	
devil	
angel	
faith	
demon	
saint	
prophet	

WORD USE
COLLOCATIONS

11 Which of the adjectives in exercise 10 can go with these words or phrases?

a _____ thoughts
b _____ behaviour
c _____ child
d _____ day

e _____ friend
f _____ plot
g _____ acts
h _____ plan

ACTIVATE

12 Make the titles of imaginary books and films by adding *the* to the collocations in exercise 11; e.g. 'The Angelic Child.' Work in teams. Team A gives Team B a description of a 'book' or 'film'. Team B has to guess what the title is.

Example:
TEAM A: This film is about a lovely little girl, who is always helping people, and spreading happiness.
TEAM B: Is it 'The Angelic Child'?
TEAM A: Yes, it is.

WORD USE

METAPHOR AND IDIOM

13 Match the phrases in *italics* in the picture with the meanings below.

a This may surprise you, but . . .
b it suddenly started to rain heavily
c living as man and wife, without being married
d That is very surprising.
e committed adultery
f doesn't realize what real life involves
g trying to convince someone who is already convinced
h without fail, always
i honestly, believing it was all right
j the place where I feel I really belong

1 From the moment they married she was *unfaithful* to him but he never found out.

2 Look, I sold you the car *in good faith*. It's not my fault if it's fallen apart.

3 They're *living in sin*, but I suppose that doesn't mean much these days.

4 She does her exercises *religiously* every morning.

5 My father is Australian and my mother is Greek. I suppose you could say that Greece is *my spiritual home*, though I love Australia too, of course!

6 They were about to start the last game when *the heavens opened*, so that was that!

7 *Good heavens!*

8 *Believe it or not*, he has a degree in nuclear physics.

9 He's *living in a land of make-believe*.

10 Why are you telling me? You're just *preaching to the converted!*

ACTIVATE

14 Use at least two of the expressions in a conversation about one of the following:

a two friends
b a sporting event
c an art dealer who sold someone a fake picture

15 Tell a story from your religion or a religion you know about. Use as many words from this unit as possible.

FOCUS WORDS

angel	devil	monastery	saint
angelic	devilish	monk	saintly
archbishop	faithful	Muslim	say (a prayer)
belief	forgiveness	mosque	secular
bishop	heaven	nun	sermon
Buddhism	heavenly	pilgrim	shaman
cardinal	hell	pope	Shintoism
cathedral	Hinduism	prayer	shrine
chapel	Hindu	preach	sin
choir	holy	priest	sinful
Christian	hymn	prophet	synagogue
Christianity	imam	prophetic	temple
church	Islam	rabbi	unfaithful (to
confess	Judaism	reincarnation	someone)
creed	martyr	religious	vicar
demon	minister	repentance	worshipper
demonic	missionary	resurrection	

FOCUS PHRASES

believe it or not
do something religiously
Good heavens!
in good faith
land of make-believe
live in sin
preach to the converted
spiritual home
the heavens open(ed)

WORD CHECK

Refer to Focus Words and Focus Phrases only.

1 *-ly* is an interesting ending! Which words from the list add *-ly*:
   a to become adjectives?
   b to become adverbs?
2 Find the nouns which describe people. How many of them are used to refer to men and women? How many of them are only used to talk about men?
3 Work with a partner to write a short conversation in which you use all the Focus Phrases!
4 Which ten words on the list do you think will be most useful to you in the future?

11 | *Work and employment*

1 a What are the most important factors for you in choosing or keeping a job? Put the following factors in order of importance and then compare the order you have chosen with a partner's.

   i good salary or wages
   ii interesting and varied work, not boring and monotonous
  iii work which is useful to society
  iv good working conditions
   v flexible hours
  vi opportunities to meet people
  vii friendly and considerate management and colleagues
 viii opportunities to travel
  ix long holidays
   x another factor – what?

b In your opinion, which jobs or professions fit your criteria? Does the job that you have or that you hope to have fit them?

MEANING

RELATED MEANINGS

2 Look at these people at work. What jobs are they doing? If you're not sure, look at the list of Focus Words on page 108.

a

b

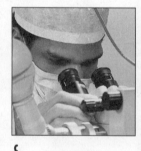
c

d

e

f

g

MEANING

CONNOTATION

3 Do their jobs fit the criteria that you have selected above? Put them in order on the lines below:

VERY BORING ⟵——————⟶ VERY INTERESTING

VERY BADLY-PAID ⟵——————⟶ VERY WELL-PAID

MEANING

RELATED MEANINGS

4 a What would you call someone who:
  i receives and pays out money in a bank?
  ii is in charge of a whole company?
  iii collects rubbish from houses?
  iv checks people's eyesight?
  v teaches at a college or university?
  vi repairs pipes, taps, etc in homes and buildings?
  vii performs tricks for audiences?
  viii does physical work involved in building, repairing roads, etc.?
  ix cleans the streets?
  x flies a plane?
  xi shows films at a cinema?
  xii checks tickets on a train?
  xiii travels round selling things?

b Which of these jobs would you most like to do? Which would you least like to do?

MEANING

SENSE RELATIONS

5 All of the above are *occupations*. But which of them can be called *professions* and which can be called *jobs*? What is the difference between a job and a profession? Put the words from exercise 4 into the appropriate box below.

Jobs	Professions

6 What is the difference between the following pairs of words?

a a *career* and a *profession*
b a *vocation* and a *job*
c a *certificate* and a *qualification*
d *skills* and *experience*

WORD USE

COLLOCATION

7 Which of these verbs can be followed by the noun *work*? Which words from exercise 6 can follow each of them?

get   find   have   follow   lose   look for

WORD FORMATION

NOUNS AND VERBS

8 a Complete the table with the appropriate verbs.

Noun	Verb
application dismissal increase interview offer promotion resignation rejection reprimand rise retirement shortlist	apply for

b Now use the verbs to fill the blanks in this passage.

Colin was eighteen. He had left school at sixteen and done two years' training in catering. There were quite a few jobs being advertised in the newspaper, and he decided to (a)_____ three of them. One of his applications was (b)_____, but the two other companies wrote back to say that he had been (c)_____, along with two other candidates. He was (d)_____ by the owner and manager of one of the companies. They asked him some tricky questions and he didn't think he did too well, but he felt that the interview for the other job went well. He was very surprised, then, that he was (e)_____ both jobs. He accepted the one with the higher salary, of course!

   Colin got on fine at first. After only three months, his salary was (f)_____ by ten per cent, and after six months he was (g)_____ to Head Chef. But then things started to go wrong. He didn't get on with the new manager and sometimes didn't accept the menus that she suggested. After a while, she called him into her office and (h)_____ him for disobeying her orders. She warned him that if his attitude continued he would be (i)_____. In the end Colin felt so unhappy at work that he decided to leave his job. He (j)_____ on 30 June and left at the end of July, just in time to take a summer holiday.

MEANING IN CONTEXT

9 Look at the charts below and on the next page. Put the nouns from exercise 8 and from the box below in the appropriate places in the stories about Angela, Ben and Sheila.

> part-time job   temporary job   contract   pension
> job description   job centre   redundancy
> Curriculum Vitae (CV)   unemployment benefit (dole)

ANGELA

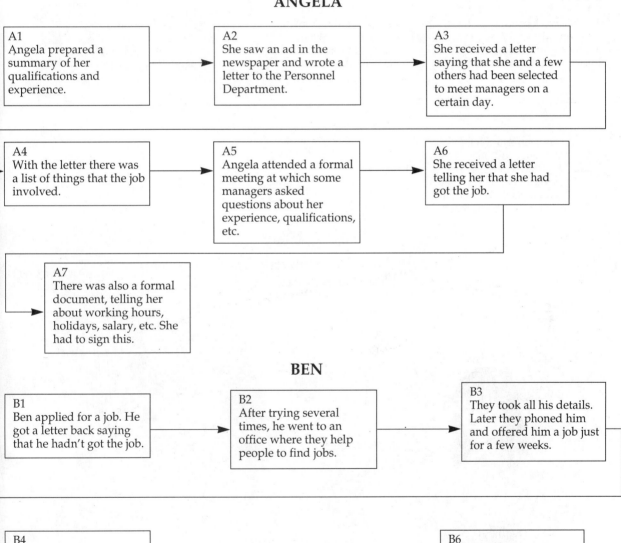

A1
Angela prepared a summary of her qualifications and experience.

A2
She saw an ad in the newspaper and wrote a letter to the Personnel Department.

A3
She received a letter saying that she and a few others had been selected to meet managers on a certain day.

A4
With the letter there was a list of things that the job involved.

A5
Angela attended a formal meeting at which some managers asked questions about her experience, qualifications, etc.

A6
She received a letter telling her that she had got the job.

A7
There was also a formal document, telling her about working hours, holidays, salary, etc. She had to sign this.

BEN

B1
Ben applied for a job. He got a letter back saying that he hadn't got the job.

B2
After trying several times, he went to an office where they help people to find jobs.

B3
They took all his details. Later they phoned him and offered him a job just for a few weeks.

B4
After this job, he got another, but it only involved working for part of the day.

B5
Ben got to the age of 65, the age when employees stop working.

B6
Now he gets money monthly during his old age from the government and from his employers.

SHEILA

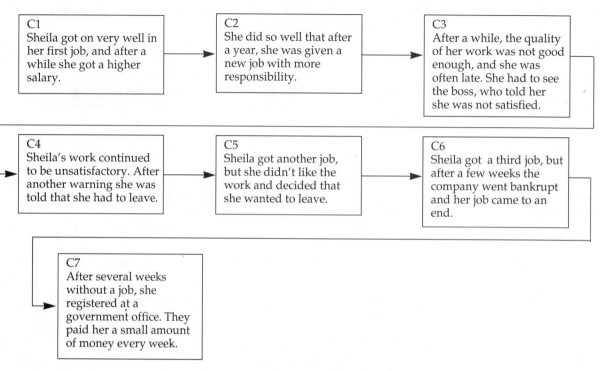

C1
Sheila got on very well in her first job, and after a while she got a higher salary.

C2
She did so well that after a year, she was given a new job with more responsibility.

C3
After a while, the quality of her work was not good enough, and she was often late. She had to see the boss, who told her she was not satisfied.

C4
Sheila's work continued to be unsatisfactory. After another warning she was told that she had to leave.

C5
Sheila got another job, but she didn't like the work and decided that she wanted to leave.

C6
Sheila got a third job, but after a few weeks the company went bankrupt and her job came to an end.

C7
After several weeks without a job, she registered at a government office. They paid her a small amount of money every week.

ACTIVATE

10 Tell the story illustrated below using words from the exercises.

WORD USE

IDIOM AND METAPHOR

11 In the following, words from this unit are used with an idiomatic or extended meaning. Explain the meaning of each.

MEANING IN
CONTEXT

12 Complete the following passage with words and phrases from the box, using a dictionary if necessary.

return to work   shop steward   ballot
on strike   dispute   sacking   pickets
lay off

Industrial action closes factory

Workers at a Romford car factory went (a)_____ yesterday following the (b)_____ of two men for allegedly punching the foreman.

The fight happened after an argument about last Saturday's football match between Millwall and West Ham. The two workers were immediately disciplined by the company and sent home. When he heard this, Don Bailey, the union (c)_____, called a meeting. The decision to take unofficial action was nearly unanimous, and (d)_____ were placed at the factory gates to discourage people from entering the works. The Managing Director said he had no idea how long the (e)_____ would continue, but that if the men didn't (f)_____ very soon, the company would be forced to (g)_____ people (h)_____ indefinitely. The union is holding a secret (i)_____ on Thursday to decide whether to take official strike action.

13 Imagine you are in the following situations. What would you do? What should you do?

a You are driving a large truck containing robots for a factory. You arrive at the gate, but there is a picket there because the workers are on strike following dismissal of 200 people because of automation.

b You are the union shop steward at an insurance company. The Personnel Director calls you into the office to ask for your help with a problem: the company is losing money and needs to lay off ten people.

ACTIVATE

14 Write a brief report to go with one of the headlines below, using vocabulary from this unit.

MANAGING DIRECTOR RESIGNS AS COMPANY CRASHES

WOMAN ACCUSES BOSSES OF DISCRIMINATION AFTER JUNIOR MALE IS PROMOTED

WOMEN SACKED FOR UNOFFICIAL STRIKE ACTION

MAN MADE MANAGING DIRECTOR AFTER 12 YEARS ON DOLE

FOCUS WORDS

apply	lay off	reprimand (v)
application	lecturer	resign
bank clerk	managing director	resignation
bank teller	offer (v)	retire
butcher	offer (n)	retirement
career	optician	rise (n)
certificate	part-time job	roadsweeper
checkout clerk	pension	sack
conjurer	pensioner	sacking
contract (n)	picket (n)	shop steward
curriculum vitae (cv)	pilot (n)	shortlist (n)
dismiss	plumber	shortlist (v)
dismissal	profession	skill
dismissive	professional	surgeon
dispute (n)	projectionist	surveyor
dustman	promote	temporary job
experience (n)	promotion	ticket collector
factory worker	qualification	traffic warden
increase (n)	raise	travelling salesman
increase (v)	receptionist	unemployment
interview (n)	redundant	benefit
interview (v)	redundancy	vocation
job centre	reject	work (n)
job description	rejection	work (v)
labourer	reprimand (n)	

FOCUS PHRASES

be/go on strike
be/go on the dole
have your work cut out
It's a good job . . .
make a good job of
make someone redundant
work out

WORD CHECK

Refer to Focus Words and Focus Phrases only.

1 How many different kinds of job are mentioned? Are there any which you would refuse to do?
2 Find at least three ways of stopping or having to give up working.
3 Write a short letter from a shop steward to a union official in which at least three of the Focus Phrases are used.
4 How many of the words with more than two syllables do not have the main stress on the second syllable? Where do they have it?

12 | *Leisure, sport and entertainment*

1 Read the questionnaire

Leisure Questionnaire

1 How much *real* leisure time (or spare time) do you have:

- ◼ each working day? _____ hours
- ◼ each weekend or national holiday? _____ hours

2 Put your top four of the following leisure time activities in order of preference
(1 = favourite, 2 = next favourite, etc).

☐ participating in some kind of sport or physical exercise – which? _____

☐ watching sport in a stadium or on TV – which sport? _____

☐ playing some other game (e.g. cards) – which?
_____

☐ reading – what? _____

☐ some kind of hobby – what? _____

☐ listening to music at home or in a concert hall – what kind of music? _____

☐ playing a musical instrument – which?
_____

☐ going to the cinema or watching videos

☐ going to the theatre or opera

☐ watching TV – which programmes?
_____

☐ dancing – where? _____

☐ going to cafés, restaurants, etc. with friends

☐ visiting new places

☐ other – what? _____

2 Compare your answers with a partner's. What are the main similarities and differences between the ways in which you like to spend your leisure time?

WORD BUILDING

COMPOUND WORDS

3 What are these people's hobbies called?

Example: John weaves baskets: *basket-weaving*

a Mary arranges flowers for display.

b George collects stamps from different countries.

c Beatrice paints with oil-paints.

d Susan climbs rocks.

e Dave skis on water.

f Robert makes model planes.

USING DICTIONARIES

DEFINITIONS

4 How are these materials and pieces of equipment used? In what hobbies might you use them?

magnifying glass   tripod   needle   rod   easel   album
wetsuit   loom   clay   wool   glue   net

5 What do these people's hobbies involve? Use a dictionary where necessary.

> *train-spotter   pot-holer   angler   gambler   canoeist*

ACTIVATE

6 In your opinion, which of the hobbies in exercises 3, 4 and 5, and which others, are:

a most suitable for old people?
b most suitable for disabled people?
c least suitable for men?
d least suitable for women?
e best for children under ten?
f most satisfying?

7 a Are you artistic? Are any members of your family or any of your friends artistic? In what ways? Use words from the box.

> *play a musical instrument   paint   draw   sing   act   dance*

   b In your experience, do artistic people have a special physical appearance? If so, what do they look like?

8 Put the musical instruments being played by this band in order of loudness (1=loudest, 9=quietist). Which three do you prefer, in what order?

WORD FORMATION
SUFFIXES

9 Complete the table, using words with the endings *-ist, -er, -or,* etc. where necessary.

A person who:	Noun
plays the piano	
plays drums	
plays a violin	
plays a trumpet	
plays football	
plays tennis	
rides a bicycle	
collects stamps	
skis	
jumps from a plane using a parachute	
makes sculptures	
takes photographs	
plays chess	

MEANING
RELATED MEANINGS

10 In which sports do people do the following?

a wear goggles
b ride on boards
c get knocked out
d strike out
e do the crawl
f make pit-stops

11 Which sports are played (and watched) in the following places?

course   stadium   court   pool   ring   track

MEANING
CONNOTATION

12 Which of the adjectives and expressions in the dialogue refer to enthusiasm for a sport or hobby, and which refer to ability? Put the italicized words and expressions in the appropriate box. Then tick, the strongest expressions in each box.

DON: What are you doing this weekend, Sandra? Off to the beach again? You're a *keen* windsurfer, aren't you?

SANDRA: Yes, I am, but this weekend we're going to the opera in London. My friend George is a real opera-*lover*.

DON: An opera-lover? I thought you said he was *mad about* modern jazz.

SANDRA: He's *keen on* all sorts of music . . . and quite a *gifted* pianist too. Are you *musical*, Don?

DON: I listen to a lot of music at home. I'm a bit of a Mozart-*freak*, I suppose. I've been collecting records and compact discs of his major works for the last two years. I play the clarinet a bit. But I'm *no good at* it . . .

SANDRA: And what about sport? You look quite athletic . . .

DON: I used to be an *obsessive* tennis player, but I gave it up when I broke my ankle last year.

SANDRA: Oh, I really *love* tennis . . . George says I'm *a natural*. Shall we have a game sometime?

DON: Well . . . I'm really *rusty*. I'll have to get a bit of practice first . . .

SANDRA: Don't be silly . . . I'm only *a novice*. We'll just have a friendly game.

DON: OK. As long as you promise not to humiliate me . . . I don't trust people who talk about 'friendly games'! . . . I've got to go now: there's an exhibition of paintings by Julie Croft, a friend of mine, opening tonight . . .

SANDRA: Is she *talented*?

DON: I'm no *expert*, but I think her work is brilliant . . . and she's only a Sunday-painter. See you on Monday.

SANDRA: OK. Don't forget to bring your racket. We'll have a game after work . . .

DON: It might rain . . .

Enthusiasm	Ability

ACTIVATE

13 Look at the pictures below. What leisure activities and hobbies do you think these famous characters enjoyed?

Count Dracula

The Mona Lisa

Goliath

Marie Antoinette

FOCUS WORDS

act	flute	painting	stamp-
album	footballer	parachutist	collector
angler	gambler	photographer	strike out
artist	gifted	piano	talented
artistic	glue	pianist	tennis-player
chess player	goggles	pitstop	track
clarinet	guitar	pool	train-spotter
clay	guitarist	pot-holer	tripod
course	keen	ring	trombone
court	knockout	rock-climbing	trumpet
cyclist	loom	rod	trumpeter
dance	magnifying	rusty	violin
design	glass	saxophone	violinist
double bass	model-	sculpture	water-skiing
draw	making	sculptor	wetsuit
drawing	musical	sing	windsurf
drum	needle	sketch	windsurfing
drummer	net	skier	wool
easel	novice	skiing	
expert	obsessive	stadium	
flower-	oil-painting	stamp-	
arranging	painter	collecting	

FOCUS PHRASES

be a natural

be a (Mozart/theatre) freak

be a (Mozart/theatre) lover

be good at

be keen on

be knocked out by

be mad about

be no good at

do the crawl/breaststroke

WORD CHECK

Refer to Focus Words and Focus Phrases only.

1 Look at the list and identify the hobbies and other leisure activities that involve physical exercise of some kind.
2 Which of the tools and instruments are usually made mainly of wood? Which mainly of metal? What are the others made of?
3 Take the roles of a famous sculptor, a famous painter, a famous musician, and a famous dancer. Hold a balloon debate. All of you are in a balloon which is losing air and can only support the weight of one person. Discuss who should be thrown out of the balloon and who should survive.
4 Talk about someone you know well using at least three of the Focus Phrases.

MEANING

1 Choose some of the words from the box to name the animals in the picture.

> donkey   scorpion
> crocodile   parrot   cobra
> peacock   tiger   lizard
> monkey   turtle   spider
> wolf   whale   shark
> hedgehog   dolphin
> tortoise   frog   fox

2 Look at the names of the animals which aren't in the picture. Are these animals similar to any that are in the picture? In what way?

MEANING
CONNOTATION

3 Which of the animals in the list is in your opinion:

a the most dangerous?   **e** the most useful?
b the least dangerous?   **f** the most intelligent?
c the most beautiful?   **g** the best?
d the ugliest?   **h** the worst?

Why?

MEANING
RELATED MEANINGS

4 a Which of the animals in the list has the following?

> a shell   fins   a beak   prickles   a tail   teeth

b Which of them are poisonous?

5 Complete the table with the names of the animals in the list.

Reptiles	Mammals	Amphibians	Birds	Fish	Insects

ACTIVATE

6 a Think of three animals that you like or dislike. They do not have to be from the list above. How would you describe each of them and their behaviour to someone who had never seen or heard of them before?

b Work in groups. One of you thinks of an animal, and the others try to guess from his/her description which animal he or she is thinking of. They may ask him/her questions, which he or she must answer truthfully if possible.

7 Work with a neighbour. Design a questionnaire to find out who in the class has pets, who had pets as a child, what kind of pets they have or had, what their favourite animal is, etc.

MEANING

RELATED MEANINGS

8 Complete the table with the missing words.

Neutral	Female	Male	Young
dog		dog	
cat	cat	tomcat	
			tadpole
		drake	
horse			foal
chicken	hen		
	vixen	dog	
cattle (*plural*)	cow		
	doe	stag	
	ewe		

WORD USE

COLLOCATION

📖**9** Complete the table. (See also Part A, Unit 4 of Book 1)

Animals	Noise	Animals	Way of moving	Animals	Home
pig	grunt	horse	gallop	birds, insects	nest
	whinny		crawl		lair
	roar		slither		burrow
	purr		bound		stable
	bark		pounce		kennel
	crow		dart		sty
	sing		hover		den
	howl		strut		hive

ACTIVATE

10 Ask one another questions like this:

What animal lives in a stable, whinnies, gallops and is a foal when it's young?

11 If you could be reborn as an animal, what animal would you like to be? Discuss the reasons for your choice with a partner.

SOME OF THE WORLD'S EXTINCT ANIMALS

a

b

c

d

e

12 Many wild animals are threatened by extinction due to over-hunting and changes in the environment caused by man. Which of these statements do you agree with? Which do you disagree with? Discuss your opinion with a partner, and add any other statements that you agree with.

a More animal reserves should be created and more work should be done to help endangered species to breed in captivity.
b We can't afford to worry about animals when millions of human beings are starving.
c We shouldn't be too worried about certain species becoming extinct, there are so many species which remain.
d We are the main threat to wildlife; there should be much stricter laws to protect the habitats of wild animals.

13 Read the text opposite. How has man damaged the animal and plant life of Mauritius in the writer's view?

Gerald Durrell (left) is a British zoologist. In 1958 he established the Wildlife Preservation Trust on the island of Jersey to help endangered species by breeding them in captivity.

*The following extract is taken from his book **Golden Bats and Pink Pigeons,** and it describes Durrell's first visit to the island of Mauritius in the Indian Ocean.*

. . . There, on this speck of volcanic soil in middle of a vast sea, a complete, unique and peaceful world was created slowly and carefully. It waited there for hundreds of thousands of years for an annihilating invasion of voracious animals for which it was totally unprepared, a cohort of rapacious beasts led by the worst predator in the world, *homo sapiens*. With man, of course, came all his familiars: the dog, the rat, the pig, and, in this instance probably one of the worst predators next to man, the monkey.

In an incredibly short space of time, a number of unique species had vanished: the dodo; the giant, black flightless parrot; the giant Mauritian tortoise, followed rapidly by the Rodrigues tortoise; and that strange bird, the solitaire. The dugong, which used to throng the reefs, vanished, and all that was left of a unique and harmless fauna was a handful of birds and lizards. These, together with what is left of the native forest, face enormous pressures. Not only is Mauritius one of the most densely populated parts of the globe, but as well as dogs, cats, rats and monkeys a number of other things have been introduced in that dangerous, unthinking way that man has. There are, for example, twenty introduced species of birds . . ., there is the sleek and deadly mongoose and, less damaging but still out of place, the hedgehog-like tenrec from Madagascar. Then there are the introduced plants and trees, so that the native vegetation is jostled and strangled by Chinese guava, wild raspberries, privet and a host of other things. In the face of all this, the indigenous flora and fauna of Mauritius can be said to be hanging on to its existence by its fingernails.

MEANING
WORDS IN CONTEXT

14 a Using a dictionary if necessary, find the various different words in the text which Durrell has used instead of the following.

> *plants   animals   disappeared   world*

b Which words in the text have the following meanings?

   i very destructive
   ii an animal which kills other animals for food
   iii with a very large appetite
   iv to crowd around
   v a small quantity

15 Complete the following sentences on the basis of the information in the text.

a Before the arrival of man and domesticated animals in Mauritius, the island _____.

b Great pressure is put on the remaining species of birds and lizards because _____.

c Imported plants like the Chinese guava also cause difficulty because _____.

d Durrell uses words like 'incredibly', 'enormous' and 'unthinking' in order to _____.

16 Using some of the words and expressions in the text, write a few lines about the way in which man has treated the environment and animal and plant life in your country. What do you feel should be done now? Get a neighbour to read through what you have written.

17 In the text, the mongoose is described as 'sleek and deadly'. Use adjectives from the box and some of your own words to describe other animals in this unit.

> *talkative   clever   cunning   deadly   affectionate   stealthy*
> *playful   huge   frightening   colourful   stubborn   timid*

MEANING

RELATED MEANINGS

18 Match the descriptions with the places shown in the photographs below and on the next page.

a It's extremely hot and humid, but you are protected from the sun by the thick and luxuriant canopy of branches overhead, and the *jungle* resounds with the calls of exotic birds and the noises of animal life in the *undergrowth*.

b The majestic *peaks* rise above the sweet-smelling pine *forest*; the air is invigoratingly pure, and the *streams* run with clear water.

c The sun beats down relentlessly; except at the rare *oasis*, there is no shade – just undulating *dunes* as far as the eye can see, peopled only by the occasional mirage.

d The dry grass around the *swamp* sways in the hot breeze, while antelope graze, ever fearful for the predators who may be watching from the shade of the few trees that dot the *bush*.

e Breakers crash against the *cliffs* that rise above the *shore*, throwing spray into the air, while gulls and pelicans circle above the *rocks* looking for fish in the grey *ocean*.

f The leaves are beginning to turn golden, and the small mammals that inhabit the *woods* and the *fields* are gathering food as they prepare for hibernation; birds swoop over the *hills* in the distance, heading for Africa.

19 a What kind of climate would you expect to find in the places shown?

temperate	arid	subtropical	tropical	arctic

b What animals would you expect to find living in each of these environments?

20 Place the words in *italics* from exercise 18 on the following lines.

Land formation	MOST BARREN <————————> LEAST BARREN
	FLATTEST <————————————> HIGHEST
Vegetation	MOST LUXURIANT <———> LEAST LUXURIANT
Water	LARGEST <————————————> SMALLEST
	SAFEST <————————> MOST DANGEROUS

ACTIVATE

21 Imagine that you have found yourself in the most beautiful place that you have ever seen. Write a letter to your family describing it.

FOCUS WORDS

amphibian	drake	kitten	shell
annihilate	duck	lair	shore
bark	duckling	lamb	sing
beak	dune	lizard	slither
beast	ewe	mammal	spider
bitch	fauna	mare	stable
bound	fin	monkey	stallion
bull	flora	moorland	stream
burrow	foal	nest	strut
bush	forest	ocean	sty
calf	fox	parrot	swamp
chick	frog	peacock	tadpole
cliff	gallop	pounce	tail
cobra	globe	predator	throng
crawl	grunt	prickles	tortoise
crocodile	handful	puppy	turtle
crow	hedgehog	purr	undergrowth
cub	hill	ram	vanish
dart	hive	reptile	voracious
deer	hover	roar	whale
den	howl	rock	whinny
desert	insect	scorpion	wolf
dolphin	jungle	scrub	
donkey	kennel	shark	

WORD CHECK

Refer to Focus Words only.

1 There are many nouns in the list. Which do you feel positive about, which do you feel negative about, and which are neutral in your view? Do other people agree with you?

2 Make up sentences about two different animals from the list.

3 Which five of the new words in the list do you find most interesting? Why?

4 Look at the verbs in the list. How many of them can be followed by a direct object (e.g. sing *a song*)? What would usually follow the other verbs?

14 | *Towns and cities*

1 Choose five words from the box below. Use a dictionary to help you write a sentence for each word, starting with *I* or *we*, showing what each word means.

> breathes fogged-up smack groan shrunk snarled
> gasp clank-rattle crackle mangled

2 a Which of the words in exercise 1 can describe noise? Which cannot?
b Where would you put the 'noise' words on this line?

QUIETEST ◄─────────────────────► LOUDEST

3 Which picture best matches the poem? Why?

The noise of the city in the morning
breathes through the gap in the fogged-up

window: it is the hydraulic smack of doors
and the relentless groan of speeding drivers

shrunk behind the glasses of their routine
on another freeway into somewhere,

snarled in the town tangle of the monster.
A rush of the air gasp in the cherry

sky and the clank-rattle on the rails
heralds happiness and horror with the crackle

of people, moving, moving anywhere, giving
the mangled concrete a reason in the dawn.

Peter Hedley

4 In groups give the poem a title. Decide on an adjective to describe the poem's mood.

5 In groups decide on five adjectives to describe living in cities and five adjectives to describe living in the country.

Living in cities	Living in the country

MEANING

RELATED MEANINGS

6 Put the following in order of size and importance. What do they all mean?

> *village   country   settlement   region   town   county*
> *capital   metropolis   state   city   hamlet   province*

7 All of the words in the box refer to an area of a town or city. What do they mean? Do they have a positive, negative or neutral connotation?

| *district* | *quarter* | *shanty town* | *ghetto* | *slum* |

WORD USE

COLLOCATIONS

8 Which words from column B can go with which words from column A? Use a dictionary if necessary.

A	**B**
housing	*area*
office	*precinct*
flats	*site*
apartment	*estate*
shopping	*block*
building	*site*
housing	*development*
industrial	*mall*
residential	*centre*
commercial	

ACTIVATE

9 Describe the photographs below. Would you like to work in the places shown?

USING DICTIONARIES

DEFINITIONS

a *rural*
b *rustic*
c *urban*
d *suburb*
e *suburban*
f *outskirts*

10 Match the words with their dictionary definitions. Check your answers in a dictionary.

iii) of or like the countryside; concerning country or village life

i) outer areas or limits

ii) an outer area of a town or city where people live

v) *often apprec* typical of the country, esp. in being simple and unspoiled by modern developments

iv) of a town or city

vi) *often derog* of, for, or in the suburbs, esp. as considered uninteresting or unimaginative

11 Complete the following sentences with the most appropriate word from exercise 10.

a Shanty towns are frequently found on the _____ of big cities.

b The decline of the inner cities often produces _____ squalor.

c Houses in this particular tree-lined _____ of London have shot up in price.

d Welsh people are fed up with English city dwellers buying their homes because of their _____ charm, thus putting the prices beyond the locals' reach.

e Picture the typical _____ scene; the little squares of grass, the shining cars lovingly polished by their owners on Sundays and the sheer tidiness of it all. Anything would be better than that!

f One of the charms of this particular village is its idyllic _____ setting deep in the Somerset countryside.

ACTIVATE

12 Using as many words as possible from exercises 5 to 10, describe a city, town or village that you either love or hate. Say why you feel this way.

MEANING

13 Read the text. Find the words in it to match the numbers in the

When he dreamed of home he saw the village green, the pub where he used to wait for his father on a summer evening, the village schoolhouse, the cottage where he used to live, the solid church steeple, and in his ear he could still almost hear the creak of the sails on the old windmill. What was that distant hum of conversation in the little shop? He could almost smell the warmth of the community, wrapping him in security, the scent of mown hay on the wind, the stroking of the brittle breeze – and boredom, a kind of dull imprisonment stretching on into the future, burying him in the brown earth, cutting off his escape. That's why he had come to this place of excitement and opportunity. Why then did he feel so like an alien, unwelcome and out of tune?

14 Answer these questions.

a Who is 'he'? Where is he? What is this paragraph about?

b Which of the places mentioned in the text could also be found in a town or city. Which could not?

c List five things you would expect to find in a village in your country.

15 What do the phrases in italics mean?

a It's become a *ghost town.*

b You can't speak to her, I'm afraid. She's *out of town* at the moment.

c Let's really *go to town* on this project.

e Let's go and *paint the town red*!

d Who's for a really good *night on the town*?

f She's really *slumming it* at the moment.

g It's not a huge company, only a *cottage industry*.

ACTIVATE

16 Write to a penfriend, inviting her or him to come and stay. Describe the place where you live and work/study. Say where it is and whether you like it or not.

17 Choose one of the pictures in exercise 3 and describe the scene you see there.

FOCUS WORDS

apartment (block)	green	shanty town
area	hamlet	shopping mall
block	housing estate	shopping precinct
block of flats	industrial estate	site
building site	mall	slum
capital	metropolis	state
church	office block	suburb
city	outskirts	suburban
commercial	province	town
cottage	pub	urban
country	quarter	village
county	region	village green
development	residential	village schoolhouse
district	rural	village shop
estate	rustic	windmill
ghetto	settlement	

FOCUS PHRASES

cottage industry	out of town
ghost town	paint the town red
go to town on (a project)	slum it
night on the town	

WORD CHECK

Refer to Focus Words and Focus Phrases only.

1 Find all the nouns or noun phrases which refer to a building.
2 Think of at least two situations you have been in and describe them using at least two Focus Phrases.
3 List all the two-word noun phrases in the Focus Words. Now look at your list and answer these questions.
   a How many stressed syllables do they have?
   b Where does the main stress occur?
4 Which words describe buildings that you frequently visit (but do not live in)? Which words describe places or areas that you frequently visit, but do not live in?

15 | *Stores, shops and services*

1 Complete this small questionnaire with a partner.

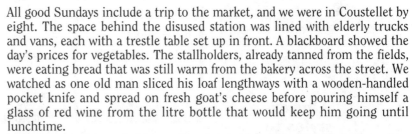

1 How often do you go shopping?	_____ Why?_____
2 Where do you do most of your shopping?	_____ Why?_____
3 What shopping do you like doing least?	_____ Why?_____
4 What shopping do you like doing best?	_____ Why?_____

2 Read the text and answer the questions below.

All good Sundays include a trip to the market, and we were in Coustellet by eight. The space behind the disused station was lined with elderly trucks and vans, each with a trestle table set up in front. A blackboard showed the day's prices for vegetables. The stallholders, already tanned from the fields, were eating bread that was still warm from the bakery across the street. We watched as one old man sliced his loaf lengthways with a wooden-handled pocket knife and spread on fresh goat's cheese before pouring himself a glass of red wine from the litre bottle that would keep him going until lunchtime.

The Coustellet market is small and not yet fashionable. Customers carry baskets instead of cameras, and only in July and August are you likely to see the occasional haughty woman down from Paris with her Dior track suit and small, nervous dog. For the rest of the season, from spring until autumn, it is just the local inhabitants, and the peasants who bring in what they have taken from the earth or the greenhouse a few hours earlier.

We walked slowly along the rows of tables, admiring the French housewife at work. Unlike us, she is not content merely to look at the produce before buying. She gets to grips with it – squeezing aubergines, sniffing tomatoes, snapping the matchstick-thin green beans between her fingers, tasting cheese and olives – and, if they don't come up to her private standards, she will glare at the stallholder as if she has been betrayed before taking her custom elsewhere.

At one end of the market, a van from the wine co-operative was surrounded by men rinsing their teeth thoughtfully in the new rosé. Next to them a woman was selling free-range eggs and live rabbits, and beyond her the tables were piled high with vegetables.

We bought red peppers to roast and big brown eggs and basil and peaches and goat's cheese and lettuce and pink-streaked onions. And, when the basket could hold no more, we went across the road to buy half a yard of bread. The bakery was crowded and noisy, and smelt of warm dough and the almonds that had gone into the morning's cakes. While we waited, we remembered being told that the French spend as much of their income on their stomachs as the English do on their cars and stereo systems, and we could easily believe it.

a What differences are there between the way you shop and the scene described here?

b What impression of the scene and the people is the writer trying to convey? Do you like it?

c Would you like to shop at the same place? Why? Why not?

d Make lists of words from the text under the following headings: *people who sell things; places where things are sold; food*

MEANING

3 Look at the advertisements and notices. Which of the following places might you see them in?

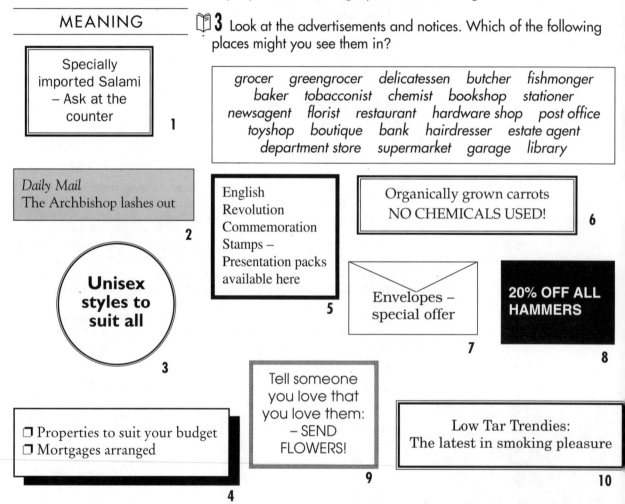

Specially
imported Salami
– Ask at the
counter

1

grocer   greengrocer   delicatessen   butcher   fishmonger
baker   tobacconist   chemist   bookshop   stationer
newsagent   florist   restaurant   hardware shop   post office
toyshop   boutique   bank   hairdresser   estate agent
department store   supermarket   garage   library

Daily Mail
The Archbishop lashes out

2

English
Revolution
Commemoration
Stamps –
Presentation packs
available here

5

Organically grown carrots
NO CHEMICALS USED!

6

**Unisex
styles to
suit all**

3

Envelopes –
special offer

7

**20% OFF ALL
HAMMERS**

8

❑ Properties to suit your budget
❑ Mortgages arranged

4

Tell someone
you love that
you love them:
– SEND
FLOWERS!

9

Low Tar Trendies:
The latest in smoking pleasure

10

Choose any three of the places. Make a list of as many things as possible that you can buy there.

4 We can say *grocer* (= the person or the shop) or *grocer's* (= the shop). How many of the words from the box in exercise 3 can be treated the same way?

5 Where do the following people work? Put as many of them as possible in the chart on page 135. Then try to think of other people who work in shops and services to add to the chart

a   a *shop assistant*
b   a *manager*
c   a *counter clerk*
d   a *cashier*
e   a *check-out person*
f   a *store detective*

g   a *customer*
h   a *salesperson*
i   a *street trader*
j   a *mechanic*
k   a *(head) waiter*
l   a *security man/woman*

ACTIVATE

6 Of all the places mentioned in this unit so far, where would you be happy to work and where would you not like to work? Which jobs would you like/not like? Why?

___

WORD USE

METAPHOR AND IDIOM

7 What is the missing word which will fit into all of the blanks in the phrases in italics?

I don't know what's the matter with her. She seems to be *all over the* a) _____.

Before deciding on which course to take, why not d) _____ *around* a bit.

You'll never be allowed in. It's a closed i) _____.

Oh yes. He's *set up* b) _____ with Jane, and her husband is going to divorce her.

I want a reduction! This material is clearly e) _____ *soiled*.

The managers are all in agreement, but I doubt if you'll get a consensus on the f) _____ *floor*.

He's such a bore. He's always g) *talking* _____. He can't talk about anything else.

8 Match these meanings with the words and phrases in exercise 7.

a   the place where all the manual work takes place; the workers
b   look at the alternatives before choosing
c   discussing issues to do with work
d   looking but not buying
e   totally disorganized
f   stealing from shops
g   started to live with
h   an organization that is completely exclusive
i   used for display in the shop, so dirty or damaged

9 Make a dialogue using at least one expression from exercise 7, one place from exercise 3 and one person from exercises 4 and 5.

___

WORD USE

RELATED MEANINGS

10 What is the difference between the following pairs of words? Use them to fill the blanks in the sentences below.

a *lend* and *borrow*
b a *bargain* and a *discount*
c a *loan* and *hire purchase*
d *in credit* and an *overdraft*
e to *withdraw* and to *deposit*
f a *cheque book* and a *paying-in book*
g to *save* and to *pay back*
h a *credit account* and an *expense account*
i a *credit card* and a *cash card*
j to *part-exchange* and to *pawn*

1 When you want money you _____ some from the bank; when you put your money into the bank you _____ it.

2 He pays for all his meals and hotels on the firm's _____; he has a _____ at Harrods so that he can buy what he wants even if he doesn't have any cash.

3 You _____ someone money which is yours and which they will give you back; that person _____ the money from you.

4 If you pay in cash they give you a 30% _____; if you look around you can often find a _____, especially in markets.

5 The bank gave him a _____ to buy a car and he'll pay it back in five years; she is buying her car in instalments by the _____ method.

6 When you keep money for the future you _____ it; when you return money that you have borrowed you _____.

7 When you give something to a special shop temporarily in exchange for money you _____ it, hoping to get it back if you can raise the money; when you give something as part of the payment for something else you _____ it.

8 A _____ is the one you fill in to put money into the bank; a _____ is used for taking money out of the bank or paying bills.

9 When you have a lot of money in the bank your account is _____; when you have spent more than you have in the bank you have an _____.

10 You can often pay for things with a _____; but when you go to a cash machine to get money you need a _____.

ACTIVATE

11 Role-play the following situations.

a You visit your bank to request an overdraft.
b You are in a car showroom to look for a new car.
c You are in a pawnshop because you need to pawn something
d You are in a bank because you want to open an account.

MEANING

12 a Put these professions in the correct place in the chart.

| *police officer   doctor   firefighter   medical orderly* |
| *social worker   surgeon   constable   specialist* |
| *postal delivery worker   nurse   administrator   sergeant* |
| *sister   health visitor   dustman/refuse collector   milkman* |
| *hospital porter   postman   ambulanceman   detective* |

Health service	Postal service	Social services	Sanitation services	Police force	Fire service	Other emergency services	Other services

b Can you add any more words?
c Who gets paid most and who gets paid least?

13 Who is being talked about in the following sentences? Choose a word from exercise 12. (You may have to make it plural or change the sex.)

a She went in through the window and got the boy out, even though the place was full of smoke. She didn't even have her breathing apparatus on!
b The boy next door kept getting beaten up by his father, so that's why she came round.
c He uses his bike for his deliveries. It must be pretty miserable in the winter.
d I can hear the bottles clinking as he comes up to the door, every morning at five thirty.
e When she put the handcuffs on me I was humiliated. I mean, I only took a pair of stockings.
f It's really irritating. They never seem to take everything. They always leave boxes and things behind.
g He examined my father for only a few seconds before calling the emergency services.

h If they hadn't got him to hospital so quickly he would have died.
i The care he received in hospital was fantastic. One of them was especially kind and gentle.

WORD USE

14 Complete these sentences, using words from exercise 12. You can use the same words more than once.

a _____ *fought to save the lives of* the victims.

b _____ *tackled the blaze.*

c _____ *ferried people to hospital*

d _____ *cleared* the piles of rubbish.

e _____ *arrested* the rioters.

f _____ *delivered* two extra *pints.*

g _____ *held back* sightseers.

ACTIVATE

The Bridge Street disaster

15 Bridge Street is the central street of a small town called Barnford. It has banks, flower shops, stationers, etc. and even a small supermarket and a garage.

Decide which shops or other places the following people were in and what they were doing there at approximately 11.30 yesterday morning.

Mabel	(trying to start up her own business)
Keith	(having trouble with his car)
old Mr Tubbs	(needs something for his cough)
Stephen	(wants to send something to his girlfriend because it's Valentine's Day)
Tracey	(doing the weekly shop for the family)
Jack and Katie	(the 12-year-old Towaski twins spending pocket money on pens, paper, etc.)
Ronald	(wants to cook a fish casserole tonight)
Anne	(a nicotine addict)

Example:
Mabel was talking to the bank manager. She was asking for an overdraft.

16 At 11.30 a petrol tanker went out of control in Bridge Street and crashed into the supermarket. Look at the pictures opposite. Make statements about what happened in Bridge Street and elsewhere after the accident, using words and expressions from exercises 12 and 14.

Example:
Fire officers from the region tackled the blaze.

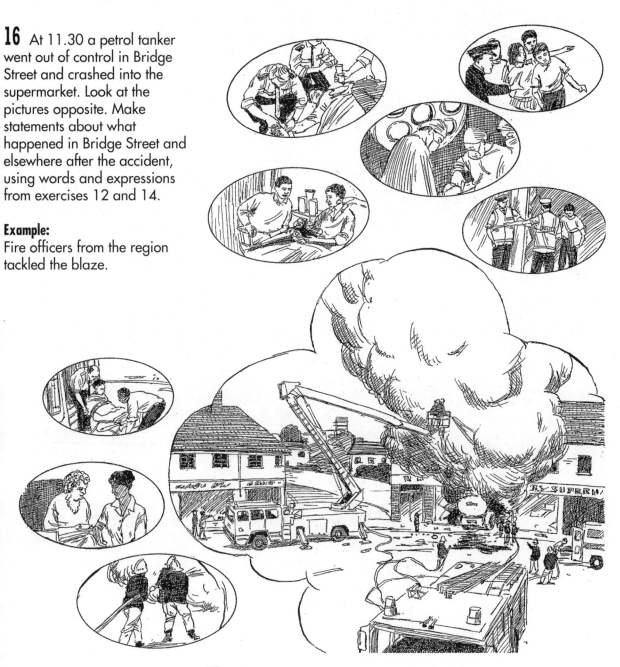

17 Use the information in exercises 14 and 15 to write an account of the disaster as one of the following:

a a letter to a friend
b a newspaper article
c a radio news bulletin

FOCUS WORDS

account	delicatessen	library	sanitation
administrator	department	loan	services
ambulanceman	store	manager	save
arrest (v)	deposit (v)	mechanic	security
baker	detective	medical	man/woman
bank	discount	orderly	sergeant
bargain	doctor	milkman	shop
bookshop	dustman	newsagent	shop assistant
borrow	expense	nurse	shoplifting
boutique	account	overdraft	shop-soiled
building	fire fighter	part exchange	sister
society	fire service	(v)	social services
butcher	fishmonger	pawn (v)	social worker
cash card	florist	pay back (v)	specialist
cashier	garage	paying-in book	stationer
check-out	greengrocer	police force	store detective
person	grocer	police officer	street trader
chemist	hairdresser	postal delivery	supermarket
cheque book	hardware shop	worker	surgeon
constable	health service	postal service	tobacconist
counter clerk	health visitor	post office	toyshop
credit	(head) waiter	postman	waiter
credit account	hire purchase	restaurant	window
credit card	hospital porter	salesperson	shopping
customer	lend		withdraw (v)

FOCUS PHRASES

all over the shop	hospital	shop floor
be in credit	fight to save lives	tackle a blaze
clear rubbish	hold (people) back	talk shop
closed shop	set up shop with	
ferry (people) to	shop around	

WORD CHECK

Refer to Focus Words and Focus Phrases only.

1 Using words from the list say where you could go if you wanted:
   a food **b** money **c** other items (not services)

2 Find the names of all the occupations in the list. List them in order from most dangerous to least dangerous.

3 A policewoman has a milkman for a brother. Write one sentence for each of them about an extraordinary day in which they did unusual things. Use as many Focus Phrases as possible.

4 How many words in the list are similar to words in your language? Do they mean the same as the words in your language?

16 *The home and accommodation*

1 a When you choose a home to rent or buy, which of the following points is or would be more important for you? Write 1, 2 and 3 beside the three most important ones.

1 _____ neighbours, and possibilities for social relations

2 _____ ease of cleaning and maintenance

3 _____ location

4 _____ lack of noise

5 _____ garden and views

6 _____ size and number of rooms

7 _____ age and condition

8 _____ other: what? _____

b Compare your ideas with a partner's. Do you agree?

MEANING

RELATED MEANINGS

a cottage
b semi-detached house
c terraced houses
d villa
e detached house
f bungalow
g mansion
h hut
i farmhouse

2 Match the pictures with the words on the left.

3 Use the words in the box to label the plan.

> basement flat   maisonette
> studio flat   second floor flat
> bedsitter   penthouse flat
> ground floor flat   balcony

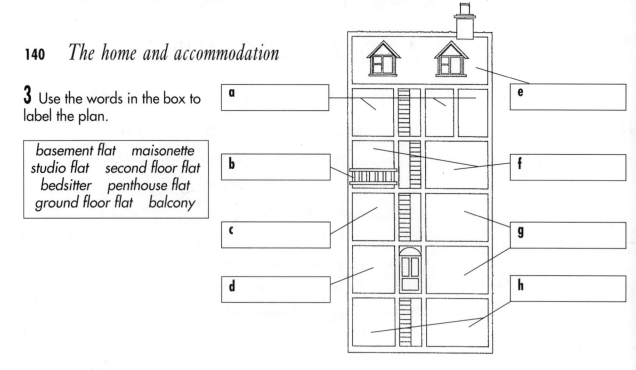

ACTIVATE

4 Which of the kinds of home in exercises 2 and 3 are most common in your country? Are they similar to or different from similar kinds of home in other countries you know? What are the main differences?

5 Imagine you have decided to go to study in Britain for two or three years. What would you do about accommodation? Which of the following would be the most important <u>two</u> considerations for you? Compare your priorities with a partner's.

a distance from college   **d** noise
b cleanliness   **e** comfort
c price   **f** other _____

USING A DICTIONARY

DEFINITIONS

6 All of the words below can be used instead of *live*. Using a dictionary if necessary, match them with their definitions.

a inhabit   **e** reside
b occupy   **f** squat
c settle   **g** stay
d lodge   **h** dwell

> **1** to start to live in a place (after moving from somewhere else)
> **2** [of large groups of people or animals] to live in a country or area
> **3** to live in a place for a while as a visitor or guest
> **4** [*formal*] to have one's home in a place
> **5** to be in (a house or room)
> **6** [*literary or old use*] to live in a place
> **7** to stay in someone else's home in exchange for paying rent
> **8** to live in an unused building without permission and without paying rent

7 Use the verbs above to complete the following sentences.

a When Clare was a student at university, she _____ with two old ladies for a year. The rent was very reasonable.
b If you come to Boston for a few days, you can _____ with us. We have plenty of space.
c The Tuaregs _____ parts of Northern Africa.
d The homeless couple broke into the empty house and _____ there for six months. Then the owner forced them to leave.
e After the war, the Van Dongs left Vietnam and eventually _____ in Bordeaux.
f That house doesn't seem to be _____. There are no curtains in the windows, and I've never seen anyone go in or out.

MEANING IN
CONTEXT

8 Complete the following with appropriate words from the box, using a dictionary if necessary.

> let   rent (v)   rent (n)   deposit   evict   landlord   landlady
> owner   tenant   contract/agreement   host   guest
> hospitality   agency

❝We spent six months in London in 1988. Finding a home was hard. For the first week, we were a) _____ of the parents of a friend of mine. They were very kind and showed us great b) _____. Our c) _____ also helped us look for a place to live and put us in touch with an d) _____ which specializes in short-term accommodation. On the fourth day we went to visit a two-bedroomed flat in Fulham which was to e) _____. We liked it a lot, but the f) _____ told us that she had promised to g) _____ it to another couple the day before. They had had trouble with the h) _____ of the flat where they were living: he wanted to increase their i) _____ by 30 percent, and they were refusing to pay, so he was going to j) _____ them. That's why they needed another home. We were very worried when we heard this, and we learnt that it is very important to read your k) _____ or lease carefully before signing it. Then your rights as a l) _____ can be protected.
Anyway, the next day we heard that the flat in Fulham was available after all, so we hurried back to the agency, checked the m) _____ carefully, and paid a n) _____ of £400, as well as the first month's o) _____ – another £400. Living in London was going to be pretty expensive. ❞

9 Look at the verbs in the following sentences. Then complete them using nouns with these endings:

> People   -er/-ier   -ent/-ant
> Places: -ing   -ence   -ment   -ation

a A person who *lodges* with a family is their

_____.

b The large home which a rich family *resides in* is their

_____.

c The person who *occupies* a home, even if only for a short time, is the _____.

d The place where a person *lodges*, usually for a short period, is called his or her _____ in formal English, or *digs* in informal British English.

e People who *squat* in empty houses without the owners' permission are called _____.

f A place where a group of people decide to *settle*, for example in a jungle or uninhabited area, is called a

_____.

g The people who *inhabit* a country or city are called its

_____.

h People who went to a newly developed part of a country to *settle* there were often called _____.

10 a Fill in the table describing your current home (or a home you know well). Describe its rooms, its atmosphere, its location, any special features or views, etc. and the people who live there. Is it similar to your ideal home? If not, what would your ideal home be like?

	Present home	Ideal home
Type of home		
People who live there		
Location		
Rooms		
Atmosphere and special features		

b   Compare the description of your ideal home with a partner's

11 Read the following advertisements for homes taken from a British estate agent's publicity. Assuming you had the money, which home, if any, would you want to look at and why?

Spacious Victorian terraced house enjoying views across the city. *Handy* for local shops, buses, schools, etc. Porch, entrance hall, 2 *impressive* reception rooms, kitchen/breakfast room, bathroom with shower, 3 bedrooms, gas central heating, small but *delightful* garden.

Southern outskirts of the city: a *double-fronted pre-war* semi-detached 3-bedroomed house in a quiet tree-lined road. *Convenient* for local shops and city buses. *Period* hall, *good-sized* lounge, dining room, utility room/storeroom, electric storage heaters, double-glazing, *charming mature* garden, garage.

A *purpose-built* upper floor flat located in one of the city's *prime* residential areas, some 10 minutes' walk from the city centre and railway station. *Close* to local shops and canal path walks. Commanding *superb* views over the city and surrounding hills. Gas central heating, hall, 6m x 4m living room, bathoom, 2 double bedrooms with wardrobes, garage.

A very *well-proportioned* detached bungalow, *not far* from the city centre, containing a *luxury* kitchen, an impressive *open-plan* living room with a fireplace, 4 double bedrooms, and 2 bathrooms. Gas central heating, *fair* decorative order throughout, large *secluded* garden, and double garage.

12 The following adjectives are all taken from the advertisements above. Put them in the table according to whether their meanings relate to size, distance, age or quality.

spacious   fair
purpose-built   good-sized
prime   superb
double-fronted   pre-war
close   period   impressive
luxury   open-plan
mature   well-proportioned
not far   secluded   handy
convenient   charming

Size	
Distance	
Age	
Quality	

📖 **13** Using a dictionary if necessary, find one other compound word beginning with each of the following.

a good-   **b** open-   **c** well-   **d** purpose-   **e** double-

ACTIVATE

📖 **14** Use vocabulary from the advertisements to prepare a new advertisement for a house or flat you know well (or for an imaginary flat/house) to put on the class noticeboard. Remember that you can exaggerate its advantages and understate its disadvantages. Aim to get as many people interested as possible!

WORD USE
_____
METAPHOR AND IDIOM

📖 **15** Can you work out what these expressions mean?

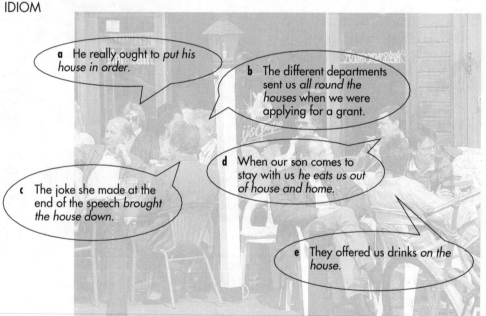

a He really ought to *put his house in order*.

b The different departments sent us *all round the houses* when we were applying for a grant.

c The joke she made at the end of the speech *brought the house down*.

d When our son comes to stay with us *he eats us out of house and home*.

e They offered us drinks *on the house*.

WORD USE
_____
PROVERBS AND SAYINGS

16 Put the words in the following in the correct order to make famous sayings and lines from songs about home. Are there similar sayings and quotations in your language?

a where/is/home/is/the heart
b wish/homeward/were/ bound/I/I
c home/keep/fires/burning/ the
d no/home/like/there's/ place
e heart/absence/the/fonder/ makes/grow
f home/home/sweet

FOCUS WORDS

agency	double-fronted	landlord	residence
agreement	double-	let	secluded
balcony	glazing	living room	second floor
basement flat	drawing room	lodge	semi-detached
bathroom	dwell	lodger	house
bedroom	estate agent	lodging	settle
bedsitter	evict	lounge	settler
breakfast	fair	luxury	settlement
room	farmhouse	maisonette	spacious
bungalow	flat	mansion	squat
central heating	floor	occupy	squatter
charming	good-sized	occupant	stay
classroom	ground floor	open-plan	storeroom
close	guest	owner	studio flat
contract	hall	penthouse flat	study
convenient	handy	period (*adj*)	superb
cottage	hospitality	porch	terraced house
delightful	host	pre-war	utility room
deposit	hut	prime	villa
detached	impressive	purpose-built	well-
house	inhabit	rent	proportioned
digs	kitchen	reside	
dining room	landlady	resident	

FOCUS PHRASES

all round the houses
bring the house down
eat someone out of house and home
on the house
put your house in order

WORD CHECK

Refer to Focus Words and Focus Phrases only.

1 Of all the kinds of room mentioned, which do you feel most comfortable in? Why?

2 There are several compound words in the list. Which have the stress on the first part and which have the stress on the second part? Do there seem to be any rules?

3 Make up a short story with someone else in the class in which you use all the Focus Phrases.

4 Which words in the list do you find:
   a strangest? Why?
   b hardest to pronounce? Why?

1 Look at the floorplan of the flat. With a partner, decide what furniture you would need to make it comfortable. List the items in the table below.

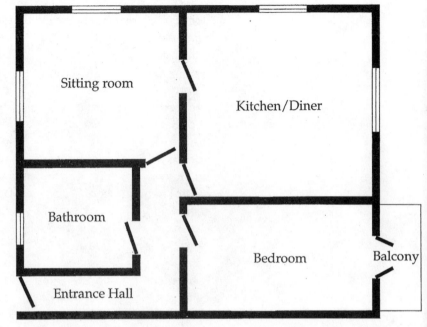

Sitting room	Bedroom	Kitchen	Bathroom	Entrance hall

MEANING IN CONTEXT

2 Look at this picture of a second-hand furniture shop. Use the words in the box below to label the items in the picture. Then say which room(s) each piece of furniture would normally be used in.

> sideboard
> chest of drawers
> dressing table   stool
> dresser   bunk-bed   hat-
> stand   divan bed

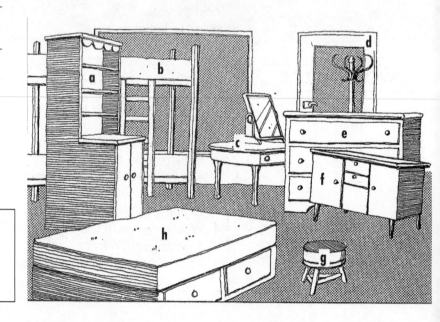

MEANING

RELATED MEANINGS

📖 **3** Using a dictionary if necessary, explain the differences between the following similar items.

a an *armchair* and an *upright chair*
b a *king-size bed*, a *double bed* and a *sofa-bed*
c a *coffee table*, a *dining table*, a *bedside table* and a *desk*
d a *fitted cupboard* and a *wardrobe*
e a *bookcase*, a *bookshelf* and a *mantelpiece*
f a *refrigerator*, a *freezer* and an *icebox*
g a *washbasin* and a *sink*
h a *washing machine* and a *dishwasher*
i a *cooker*, an *oven* and a *toaster*
j a *cushion* and a *pillow*
k a *sheet*, a *blanket* and a *duvet*

WORD USE

COLLOCATION

4 Match the adjectives with the pieces of furniture. Tick the boxes. What does each phrase mean?

	chair	table	bed	bedroom
double				
single				
dining				
breakfast				
folding				

ACTIVATE

5 Complete the following with appropriate words and phrases.

a Mary hung _____ in the wardrobe.

b On her bedside table, there were _____ .

c After the party, the sink was full of _____ .

d Before the meal George took _____ out of the sideboard.

e Although the sofa was quite hard, it was comfortable because there were some soft _____ on it.

f Mary sat at her dressing table in order to _____ .

g There was a wide mantelpiece above the _____ . On it, there were _____ .

h David went into the bathroom and washed his hands in the _____ .

ACTIVATE

6 a Look at these items of
furniture. What are they?
Would you like to have
any of them in your
home? Why/why not?

b With a partner, work out
a very 'fashionable'
design for some other
piece(s) of furniture. Draw
your design, and produce
some notes to describe it.
Then put it on the
classroom notice board.

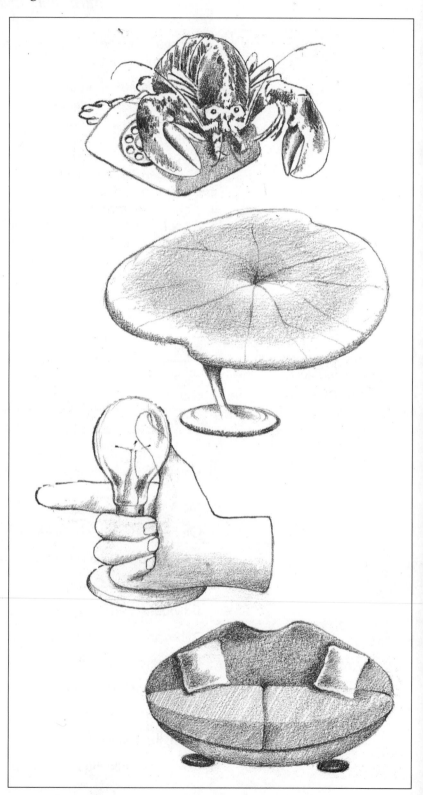

MEANING

RELATED MEANINGS

7 Imagine you and a partner have just bought the house in the picture for a very low price. Now you want to improve it. Use the verbs below to plan what needs to be done.

> *mend   repair   fix*
> *improve   replace*
> *change   rebuild   remove*
> *paint   clean*

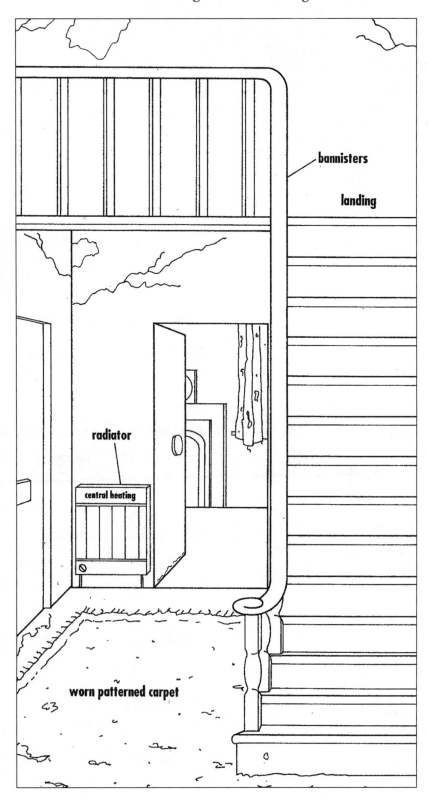

bannisters

landing

radiator

central heating

worn patterned carpet

8 Have you ever decorated a house or a room yourself? Would you like to? What are the advantages and disadvantages of *Do-it-yourself (DIY)*? Work with a partner to fill in the table.

Advantages	Disadvantages
not so expensive	

MEANING

SENSE RELATIONS

9 Using a dictionary if necessary, make pairs of opposites using the words in the box.

> bright   gloomy   well-maintained   out-dated   neglected
> ugly   modern   attractive

10 Use appropriate words from the box to complete the following.

a The Greens don't like their new house very much. It is

_____ because there are so few windows, and it's quite

small.

b Although the car is four years old, it's _____. The owners

have serviced and cleaned it regularly.

c A: These flats that were built in the 1960s look terribly

_____ and depressing from the outside, don't they?

   B: Yes, but when they are redecorated like Marjorie's, they can

be very _____ inside.

d The town looks lovely and _____ in the morning sunshine.

e She finds her parents' attitudes very _____. In fact, she

says they are nineteenth century attitudes.

ACTIVATE

11 Write a description of the room you are working in now, for example as part of a letter to a friend. What condition is it in and what impression does it make on you? Why? Compare your description with a partner's. Then describe a room that you like very much.

MEANING
RELATED WORDS

12 Here are some of the things you would probably need if you were decorating a room. Match the words on the left with the appropriate pictures on the right. Then decide whether you would use them for preparation or for decorating, and complete the table.

1 paint
2 paintbrush
3 roller
4 scissors
5 bucket
6 sponge
7 wallpaper
8 step-ladder
9 sandpaper

Preparing	Decorating

ACTIVATE

b Now discuss what needs to be done, and who will do what. Use expressions like these:

The windows need cleaning. We'll have to paint the ceiling white. We must have/get the door fixed.

13 a Imagine you are moving into a small unfurnished flat with a partner. There is torn flowery wallpaper in the main room, and dirty orange paint on the woodwork. The paint on the ceiling is peeling. How would you redecorate it? Discuss colours and styles and complete the table.

	walls	ceiling	floor	windows	lighting	doors
Main room						
Bedroom						
Kitchen						
Bathroom						

FOCUS WORDS

armchair	desk	king-size bed	sheet
banisters	dining	landing	shutters
bedside table	dishwasher	letter box	sideboard
blanket	divan bed	mend	single-
blind (n)	double bed	modern	sink
bookcase	dresser	neglected	sofa
bookshelf	dressing table	old-fashioned	sofa-bed
bright	duvet	oven	sponge
bucket	fence	paint	stairs
bunk-bed	fireplace	paintbrush	step-ladder
carpet	fitted	pillow	steps
ceiling	cupboard	put on	stool
central heating	fix	rebuild	toaster
chest of	folding	refrigerator	upright chair
drawers	freezer	remove	wallpaper
chimney	gate	replace	wardrobe
coffee table	hang	roll (of paper)	washbasin
cooker	hat-stand	roof	washing
cupboard	hedge	rug	machine
curtains	icebox	sandpaper	well-
cushion	improve	scissors	maintained

FOCUS PHRASES

armchair socialist/
   revolutionary etc
be curtains for (someone)
go through the roof
have something

mended/repaired/painted
need painting/repairing
sit on the fence
smoke like a chimney

WORD CHECK

Refer to Focus Words and Focus Phrases only.

1 How many items are there in the list which are or were originally composed of two words? Divide them into the following categories:

Purpose or use	*Location*	*Other*
e.g. teapot	e.g. back door	
(= a pot for tea)	(=a door at the back of the house)	

2 In the words you have listed in exercise 1, is the main stress on the first part or the second part? Are there any rules about this?

3 With a partner, prepare a conversation involving five of the Focus Phrases.

4 Which ten new words on the list do you think will be most useful to you in the future? Why?

18 | *Housework*

1 Read this following 'job description' quickly. What are your reactions to it? Do you find it funny? Does it make you think? Does it ring true?

OCCUPATION:
HOUSEWIFE

☐ JOB DESCRIPTION:
You will be expected to 'live in' at the place where you work and provide cleaning, cooking, shopping, laundry, nursing, psychotherapy, teaching, entertainment and secretarial services for the others living there.

☐ HOURS:
You will be on call 24 hours a day, 365 days a year, but your 'regular work' will take between 50 and 100 hours per week, depending on the age, health and number of children or disabled people in the house, the standards of work demanded by the employer and the size and condition of the house.

☐ PAYMENT
The employer provides an allowance called 'housekeeping money' and the State provides 'child benefit'. This money is for essential expenses such as cleaning utensils and food. There is no payment for your labour as a housewife.

☐ HOLIDAYS
Your duties will be easier if the holiday is taken in a hotel, but you will often be expected simply to do your normal work in strange surroundings while other members of the household enjoy their leisure.

☐ WORK HAZARDS
You will be one and a half times more likely to die of cancer than women in paid employment. Insomnia, dizziness, headaches, nightmares and anxiety ('housewife syndrome') are much more common among housewives than among women in paid employment.

☐ JOB SECURITY
Your job will be continuously and increasingly threatened by divorce. Two out of three marriages today are expected to end in divorce. One year after divorce, the housewife's standard of living drops by 73%, while that of her ex-employer rises by 42%.

☐ FRINGE BENEFITS
Your board and lodging will usually be provided, but you will normally be expected to share a bedroom (and bed) with your employer.

2 The 'job description' mentions many of the problems faced by the average housewife in many countries. List at least three of the problems. Are men to blame for them? Which is the most serious?

MEANING IN CONTEXT

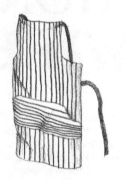

MEANING

RELATED MEANINGS

*ironing   bed making
vacuum cleaning   washing
cooking   dusting
washing up   window
cleaning   shopping
polishing*

ACTIVATE

3 Find words or phrases that are similar in meaning to the following words from the text.

Example:

Paragraph 1 –

laundry: *washing*

Paragraph 2 –

on call: _____

Paragraph 3 –

utensils: _____

Paragraph 4 –

household: _____

Paragraph 5 –

nightmares: _____

anxiety: _____

4 *Chore* is another word for a job which is regular and unpleasant. It is often used for jobs around the house. Each of the speakers below is talking about one of the chores in the box. Which one?

a Put the dishes in the sink.
b I'd better turn it inside out first or it may go shiny.
c I can't really put them outside. It looks like rain.
d Can you get me a trolley? They're over there, look.
e I think I'll need that big saucepan. Can you reach it?
f The bag's full. That's why it isn't picking up all the dirt.
g You've left finger-marks on the outside and the inside.
h You've missed part of the mantelpiece. I'll move the ornaments.
i You can see your face in this table now – not that you'd want to!
j I usually change the sheets and pillow cases on Wednesdays.

5 a Which of the chores above do you/would you find most unpleasant? Why?
b Which of the chores have you done:
very often? _____
often? _____
occasionally? _____
c Which have you never done? _____
Why not? _____

WORD USE

WORDS TOGETHER

mop rinse dry up
stir sweep wipe
scrub beat scorch
soak wring fold drain
scour chop press

sponge broom brush
bucket ironing board
cloth detergent
dustpan chopping board
bowl tea towel

6 a Each noun and each verb in the boxes relates to one or more of the chores in the table below. Group them together by listing the words in the most relevant columns.

	Cleaning the floor	Washing up	Washing a sweater	Ironing a blouse	Making dinner
Verbs					
Nouns					

b Using a dictionary if necessary, match each noun with at least one verb to describe part of a chore.

MEANING

RELATED MEANINGS

7 Complete the following with words from exercise 6.

a Oh dear, the iron was too hot. Look, I've _____ your blouse. Do you think anyone will notice?

b This floor is very dirty. Can you bring me a fresh _____ of water? I want to rinse the _____ again.

c The collar of this shirt is so dirty I'll have to _____ it in a _____ of hot water for half an hour, and then _____ it with a brush.

d Thanks for washing the dishes. We haven't got time to _____ them _____. Let's just leave them there to _____.

e Can you _____ the ironing board and put it away? I've finished the ironing now.

f First _____ two eggs in a _____. Then _____ three mushrooms into small pieces and add them, with some milk and salt . . .

ACTIVATE

8 Imagine a child is helping you do the following chores. He/she has never done any of them before. Give him/her exact instructions.

a washing up some knives, forks and spoons
b ironing a T-shirt
c washing a pair of very dirty socks
d boiling an egg
e making a bed
f polishing a wooden table

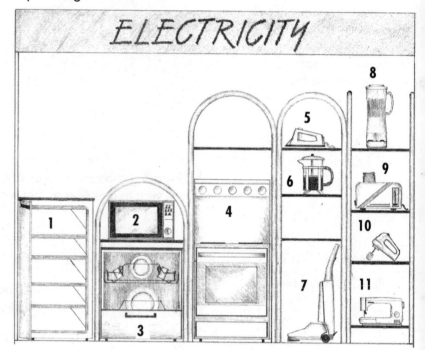

9 Look at the shop-window above. All but two of the appliances below are shown in the window. Put the correct number beside each word.

__ cooker
__ dishwasher
__ blender
__ sewing machine
__ washing machine
__ iron
__ beater

__ vacuum cleaner
__ microwave oven
__ coffee machine
__ toaster
__ fridge
__ freezer

Which appliances are used for which chores in exercise 6? What else are they used for?

ACTIVATE

10 With a partner, decide which *three* appliances (not just those from exercise 9) deserve prizes for being the most useful inventions for the household. Give reasons.

WORD USE

IDIOM AND METAPHOR

11 In the following sentences, phrases borrowed from housework are used to talk about quite different things. What?

a Ironfist Ivan is *all washed up*. I don't think he'll fight again.

b It's Denise's fault if she is having problems at work. She's *made her bed*. Now she'll *have to lie on it*.

c I managed to *iron out* my problems with Mary last night.

d I don't think it's a good idea for you and Dave to *wash your dirty linen in public*.

e Julia didn't feel like going to Sally's party so she *cooked up* some excuse.

g The company has *dusted off* that development plan I drew up three years ago.

f I need to *polish up* my French before we go to Paris.

ACTIVATE

12 Brenda and Bob Mason have been married for ten years. She has been working as the kind of housewife described in the job description on page 153. She has finally decided to take a full-time job and to try to persuade her husband to share the household chores. At first he is rather surprised . . . With a partner continue the dialogue in which Brenda gradually succeeds in convincing her husband to take help around the house.

BRENDA: Bob, I've been thinking: I'd like to go back to work. The children are at school most of the day and . . .

BOB: Hold on, hold on . . . just a minute. You don't need to go to work. My salary is pretty good and . . .

BRENDA: I've made up my mind. In fact, I'm going for some interviews next week . . .

FOCUS WORDS

anxiety	detergent	microwave	stir
beat	dishwasher	oven	sweep
bed-making	dry up	mop (v)	tea towel
blender	dust (v)	nightmare	toaster
bowl	dustpan	polish (v)	utensils
broom	fold	press	vacuum
brush	freezer	rinse	cleaner
bucket	fridge	scorch	vacuum
chop	household	scour	cleaning
chore	housewife	scrub	washing
cloth	housework	services	wash up
coffee	iron (n)	sewing	window
machine	iron (v)	machine	cleaning
cooker	ironing board	shop (v)	wipe
chopping	laundry	soak	wring
board		sponge	

FOCUS PHRASES

be all washed up
be on call
cook up (an excuse)
do the ironing/washing/cleaning/dusting etc.
dust off (a plan/an idea/a project)
make the beds
polish up (a language, etc.)
You've made your bed, so lie on it.
wash your dirty linen in public

WORD CHECK

Refer to Focus Words and Focus Phrases only.

1 Which of the appliances and pieces of equipment in the list of Focus Words are usually made of metal? What are the others usually made of?
2 Find all the chores in the list. Work with a partner to list them in order of unpleasantness (1 = most unpleasant, etc.)
3 Look at all the verbs in the list. Which are *irregular* in the past simple form? Put the others in one of the following groups, giving your reasons:
-ED ending pronounced /t/ , /d /or /id /

4 Write a short story using at least four of the Focus Phrases about a man whose wife has to go into hospital for two weeks.

19 *Preparing and eating food*

1 a Write a diary of what you have eaten and drunk in the last 24 hours. Be honest!

Example:

```
OOOOOOOOOOOOOOOOOOOOOOOOOOOOOOO

  Yesterday :

  2 P.M.  mushroom Omelette,
           bread, water
  4 P.M.  apple, chocolate, coke
           etc.


```

b Show your diary to other people. What are the main differences and similarities between your diary and theirs?

2 Discuss these questions with a partner.

a What time(s) of day (and night) do you feel hungriest?
b How do you feel physically and emotionally when you are really hungry?
c What activities make you feel particularly hungry or thirsty?
d How many times per day (and night) do you eat and drink?
e How do you feel *after* eating and drinking?

MEANING IN
CONTEXT

3 Read the extract on the next page which is taken from *Oliver Twist* by Charles Dickens, and answer the questions that follow it.

The extract is taken from the beginning of the novel. Oliver, an orphan, is nine years old, and has recently been taken to the workhouse for poor people, where conditions are particularly hard.

. . . The room in which the boys were fed was a large stone hall, with a copper* at one end: out of which the master, dressed in an apron for the purpose, *ladled* the gruel* at mealtimes. Of this festive composition each boy had one bowl, and no more – except on occasions of great public rejoicing, when he had two ounces and a quarter of bread besides.

The bowls never wanted washing. The boys polished them with their spoons until they shone again; and when they had finished this operation (which never took very long, the spoons being nearly as large as the bowls), they would sit staring at the copper, with such eager eyes, as if they could have *devoured* the very bricks of which it was composed; employing themselves meanwhile, in *sucking* their fingers most *assiduously,* with a view to catching up any stray *splashes* of gruel that might have been on them. Boys have generally excellent appetites. Oliver Twist and his companions suffered the tortures of slow *starvation* for three months. At last they got so *voracious* and wild with hunger, that one boy, who was tall for his age, *hinted* darkly that unless he had another bowl of gruel per day, he was afraid he might some night happen to eat the boy who slept next to him. He had a wild, hungry eye and they implicitly believed him. Lots were cast who should walk up to the master after supper that evening and ask for more. It fell to Oliver Twist . . .

* copper: a large container for boiling water or food
* gruel: a thin mixture of water and oatmeal

a Match the words in italics with their meanings below.
   i wanting food very much
   ii served with a large spoon
  iii ate in a very hungry way
   iv putting in the mouth and cleaning with the tongue
   v suggested indirectly
   vi with great care and attention
  vii suffering from lack of food
 viii small amounts of liquid

b Complete the following using information from the text.

  i The boys were given a little more food when _____.

  ii The boys cleaned their bowls with their spoons because

    _____.

 iii After they had _____ for three months, one of the boys

    threatened to _____.

  iv Oliver was selected to ask for more by _____.

MEANING
RELATED MEANINGS

4 Put the words and expressions in the box in order of hungriness or thirstiness.

Not hungry ◄——————————————► very hungry
Not thirsty ◄——————————————► very thirsty

> ravenous   full up   starving   dying for a drir.k   parched
> voracious   peckish   dry   stuffed   could eat a horse
> off his/her food

ACTIVATE

5 a Which other words from this list could you use to describe the feelings of the boys in the passage above?
  b Which of these words would you use to describe how you feel:
   i on a hot day, after a lot of exercise?
   ii when you wake up in the morning?
   iii in the evening on a day when you missed lunch?

WORD FORMATION 📖
NOUNS, VERBS AND ADJECTIVES

6 Complete the table with the missing words, using a dictionary if necessary.

Noun	Verb	Adjective to describe food
salt	to salt	salty
sweets		
fat		
	to taste (of)	
		filling
	to appeal (to)	
spice		

WORD USE
CONNOTATION

7 a Use adjectives from exercise 6 and from the box below to describe dishes that you know.

> sickly   delicious   appetising   tasteless   revolting   rich

  b Fill in the table with the adjectives from exercises 6 and 7a.

Usually positive	Usually negative

ACTIVATE

8 Which are the dishes people normally associate with your country? What are the main ingredients? How would you describe these dishes?

RELATED MEANINGS

---

9 Read the descriptions of different ways of cooking, and fill the blanks with the correct verbs from the box.

roast   boil   steam   bake
simmer   grill   fry

a Cook using dry heat (normally in an oven) bread, cakes, biscuits
_____

b Cook meat, coffee beans, nuts _____

c Cook under direct heat _____

d Cook in hot oil or fat _____

e Cook in hot water at 100° centigrade _____

f Cook for a long period, at just below 100°C _____

g Cook above water at 100°C _____

10 Fill the blanks using appropriate forms of the cooking words from exercise 9 and the utensils in the box below.

kettle   saucepan   frying pan   baking tin   coffee pot
cake-tin   steamer   grill pan   teapot

a Put the vegetables in a large _____ full of water, add a little salt, and _____ them for ten minutes.

b Bob poured a little oil into a _____ _____ and put it on the gas until it was hot. Then he added some onions and _____ them for a few minutes before adding the mushrooms.

c Sally had prepared the cake very carefully and had put the mixture in a round _____. When the oven was hot, she put the cake in and _____ it for an hour.

d Those are large potatoes. I know they've been cooking for 20 minutes, but I think we should put the _____ back on the cooker and let them _____ for another ten minutes on a low flame.

e A: That smells good.

B: Yes. Lunch is in the oven. We're having _____ chicken.

f A: How are we going to cook this fish?

B: It's probably easiest if we _____ it over the vegetables, which are in that large saucepan.

A: OK. Let's put the fish in this _____. It will fit on top of the saucepan, I think.

g Jack _____ some water in the electric _____ to make himself some tea.

ACTIVATE

11 Look at the picture opposite. Describe the kitchen and what the three chefs are doing in the picture, and say what you think they will do next. Would you like to eat in their restaurant?

DICTIONARY USE

DEFINITIONS

carve	grind	stir	soak
beat	crush	slice	grate
whisk	dip	marinate	chop

12 The words in the box all describe ways of preparing food. Using a dictionary if necessary, put them in the right list below and explain what differences there are between the words in each list..

Mix or move round	
Cut into pieces	
Put into liquid	
Make into powder or small pieces	

ACTIVATE

📖 **13** The pictures below show a procedure for making a mushroom omelette. Write the procedure out as a normal recipe using words from this unit.

14 Mark each of the following statements about eating A if you agree or D if you disagree. Then compare your responses with a partner's.

___ Eating is such a waste of time, effort and money. It would be better if we could simply take pills.

___ You are what you eat.

___ Eating is one of the greatest pleasures available. In the modern world we tend to eat too quickly and not well enough.

___ The problem is half the world eats too much, and the other half doesn't have enough to eat.

MEANING IN
CONTEXT

15 Read the extract on the next page. What are the names of the people in the picture? How do you know?

As usual, Miles had excelled himself in the kitchen, and the table was spread with an array of Mediterranean dishes that filled the air with a delicious aroma. However, the events of the afternoon had affected the family's appetites in different ways. Lord Belsize *tucked* in with his usual vigour, *stuffing* great chunks of avocado into his mouth and washing them down with *gulps* of white wine, while Lady Belsize *picked* daintily *at* her plate of snails with garlic sauce and *nibbled* at olives. George gazed dreamily out over the bay, occasionally *sipping* mineral water, and using his fork as a drumstick. He had obviously lost his appetite completely, and was put off by the appetizing smell of the grilled trout. Meanwhile, Jemima on his left, her pretty face tense with concentration, was resolutely *attacking* her food, as if she had been *fasting* for at least two days. She deftly separated flesh from bone and thoroughly *chewed* each mouthful of the succulent fish, occasionally *downing* a whole glass of wine. Miles himself, having put so much into the preparation of the meal, was contentedly *munching* home-made bread as he *swallowed* spoonfuls of minestrone soup with a *slurping* sound. Lord Belsize, having by now *polished off* a very large rare steak with mushrooms, *drained his glass*, *licked his lips* noisily, belched and said: 'Well, George, I'm glad to see you're not *overeating* tonight. We wouldn't want you to have indigestion on the eve of your wedding, would we, Jemima?' Jemima, looking startled, began to choke and hurried into the villa, coughing. 'Looks like something went down the wrong way,' said Miles, and *gobbled* two artichoke hearts.

MEANING

RELATED MEANINGS

📖 **16** Put the words in italics in the text into the appropriate boxes below:

	With a lot of appetite	Without appetite	Neutral
Solid food			
Liquid or near-liquid			

📖 **17** Using a dictionary, add the following words to the table above. Then say which of the words in exercise 16 are closest in meaning.

> guzzle   bolt   devour   gorge   crunch   gnaw
> bite   swallow

ACTIVATE

18 How would you describe the following, using words from exercises 16 and 17?

a a lion eating a large piece of meat
b a bird trying to eat a piece of bread
c a small girl eating a large packet of potato crisps
d a Sumo wrestler eating a huge bowl of noodles
e a horse drinking water after a long gallop
f a fat man eating his third ice cream
g a dog trying to eat a large bone
h a hungry person eating an apple

19 Explain the following phrases:

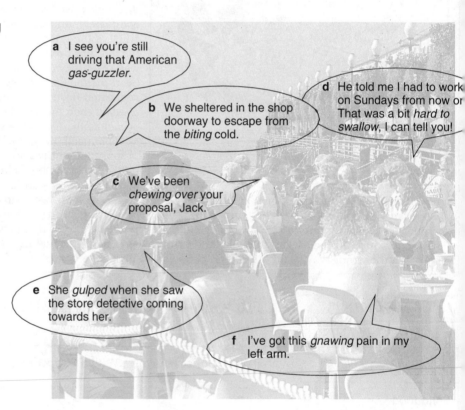

a I see you're still driving that American *gas-guzzler*.

b We sheltered in the shop doorway to escape from the *biting* cold.

c We've been *chewing over* your proposal, Jack.

d He told me I had to work on Sundays from now on. That was a bit *hard to swallow*, I can tell you!

e She *gulped* when she saw the store detective coming towards her.

f I've got this *gnawing* pain in my left arm.

MEANING
—————————
RELATED MEANINGS

20 When in England, Lord and Lady Belsize customarily have the following meals and refreshments. What order do you think they have them in? Number each of them from 1 to 6. Which of them are main meals? Which do you think is the biggest? What kinds of thing do they eat/drink on each occasion?

___ a nightcap   ___ breakfast   ___ tea
___ luncheon   ___ dinner   ___ elevenses

ACTIVATE

21 If you had the choice and the money, which famous person would you like to invite to dinner? Where would you like to have

FOCUS WORDS			
appealing	drain	luncheon	spice
appetising	dry	marinate	spicy
assiduous	elevenses	munch	splash
assiduously	fast	nibble	starvation
attack	fat	nightcap	starve
bake	filling	overeat	starving
baking tin	fry	peckish	steam
beat	frying pan	pick at	steamer
bite	full up	polish off	stir
boil	gas-guzzler	ravenous	stuff
bolt	gnaw	revolting	stuffed
cake-tin	gobble	rich	suck
carve	gorge	roast	swallow
chew	grate	salt	sweet
chop	grill	salty	taste
coffee pot	grill pan	saucepan	tasteless
crunch	grind	sickly	tasty
crush	gulp	simmer	teapot
delicious	guzzle	sip	tuck in
devour	hint	slice	voracious
dip	kettle	slurp	whisk
down	ladle	soak	

FOCUS PHRASES

chew (something) over
hard to swallow
lick your lips

WORD CHECK

Refer to Focus Words and Focus Phrases only.

1 Which of the different verbs of preparing and cooking food can only be used with liquids or semi-liquids?
2 Find all the names of meals and put them in order of size (1 = the biggest, etc.).
3 With a partner, write a short conversation between children at a party using at least four adjectives describing the taste of food and/or drink.
4 Which of the words do you find hardest to pronounce correctly? Why?

20 *Private transport*

MEANING

1 In groups (and using dictionaries if necessary) check that you understand the meaning of the words in italics in the questionnaire opposite.

2 Complete the questionnaire in pairs.

1 What are the advantages and disadvantages of travelling by the following?

	Advantages	Disadvantages
car *motorcycle* *moped* *bicycle*		

2 If/when you buy a car what do you look for? Put the following in order of importance for you.

Feature	Importance
comfort *space* *speed* *reliability* *safety design* *road-holding* *braking* *low maintenance costs* *low fuel consumption* *price* *power* *appearance*	_____ _____ _____ _____ _____ _____ _____ _____ _____ _____ _____ _____

3 Which kind of car would you most like to own? Put the following in order.

	Order	Reason
van *jeep* *saloon* *hatchback* *estate car* *sports car* *soft-top*	___ ___ ___ ___ ___ ___ ___	_____ _____ _____ _____ _____ _____ _____

3 Compare your questionnaire results in groups.

ACTIVATE

4 Role-play: Student A is a customer. Student B is a car salesperson. A decides on the kind of vehicle he or she wants to buy and goes to the car showroom to look at one.

B has to try and persuade the customer to choose a different kind of vehicle (because it's company policy or because the company is trying to get rid of a particular kind of vehicle, for example).

Example:

B: Good morning madam.

A: Good morning. I'm interested in buying a hatchback.

B: A hatchback? Why do you want that particular type of vehicle? .

MEANING

Cars   **a** bumper
     b headlight
     c sidelight
     d numberplate
     e indicator
     f bonnet
     g windscreen
     h windscreen wiper
     i wing
     j wing mirror
     k aerial
     l rear window
     m boot
     n rear light
     o brake light

Bicycles   **a** handlebars
     b pump
     c pedals
     d chain
     e saddle
     f saddlebag
     g mudguard
     h gears
     i brake
     j wheel
     k tyre

5 Match the features shown in the pictures with their names.

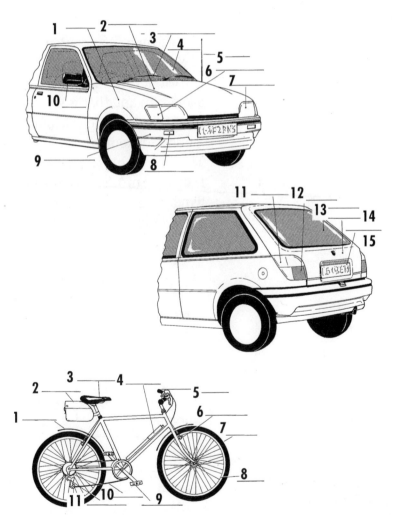

6 Design an advertisement for your car (or your friend's/relation's car). Mention features of its appearance, using as many items from exercises 1 and 5 as possible.

7 Read this insurance claim and use it to complete the chart which follows. Which words go with which? Tick the boxes.

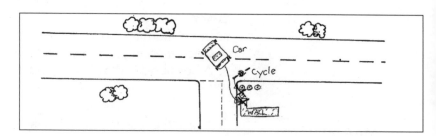

The accident was caused, I believe, because the lights on the boy's bicycle were faulty. Thus I did not see him until I had turned across the road. Obviously I had to swerve to try to avoid him and that is why I hit the wall. The boy crashed into the bollards at the side of the road. The bicycle ended up with a buckled front wheel. My car is almost a complete write-off. The headlights are smashed, the bonnet is dented and the front bumper is completely buckled. Of course the windscreen was shattered and there are two big dents in the wing. Luckily neither of us was seriously hurt.

	wing	bumper	headlight	windscreen	wheel
dented					
shattered					
buckled					
broken					
faulty					
smashed					

ACTIVATE

8 What is the problem with these vehicles? What do you think caused the trouble?

MEANING

9 a Complete the passage with the words from the box.

(rear-view) mirror   glove compartment gear lever   handbrake seat belt   steering wheel brake   horn speedometer   petrol gauge accelerator   clutch

She looked at the map one more time before putting it back in the a) _____ . It was ten past nine. She should make it just in time. She checked the b) _____ . Yes, she had plenty of petrol for the drive. She released the c) _____ , put the car in gear, and pressed down on the d) _____ . The car moved smoothly from the kerb.

Half an hour later, when she looked in the e) _____ and saw the police car she suddenly realized that she was going far too fast. The f) _____ registered 95 miles an hour. But she had to get to his house in time or a terrible wrong would be done. She gripped the g) _____ , forcing herself to be calm; in a practised routine her left foot depressed the h) _____ while her left hand enveloped the i) _____ as she changed from fourth to third in faultless synchronization. Maybe the police would leave her alone.

The car slowed, but not enough as, just ahead of her, a deer suddenly sprang up in the headlights. Her foot hit the j) _____ at the same moment as she sounded the k) _____ . Then suddenly, she was fighting desperately to control the car on the oily surface of the road – and the police were closing fast. It was at that moment that she realized she wasn't wearing her l) _____ .

b What is the story about?
c Complete the story in groups.

10 **a** Complete the table with the following verbs.

> *pull over   cycle   accelerate   speed   spin   slow down*
> *draw away   pull up   pedal   overtake   speed up   skid*
> *drive   swerve   decelerate*

Put (B) or (C) in brackets if the verb can only be used for either bicycles or cars.

stop	
start	
move in or on a means of transport	
go fast	
go faster	
go slower	
pass	
lose control	

b What is the difference in meaning between these verbs?
  i *pull over* and *pull up*
  ii *spin, skid* and *swerve*

11 In groups decide on the events of a minor accident between two vehicles. Write accident reports like the one in exercise 7 for the two drivers of the vehicle.

12 Match these adjectives with their dictionary definitions. What is the opposite of each of the words?

a dangerous
b reckless
c careless

1 not caring about possible bad or dangerous results of an action
2 not taking enough care, inattentive
3 able to or likely to cause danger

WORD USE
COLLOCATIONS

13 Which of these words can go together? Tick the boxes.

	driver	driving	vehicle	disregard	attitude	behaviour
speeding						
reckless						
careless						
dangerous						
drunken						

14 Make sentences using any two pairs of words from exercise 13.

ACTIVATE

15 Explain the following newspaper headlines. Choose one and write the accompanying story using words from this unit.

I LOST CONTROL SAYS SHOP WINDOW MOTORIST

FAMILY ESCAPES INJURY IN MULTIPLE PILE-UP

MAN DENIES HITCHHIKE KILLING

BEAUTY AND THE BOTTLE

SPEED TRAP SLOWS THEM DOWN

16 Use the facts from one story to hold a court case. What punishment should the wrongdoer(s) receive?

FOCUS WORDS

accelerate	disregard	motorcycle	shatter
accelerator	draw away	mudguard	sidelight
aerial	drive (v)	numberplate	skid (v)
appearance	driver	overtake	slow down
attitude	driving	pedal (n)	smash
behaviour	drunken	pedal (v)	soft-top
bicycle	estate car	petrol gauge	space
bonnet	faulty	power	speed (n)
boot	fuel	price	speed (v)
brake (n)	consumption	pull over	speed up
brake (v)	gear	pull up	speedometer
brake light	gear lever	pump	spin
buckle (v)	glove	rear light	sports car
bumper	compartment	rear-view	steering wheel
car	handbrake	mirror	swerve
careless	handlebars	rear window	van
chain	hatchback	reckless	vehicle
clutch	headlight	reliability	wheel
comfort	horn	road-holding	windscreen
cycle (v)	indicator	saddle	windscreen
dangerous	jeep	saddlebag	wiper
decelerate	maintenance	safety design	wing
dent (n)	mirror	saloon	wing mirror
dent (v)	moped	seat belt	

WORD CHECK

Refer to Focus Words only.

1 Find all the words in the list which refer to parts of a car.
List them in these two categories:
    a the inside of the car
    b the outside of the car

2 Write a sentence using as many words as you possibly can
from the list about
    a a very short car journey.
    b a very short bicycle journey.

3 Study the pronunciation of the **Focus Words** and list the
words which are:
    a stressed on the first syllable.
    b stressed on the second syllable.

4 Which of these words will be most useful for you in the
future, do you think? Which will you probably remember
for the longest time?

UNIT 21 Rail, air and sea travel

1 What is your favourite/least favourite form of public transport? Why?

2 What are the following items? What forms of transport do you associate them with?

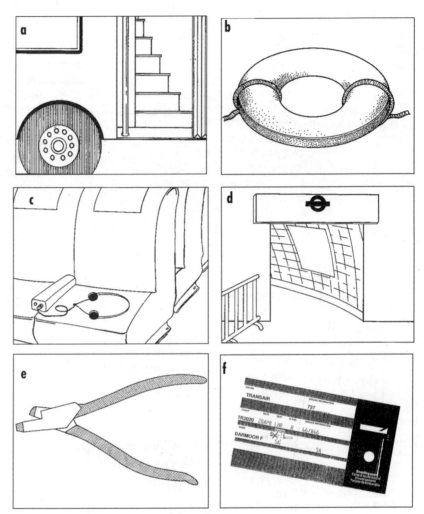

3 The following three extracts about three different journeys have lost their conclusions. Can you match the conclusions with their extracts?

He sat on one side of the *aisle*, holding the baby as the xxxxx bucketed around the sky. Outside it was hideously black. He realized that it was the worst turbulence he had even been in.

Across the aisle his wife sat rigidly, her whole body distended with fear. The American sitting next to her was watching her with a look of dazed preoccupation. He had a long pony tail and a shoulder bag and was either drugged or transfixed with fear. He leaned over to her and said 'Relax lady, it's your destiny.' She looked at him without understanding.

At that moment a bolt of lightning hit the *tail* and there was a huge crash. Everybody screamed. His baby started crying. Through the window he saw the *wings* wobbling horribly. Suddenly the American screamed 'Holy Moses, we're upside down!'

a

When the xxxxx arrived to pick them up they were relieved. The airline strike had meant that they could not get home by the usual route. They climbed aboard wearily stuffing bags into the *luggage rack* and collapsing into the high-backed seats.

The first part of the journey was dramatic as they wound their way through the mountain passes and fought the hairpin bends. Gradually the light faded until their way was illuminated only by the beam of the four *headlights* on the front of the xxxxx.

They travelled on through the night, the *driver's* face illuminated only by the dim dashboard lights. But even in that dim glow you could see him yawning.

They arrived home at ten o'clock the next morning. The door opened with a hiss of compressed air and they staggered onto the pavement bleary and uncomfortable.

It seemed a calm day. The gulls wheeled above them in a clear blue sky and there was only a gentle swell. He walked along the *deck* from the *bow* to the *stern*, smelling a mixture of engine oil and sea spray and feeling the salty wind in his hair. Everyone had told him that the Bay of Biscay was always rough but this seemed quite bearable.

He went into the xxxx's small cinema, thinking that he might as well pass the time there as anywhere else. It was dark and warm and he sank into one of the comfortable armchairs.

As he watched the film enclosed in the hot darkness, he was conscious of the rise and fall of the xxxxx. He noticed how disagreeable the cinema smelled to him and how the fragrances of the perfumes

b

i

She looked back at the driver.
'I bet you're going to have a rest.'
'Too right. I've been driving for three days without sleeping.' No wonder he had been yawning. She suddenly felt

ii sick.

c

iii Later, in the baggage hall, the American came over to him. 'Has your old lady come down yet?' 'I don't know,' he said, 'have you?'

He got out just in time, rushing over to the side where he hung, being violently sick. It was going to be a long time before he travelled that way again.

Which form of transport is involved in each case?
Have you ever been frightened or ill on one of these forms of transport?

4 Put the words from the texts which are in italics in the correct place on this chart.

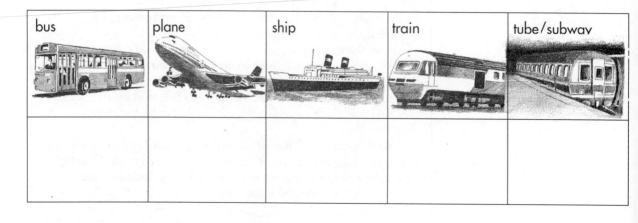

bus	plane	ship	train	tube/subway

USING DICTIONARIES
DEFINITIONS

5 Use a dictionary to complete the chart in exercise 4 with words from these three boxes. Note that some words occur in more than one column.

Features
front, back, nose, funnel, bridge, cockpit, cab, cabin, propeller, rudder, fuselage, hull, body, undercarriage, engine, locomotive, carriage, coach

Personnel
pilot, helmsman, crew, cabin crew, copilot, navigator, captain, steward, stewardess, flight attendant, guard, ticket collector, conductor, engineer, check-in clerk, driver

Verbs
take off, land, cast off, moor, move away from, leave, arrive, steer, pilot, fly, drive, skid, swerve, capsize

a What do the different 'personnel' actually have to do?
b Which job would you most/least like to have?

ACTIVATE

6 Write or tell a short story about someone who travelled on a plane, ship, bus, etc. without paying, but who got found out and had to go to court. Use at least two words from the Features box, at least one verb, and at least one word from the Personnel box.

WORD FORMATION
PARTS OF SPEECH

7 Which of the words in the box below can be:

a verbs (but not nouns)?
b nouns (but not verbs)?
c nouns or verbs with the same basic meaning in both cases?
d nouns or verbs, but with different meanings depending which part of speech they are?
e adjectives?

book	*round trip*	*reserve*	*check in*	*confirm*	*standby*
	take	*standing room*	*first class*		

8 a Read the dialogue. Do the blanks require nouns, verbs, adjectives or adverbs?

A: Are you ready for your trip to Madrid?
B: Yes, I've (1) _____ my ticket.
A: Are you just flying one-way?
B: No, I'm doing the (2) _____ . I'll be back on Wednesday.
A: Oh, I didn't realize it was such a short visit. I suppose you've (3) _____ a seat, then.
B: No, I haven't. On this flight you can't reserve your seat until you (4) _____ at the airport. So I won't be travelling (5) _____ or anything like that! But I'll be sitting in the 'No Smoking' section of course – for the first time ever!
A: Yes, that's fantastic. But you have definitely got a place?
B: Oh yes. My ticket is (6) _____ . At least it won't be like the last time when I was a (7) _____ passenger. I only got on at the last moment.
A: But you will reserve a seat on the train down to London?
B: Oh yes. Last time all the seats were (8) _____ and there was (9) _____ only. I'm not going through that again!

b Complete the dialogue with the correct words from exercise 7.
c Which of the expressions in the dialogue means
  i single
  ii return
d Use the words to complete the expressions.
  i A _____ to London please. I'm not coming back.
  ii I want a _____ ticket to Amsterdam, coming back in five days.
  iii Southampton _____ please. What time does the bus come back?

ACTIVATE

9 You are going to a travel agent's to book a holiday or a flight.

a Decide where you are going. Write four questions that you will ask the travel agent.
b Write four questions that the travel agent will ask.

Role-play your visit to the travel agent with a partner. Make sure all the questions are asked and answered.

WORD FORMATION

PARTS OF SPEECH

10 a Complete the chart with the infinitive and noun forms of these participle forms.

Infinitive	Past Participle	Noun
	delayed	
	reserved	
	confirmed	
	cancelled	

b What prefix can you use to make the following two expressions even more extreme?
  i booked
  ii crowded

11 Fill the blanks with words from exercise 10.

a When we get _____ of your booking we will let you know.
b I'm afraid the bad weather is going to _____ your flight. But it's better to be safe than sorry.
c Do you have a _____? If you don't then I think this seat is mine.

d I can't believe it! They've _____ our train. It's the second time there's been a _____ in one week.

e Excuse me, what's the _____? Why aren't we taking off?

f You can _____ a place now, madam, or you can run the risk that the train will be full and you won't get a seat.

g We apologize for the _____ of our flight. Passengers can go to the restaurant at our expense. We hope to announce a replacement flight as soon as possible.

MEANING
---

12 Fill the blanks with the words and phrases from the box. Use them only once unless otherwise stated.

> arrivals   check-in counter   customs hall   departure lounge
> gate 25   immigration (twice)   left luggage   platform six
> ticket office

1 When you travel somewhere by plane, first you go to the **a)** _____, then you go through **b)** _____ until you get to the **c)** _____, where you wait until your flight is called. Then you go to **d)** _____, for example until it is time to board the plane.

2 When you arrive at an airport you first go through **a)** _____. Then you reclaim your baggage and go through the **b)** _____, where they may check your luggage. Then it's on to the **c)** _____ to be met by friends and relatives.

3 When you travel by train you first go to the **a)** _____ to get your ticket and then to **b)** _____ to reclaim your baggage (which you deposited there because it was too heavy to carry around). Then it's time to run to **c)** _____ to catch the train.

ACTIVATE

13 Role-play a conversation in one of the following situations. Ask for directions to some of the places in exercise 12.

a You arrive late at an unfamiliar airport. Go to the information desk.

b You finally reach the check-in desk after queueing for hours. Your plane is about to go.

c Your train is about to go. The employee at the left luggage counter is being very slow in getting your bags.

d Your plane has arrived late. The immigration officer is taking his time over your passport. But you have a connecting flight in another terminal.

MEANING IN CONTEXT

airport	bus station
station	tube station

14 In which of the following places would you expect to hear these announcements (sometimes more than one answer is possible)?

a . . . is *running late* and will arrive at 12.15 . . .

b . . . *regret to announce* the *late arrival* on *platform six* . . .

c . . . *has been delayed owing to* engine failure . . .

d . . . *has been cancelled due to* instrument malfunction.

e . . . now boarding at gate 27. We *apologise for the delay which was caused by* the late arrival of the incoming plane.

f . . . this train will stop at Liverpool Street. There will be no underground service between Liverpool Street and Epping. This is due to industrial action by drivers. We *apologise for any inconvenience* this may cause.

ACTIVATE

15 Make airport or railway or bus station announcements using the expressions in italics from exercise 14.

Example:
Clear Blue Airways regret to announce the cancellation of flight CB376. This is due to the late arrival of the incoming aircraft.

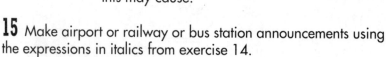

ACTIVATE

16 Describe a journey you have taken on public transport which was delayed or cancelled. Say:

a where you bought your ticket.
b what kind of ticket it was.
c why you were delayed.
d what you did about it.
e what the transport company/authority did about it.
f how long the journey took altogether.

FOCUS WORDS

airport	coach	headlights	skid
aisle	cockpit	helmsman	standby
arrivals	conductor	hull	standing
arrive	confirm (v)	immigration	room
back	copilot	land (v)	station
body	crew	leave	steer
book (v)	crowded	left luggage	stern
booked up	customs hall	locomotive	steward
bow	deck	luggage rack	stewardess
bridge	delay	moor	subway
bus	departure	move away	swerve
bus station	lounge	from	tail
cab	drive	navigator	take
cabin	engine	nose	take off
cabin crew	engineer	overbooked	ticket collector
cancel	first class	overcrowded	ticket office
capsize	flight	pilot	train
captain	attendant	plane	tube station
carriage	fly	platform (six)	tube
cast off	front	propeller	undercarriage
check in	funnel	reserve (v)	wings
check-in clerk	fuselage	round trip	
check-in	gate (25)	rudder	
counter	guard	ship	

FOCUS PHRASES

(Flight 837) has been cancelled due to (instrument malfunction).
(The aeroplane) has been delayed owing to (engine failure).
(The train) is running late.
We apologize for any inconvenience this may cause.
We apologize for the delay.
We regret to announce the late arrival of . . .

WORD CHECK

Refer to Focus Words and Focus Phrases only.

1 Play the game 'Consequences' using as many words from the lists as possible. [You play the game by writing a sentence, then folding over the paper and passing it to the next person, who can't see what you have written. That person writes the next phrase or sentence and folds the paper and so on. The story always follows the format of the example: 'Someone *met* someone somewhere, *he said, she said,* and *the consequence was . . .'*

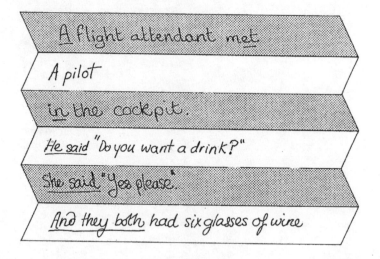

> A flight attendant *met*
>
> A pilot
>
> *in the* cockpit.
>
> *He said* "Do you want a drink?"
>
> *She said* "Yes please".
>
> *And they both* had six glasses of wine

2 Choose one of the Focus Phrases. Decide where and when it is used and then list all the Focus Words which apply to that situation.

3 The word *navigator* has a short syllable with the sound /ə/, navigator. Choose any ten other words and see how often you can find the same sound.

4 Which ten words on the list do you like best?

22 | *Streets, roads and traffic*

1 What is the difference between the following?

a being *run over*
b being *knocked off* something
c being *knocked over*
d *jaywalking*

Where are these things likely to take place?

2 The paragraphs in this instruction manual about the safest way to cross roads have become mixed up. Put the numbers 1 to 6 in the boxes to make the correct sequence.

 # THE GREEN CROSS CODE

❑ **FIRST FIND A SAFE PLACE TO CROSS, THEN STOP**
It is safer to cross at subways, footbridges, islands, Zebra and Pelican crossings, or where there is a police officer, school crossing patrol or a traffic warden.
    If you can't find any good crossing places like these, choose a place where you can see clearly along the roads in all directions. Try not to cross between parked cars. Always STOP at the kerb to give yourself lots of time to have a good look all round.

❑ **STAND ON THE PAVEMENT NEAR THE KERB**
Don't stand near the edge of the pavement. If there is no pavement, stand back from the edge of the road but where you can still see traffic coming.

❑ **LOOK ALL ROUND FOR TRAFFIC AND LISTEN**
Traffic may be coming from any direction, so take care to look along every road, and listen too, because you can sometimes hear traffic before you can see it.

❑ **IF TRAFFIC IS COMING, LET IT PASS. LOOK ALL ROUND AGAIN**
If there is any traffic near, let it go past. Then look round again and listen to make sure no other traffic is coming.

❑ **WHEN THERE IS NO TRAFFIC NEAR, WALK STRAIGHT ACROSS THE ROAD**
If there is something in the distance do not cross unless there is plenty of time to reach the other side.

❑ **KEEP LOOKING AND LISTENING FOR TRAFFIC WHILE YOU CROSS**
Once you are in the road, keep looking and listening in case you did not see some traffic – or in case other traffic suddenly appears.

3 Who are the instructions written for? Are they well written?

MEANING

Draw a picture showing as many of the things above as possible.

MEANING

RELATED MEANINGS

4 Fill in the table with the words from the box.

| road   pavement   kerb   island   traffic lights |
| pedestrian crossing   crossroads   roundabout   footbridge |
| flyover   one-way street   cul-de-sac   junction |

For the use of vehicles only	For the use of pedestrians only	For both vehicles and pedestrians

5 What's the difference between the following pairs of words? Put them in the correct sentences to find out.

a a *road* and a *street* **e** a *street* and an *avenue*
b a *road* and a *path* **f** a *path* and an *alley*
c a *subway* and an *underpass* **g** a *road* and a *way*
d a *main road* and a *side-street*

1 Both are for pedestrians but a _____ can be in the open while an _____ goes between houses or trees etc.

2 A _____ is for walking under a road; an _____ is often a road under another road.

3 A _____ is a specific thoroughfare; _____ describes the route in general.

4 A _____ usually has shops and offices on either side; an _____ is often wider and has trees.

5 A _____ is the principal thoroughfare; a _____ is less important and usually joins it.

6 A _____ can be in the town or country and usually leads to another town; a _____ is usually in a town and has shops and other buildings.

7 A _____ is for vehicles; a _____ is for people and animals to walk on.

ACTIVATE

6 Using the Instructions for The Green Cross Code as a model, write brief instructions for visitors to *your* country on:

a how to cross roads.
b what to do at roundabouts.
c what to do at road junctions.

WORD USE

METAPHOR AND IDIOM

7 Match these sentences with what people are saying in the photograph.

1 Don't disagree with me or make my life difficult again.
2 He is fooling you.
3 It should be the kind of thing we like.
4 We have a definite advantage over the other people who do the same kind of thing.
5 We should split up.
6 Why don't we start now?
7 You oppose me and I'll make your job difficult.
8 You should do things on your own – be responsible for your own actions.

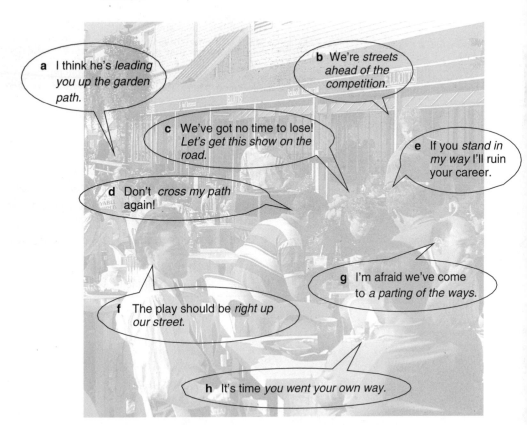

a I think he's *leading you up the garden path*.

b We're *streets ahead of the competition*.

c We've got no time to lose! *Let's get this show on the road*.

d Don't *cross my path* again!

e If you *stand in my way* I'll ruin your career.

f The play should be *right up our street*.

g I'm afraid we've come to *a parting of the ways*.

h It's time *you went your own way*.

ACTIVATE
Which of the phrases in italics
sound slightly formal when
used in speech?

8 Use any two of the expressions from exercise 7 in a quick
exchange between any of the following:

a two business people
b a policeman and a motorist
c a reporter and his/her editor
d two opposing politicians
e a radio DJ and a pop star

USING
DICTIONARIES

DEFINITIONS

9 Use a dictionary to find the meaning of the following words.

Put the words in the correct
blanks in the following radio
transcript.

> *lane   tailback   alternative routes   slip roads   clockwise
> re-surfacing   contraflow   roadworks   carriageway*

> A: . . . and we've got some gloomy news for drivers in and around north
> London.
> B: Yes, John, that's right. Owing to an accident there are long delays on the
> M25 going in an anti-(1) _____ direction between junctions 23 and 25.
> Drivers are advised to leave the motorway at exit 25.
> A: There has been a serious accident on the southbound
> (2) _____ of the M11 between junctions 7 and 8. There is a six-mile (3)
> _____ and drivers are advised to find alternative routes.
> B: On a less serious note (4) _____ are taking place on the A10 at
> Hoddesdon where the A10 joins the B119. Delays are expected all this
> week. Drivers should take (5) _____ to their destinations.
> A: And finally, because of (6) _____ work on the northbound carriageway
> of the M11 between junctions 4 and 5, a (7) _____ system is in
> operation and traffic is restricted to one (8) _____ only in both
> directions. There are long delays and there are even traffic jams on the
> (9) _____ at junction 5. So why don't you just stay at home! I would!

10 **a** Point to the problem spots on this map.
b Your partner wants to drive from Harlow to Chigwell and
you have just listened to the radio. Decide which roads they
should take to their destination.
c Give them directions. Use these expressions:

> *turn right/left   take the (first) right/left
> go straight on (for about . . .*

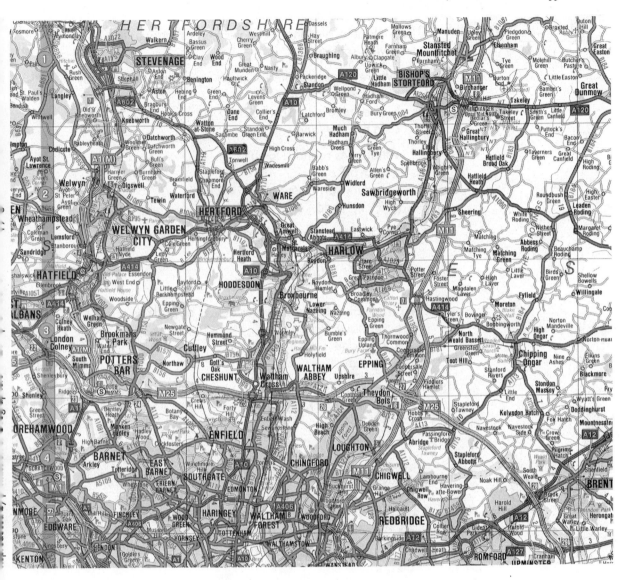

ACTIVATE

11 In groups tell each other about:

a how you feel when you get in a traffic jam.
b what you do when you get in a traffic jam.
c when traffic jams take place in your area.
d why traffic jams take place in your area.
e the worst traffic jam you've ever been in.

12 Using a dictionary choose the best answer **a**, **b** or **c** in the following sentences.

1 Where would you find a *crash barrier* on a motorway?
   a on the *central reservation*
   b in a *motorway service area*
   c in the *fast lane*

2 What goes round a town?
   a a *bypass*
   b a *dual carriageway*
   c a *ring road*

3 What normally runs along the side of motorways?
   a a *lay by*
   b a *grass verge*
   c a *hard shoulder*

4 What takes boats on water across a road?
   a an *aqueduct*
   b a *bridge*
   c a *viaduct*

5 Which roads are supposed to carry the least traffic?
   a *unclassified roads*
   b *B-roads*
   c *A-roads*

13 Discuss the advantages and disadvantages of using motorways. Talk about:

a safety   **b** convenience   **c** time

14 Read this poem by Adrian Henri.

Song for a petrol pump attendant

I wanted your soft verges
but you gave me your hard shoulder

Can you write a similar two-line poem using words from this unit?

FOCUS WORDS

alley	crash barrier	motorway	side street
alternative	cul-de-sac	service area	slip road
route	dual	one-way street	street
anti-clockwise	carriageway	path	subway
aqueduct	flyover	pavement	tailback
avenue	footbridge	pedestrian	traffic lights
A-road	grass verge	crossing	unclassified
bridge	hard shoulder	pelican	road
B-road	island	crossing	underpass
bypass	junction	re-surfacing	verge
carriageway	kerb	ring road	viaduct
central	lane	road	way
reservation	lay by	roadworks	zebra
clockwise	main road	roundabout	crossing
contraflow	motorway	route	

FOCUS PHRASES

cross someone's path
get the show on the road
lead someone up the garden path
parting of the ways
right up (your) street
stand in someone's way
streets ahead (of)

WORD CHECK

Refer to Focus Words and Focus Phrases only.

1 Think of a journey from your house to another place you go to frequently. Find words that describe things you see or experience on your journey.

2 Use at least three Focus Phrases in a three sentence story about an argument you have had at some stage of your life.

3 Find all the noun phrases which consist of two or more words. Does the main stress occur on the first word or the last word?

4 Which words or phrases from the list:
   a were new to you in this unit?
   b have you found most easy to learn?
   c will you remember for longest, do you think?

23 *Science and technology*

1 Look at these anagrams. Which areas of scientific study or of technology are in the list? (Remember that many subjects and disciplines end in -ICS or -Y. What do they mean?

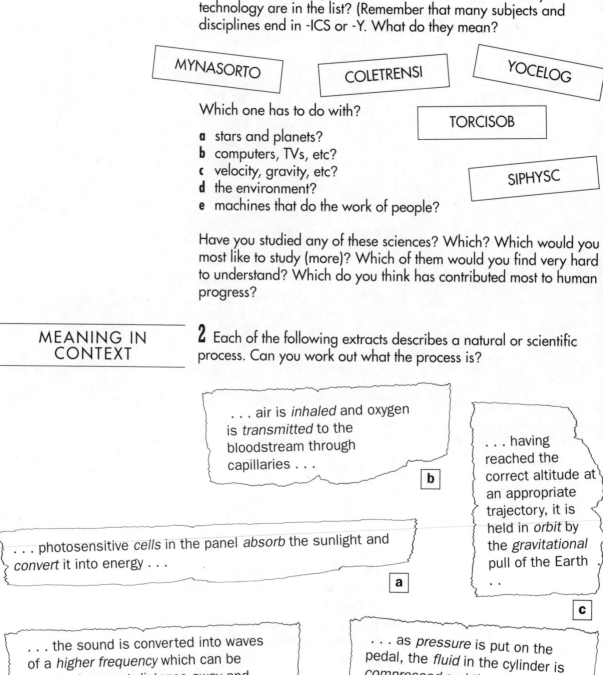

MYNASORTO

COLETRENSI

YOCELOG

Which one has to do with?

TORCISOB

a stars and planets?
b computers, TVs, etc?
c velocity, gravity, etc?
d the environment?
e machines that do the work of people?

SIPHYSC

Have you studied any of these sciences? Which? Which would you most like to study (more)? Which of them would you find very hard to understand? Which do you think has contributed most to human progress?

MEANING IN CONTEXT

2 Each of the following extracts describes a natural or scientific process. Can you work out what the process is?

. . . air is *inhaled* and oxygen is *transmitted* to the bloodstream through capillaries . . .

b

. . . having reached the correct altitude at an appropriate trajectory, it is held in *orbit* by the *gravitational* pull of the Earth . . .

c

. . . photosensitive *cells* in the panel *absorb* the sunlight and *convert* it into energy . . .

a

. . . the sound is converted into waves of a *higher frequency* which can be *received* a great distance away and converted back into soundwaves . . .

d

. . . as *pressure* is put on the pedal, the *fluid* in the cylinder is *compressed* and the discs are squeezed together *applying* friction to the wheels . . .

e

WORD FORMATION

PARTS OF SPEECH

3 Complete the following tables.

Nouns	Verbs
	inhale
	transmit
	convert
	absorb
pressure	
	compress
	apply

Nouns	Adjectives
	gravitational
frequency	
cell	
fluid	
	high

ACTIVATE

4 Describe briefly two other processes that you know about.

Examples:

taking a photograph or developing a film
transplanting a heart or a kidney

MEANING

RELATED MEANINGS

5 Look at these inventions and discoveries. Which branch of science does each belong to? Put them in order of their importance for mankind. Give reasons for the order that you have chosen.

Compare your selection with a neighbour's. What are the differences?

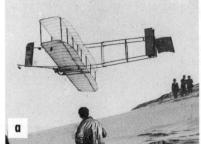
a

b

c

d

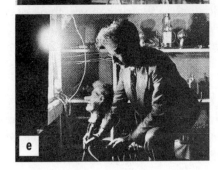
e

f

6 Hold a 'balloon debate': the class divides into pairs or groups. Each pair/group chooses one of the inventors above. They then explain why their invention is so great that their inventor should be the last one left in the falling balloon while the others jump out to save him or her.

WORD USE

7 Which invention(s) from exercise 5 does each of the following words relate to? Write the appropriate letter **a** to **f** beside each word. Then explain (if you can) what the relationship is.

___ wing   ___ charge

___ valve   ___ lift

___ test tube   ___ bacteria

___ bit   ___ cure

___ radioactivity   ___ exhaust

___ wire   ___ altitude

___ piston   ___ receiver

___ key   ___ software

___ radium   ___ energy

Use words from these lists and your own knowledge to describe how one of the inventions/discoveries works.

WORD FORMATION **8** What do the following parts of words mean?

| tele- aero- photo- micro- mono- bi- auto- hydro- |

How many words can you think of or find in which they are used? Write a brief report containing five words with different prefixes from the list above.

9 What does the word *nuclear* mean to you? Write down four words or ideas that you associate with *nuclear*. Compare your list with other people's.

WORD USE

COLLOCATION

10 Make sentences using one word from column A with one from column B in each.

A	B
achieve	atom
become	energy
extract	breakthrough
generate	mineral
split	reality
fuse	

MEANING IN CONTEXT

11 Read the following and answer the questions.

NUCLEAR FUSION BREAKTHROUGH

NUCLEAR PROMISES CHEAP SAFE POWER

By Tom Knight

The *science fiction* dream of clean, cheap, unlimited power is on its way to becoming reality.

For the first time anywhere in the world, scientists at the joint European Torus (JET) experimental fusion reactor at Culham in Oxfordshire have achieved controlled nuclear fusion – *harnessing* the reaction which powers the stars.

The success came when they put 'real' fuel inside the reactor for the first time. Previously only deuterium (a type of hydrogen) had been used in fusion experiments, but by adding tritium, they achieved a major break-through in the amount of energy which could be generated.

Fusion *research* has been going on for 40 years, but, said a JET spokesman, "It is the first time that anyone has produced any substantial amount of fusion power in a controlled fusion experiment as opposed to a bomb."

In a *conventional* nuclear reactor, heavy, unstable radioactive uranium atoms are split apart, creating lighter more *unstable* and dangerous elements such as plutonium, as well as vast amounts of heat.

By contrast, fusion relies on super-heating simpler 'clean' atoms, making them strike each other with such force that they *fuse together*. The heat has to be around 200 million degrees – 20 times the heat of the sun. With current technology the reaction can only be sustained for several seconds, producing in that time the equivalent of one million watts of electricity.

The fuels needed for fusion are plentiful. Deuterium is extracted from water, while tritium can be made inside the reactor. Just 10 grams of deuterium and 15 grams of tritium would be enough to provide the lifetime electricity needs of an average person in an industrialized country.

A commercial fusion-powered reactor could be *commissioned* by 2020.

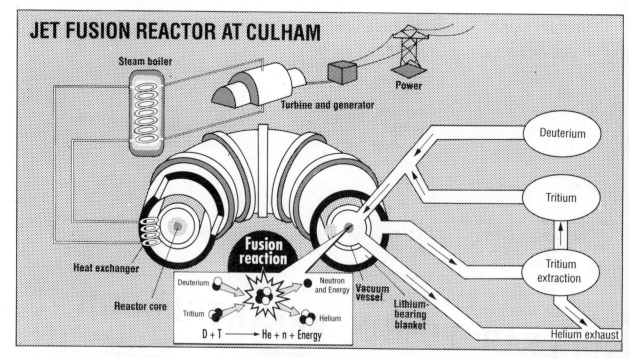

JET FUSION REACTOR AT CULHAM

a Check your answers to exercise 10 by finding combinations of words in the passage.

b What do the words in *italics* in the passage mean in this context? Find other words and expressions which have a similar meaning.

c Complete the following on the basis of the information in the passage:

The key difference between nuclear fission and nuclear fusion is that fission involves **1**_____ atoms, while fusion happens after atoms have **2**_____ to an extremely high temperature and have violently **3**_____. Both normal nuclear fission and nuclear fusion **4**_____ of energy, but the problem with conventional nuclear reactors is that **5**_____ _____.

Nuclear fission has another advantage: it isn't difficult to find **6**_____ required for it.

In the recent experiment it was only possible to

7_____ _____ for a few seconds. This is mainly because there are considerable technological problems in

8_____ 200 million degrees. However, scientists hope to be able to **9**_____ by the year 2020. If they succeed, the human race will be on the way to **10**_____ .

12 Complete the following on the basis of information in the passage.

a Stars like the sun are _____ by nuclear fusion.

b Because tritium was added to deuterium in the fusion experiment, _____.

c Although bombs involving fusion power have been built, there are not yet any _____.

d The main source of deuterium is _____, but tritium cannot _____.

e Very small amounts of these chemicals _____ _____.

USING A DICTIONARY

DEFINITIONS

13 Make sure you understand the words in *italics*. Then do the following quiz.

SCIENCE QUIZ

WIN A TRIP TO THE MOON IN 2005!

Just answer these simple questions:

1 Which of the following are solids, which are liquids, and which are gases?

GOLD   OXYGEN   ICE
SULPHURIC ACID   MERCURY

2 Which of the substances in 1 are 'elements'? Which are 'compounds' of more than one element? Which are metals?

3 Which can be melted? Which can be liquefied?

4 Which is bigger, a molecule or an atom?

5 What is a nucleus? Where would you find one?

6 How many planets are there in the solar system?

7 What is the chemical formula for water? What is CO_2?

8 What is the 'greenhouse effect'?

ACTIVATE

14 Write four quiz questions of your own on science and technology using vocabulary from this unit and other words that you know. You must know the answers to your own questions! Then use them, together with other people's questions, in a classroom quiz.

WORD USE

IDIOM AND METAPHOR

15 Complete the following expressions with words selected from those in *italics* above.

a They couldn't understand what was happening: it was as if they were from a different _____.

b There isn't an _____ of truth in the rumour that she's leaving her husband.

c There's no set _____ for being successful at public speaking – some people are and some aren't.

d There's an _____ of truth in what you say about our company's financial difficulties.

e The research is best done by a small _____ of people working intensively together.

FOCUS WORDS

absorb	compress	generate	photo-
absorption	compression	gravity	photosensitive
aero-	connect	gravitational	physics
aeronautics	convert	hydro-	piston
altitude	conversion	hydrofoil	planet
apply	cure	inhale	receiver
application	current	inhalation	robotics
astronomy	disconnect	lift	software
atom	ecology	liquefy	solar
auto-	electronics	magnet	split
automatic	element	melt	sterilize
bacteria	exhaust	micro-	tele-
bi-	extract	microchip	telescope
bifocal	fluid	mineral	test
bit	focus	molecule	valve
cell	formula	mono-	wing
cellular	frequency	monorail	
charge	frequent	nucleus	
compound	fuse	orbit	

FOCUS PHRASES

achieve a breakthrough
atom of truth
become reality
element of truth
greenhouse effect
set formula

WORD CHECK

Refer to Focus Words and Focus Phrases only.

1 Which words in the list are similar to words in your own language? Do they have the same or different meanings?
2 Look at all the words with three syllables or more. Which have the main stress on the first syllable, and which have it on the second syllable?
3 How many of the words in the list describe objects that you can see?
4 Write a short paragraph using at least four of the Focus Phrases.

The environment and the future

📖 1 a Look at the following with a neighbour, and check that you
    understand the words in *italics*, using a dictionary if necessary.
    Discuss what you think the answers to the questions are.

The number of *nuclear reactors*
planned or operating in *industrialized*
countries and Eastern Europe is 586.
How many are planned or operating in
the whole of the rest of the world?
More than 500, between 100 and 500,
or less than 100?

The amount of petroleum used on an
average day by a Pakistani is 0.136
kilos. How much is used by a
Canadian: 0.5 kilos, between 1 and 3
kilos, or more than 10 kilos?
_____

UK taxes allocated to research into
nuclear power in 1991-92 were £94.1
million.
How much do you think was allocated
to *solar power* research: more than
£100 million, less than £5 million, or
around £10 million? _____

What do you think the lowest
reckoning of the area of the world's
tropical forests felled each working
day in 1991 was: over 1,000 square
kilometres, between 400–700 sq. kms,
or between 200 and 400 sq. kms?
_____

In 1991, how much oil was being
discharged into the world's seas each
working day by *oil tankers*: about 100
tonnes, 10,000 tonnes or between,
3,000 and 5,000 tonnes? _____

What percent of the world's
water is *drinkable* (i.e. not salty):
over 20%, around 3%, or less
than 1%? _____

How many *satellites* have been
launched into space since 1957:
about 3,000, about 12,000, or less
than 1,000? _____

b Look at the real answers on page 204. How many did you get
   right? Which did you find most surprising? Which is most
   worrying for you?
c Which other facts would you like to know about the environment
   and natural resources? Why?

MEANING IN CONTEXT

📖 **2 a** Which words in the statements above mean the following?

| dispose of   budget for   cut down   calculation |

b *solar* means 'relating to the sun'. What words, also ending in -*ar* mean 'relating to the moon' and 'relating to the stars'?

c *drinkable* means 'can be drunk'. Find words ending in -*ble* which mean: 'can be eaten', 'can't be eaten', 'can't be touched', 'can be disposed of', and 'can't be thought about'.

d Satellites can be *launched*. Which of the following can also be *launched*?

| a career   a boat   a publicity campaign   a disaster |

MEANING

RELATED MEANINGS

3 Match the verbs in column A with their opposites in column B.

A	B
create	damage
save	neglect
care for	pollute
improve	destroy
purify	waste

WORD FORMATION

PARTS OF SPEECH

4 Complete the following table with nouns and adjectives related to the verbs listed.

Verb	Noun	Adjective
waste	waste	
damage		
improve		xxxxxx
neglect		
destroy		
pollute		xxxxxx
create		
purify		
congest		

Which endings have you used to make nouns?
Which endings have you used to make adjectives?

5 Complete the following using the appropriate form of one of the words in *italics* from the paragraph above, and a verb from the box.

reduce	control	harness	affect	improve	provide	repair

Example:

The recycling of certain kinds of waste is now common practice. Glass, paper and most metals are now _____ at special plants. But many more such plants need to be _____.
Answer: *recycled, provided*

a Air *pollution* is a huge problem in most of the world's big cities, and people complain about it constantly. However, what _____ the air most is the exhaust from the vehicles which those same people drive. One solution would be to _____ strictly the amount of driving people can do in cities.

b Cars *emit* poisonous gases such as carbon monoxide and carbon dioxide. Steps are being taken to _____ these _____ by fitting new cars with 'catalytic convertors' which make most of the gases harmless.

c Thousands of hectares of the world's rainforests are *destroyed* every year. This _____ of the rainforests is expected to _____ the global climate, as well as wildlife, in various ways.

d Scientists now believe that the ozone layer is being *damaged* by the chemicals in certain common products, such as deodorants and hairspray, and the chemicals given off by air-conditioners. The _____ caused to the ozone layer can never be _____.

e Everyone knows that nuclear waste can *harm* the environment. But until it becomes possible to _____ the natural energy of the sun, the wind and the waves, it will be impossible to meet man's energy needs without producing _____ waste of one kind or another.

f As cities become more *congested* with traffic, local councils tend to widen streets and try to _____ the flow of traffic. Of course, this encourages more people to drive in the city, and the _____ increases again.

ACTIVATE

6 With a partner, write the text for *three* street posters to be used in environmental campaigns. Then design one of these posters.

7 Read the following questionnaire and try to answer the questions (see page 204 for answers).

HOW GREEN ARE YOU?

There is more to being green than recycling your newspapers and using unleaded fuel. Here is a chance to test your ecological intelligence

1 Which uses the most energy?
   a a fridge
   b a cooker or stove
   c a washing machine

2 What is the best way to make cars *ecologically safer*?
   a buying a car with a catalytic converter
   b using unleaded petrol
   c buying a more *fuel-efficient* car

3 Which of the following does not damage human health?
   a aspirin
   b roast beef
   c excessive intake of vitamin C

4 Which uses the most water in the home?
   a the toilet
   b the bath
   c the washing machine
   d the dishwasher

5 Which of these statements about '*ozone friendly*' aerosol cans is true?
   a they contain no *ozone-damaging* propellants
   b they are *biodegradable*
   c they are *recyclable*

6 Which is the best way of improving the quality of drinking water?
   a buying bottled water
   b collecting rainwater
   c lobbying for a dual water supply
   d boiling tap water

7 Which is the best way to dispose of waste?
   a burning it in incinerators that generate energy
   b recycling
   c composting

8 Which is the most *environment-friendly* form of energy?
   a nuclear power
   b coal
   c gas
   d oil

adapted from *New Internationalist* January 1990

MEANING
CONNOTATION

8 Explain the adjectives in *italics* and put them in the two boxes below.

Good	Bad

WORD FORMATION
COMPOUND WORDS

9 Match words from column A with words from column B to make phrases related to the environment.

A	B
ozone	*effect*
global	*pollution*
rain	*layer*
food	*explosion*
air	*rain*
greenhouse	*shortages*
acid	*forests*
population	*warming*

WORD USE
WORDS TOGETHER

10 Complete the sentences below by beginning with one of the phrases from exercise 9, and using appropriate forms of verbs from the box.

> *cause play   protect   make   affect   result*

a . . . life in our cities unhealthy.
b . . . people in several countries in Subsaharan Africa.
c . . . many fish in the lakes of Northern Europe to die.
d . . . from the accumulation of carbon dioxide and other man-made gases in the atmosphere, which absorb and reflect more of the sun's heat than is normal.
e . . . an important role in the climate patterns of the whole world.
f . . . us from the adverse effects of ultra-violet radiation.

MEANING
RELATED MEANINGS

11 The words in the box all have similar meanings.

> *spoil   ruin   harm   damage   destroy   mar*

a Use a dictionary if necessary to arrange them in order on the line below.

WEAKEST ◄————————————————► STRONGEST

b Which would you be most likely to use to talk about the following?
   i a car after a slight accident
   ii a day of your holiday when things went badly
   iii a building after a bad storm
   iv a building after heavy bombing
   v people's lungs in a polluted city
   vi a meal after too much cooking
   vii a view from the top of a hill after the building of a road
   viii a businessman or woman who is bankrupt

12 These nouns all refer to different kinds of waste. Match them with their definitions.

garbage refuse scrap litter trash junk debris sewage

a something worthless or of low quality
b waste material to be thrown away
c the remains of something broken into pieces or destroyed
d old useless things
e small things, usually paper, that have been thrown away
f waste material of any kind
g liquid waste from people's houses and buildings
h rubbish collected or thrown away from people's houses
i waste metal

Which two words are mainly used by Americans instead of *rubbish*?
Which of these nouns can also be used as verbs? What meanings would the verbs have?

ACTIVATE

13 Role-play

You live in a city with a population of 150,000. A new plan for dealing with rubbish is under intense discussion because the Ministry of the Environment has told the city council that the current inadequate facilities must be closed in two years. The main plan under discussion is as follows.

A ten-hectare site, near the railway line but in a residential suburb, will be equipped with facilities for sorting different kinds of waste – glass, paper, metal, etc – for recycling. Once sorted the materials will be taken away by train for recycling. In addition, there will be a large incinerator for non-recyclable waste. The incinerator will be used to generate electricity for the surrounding residential area.

You and others in the class are attending a public meeting on the project to express and listen to the various opinions. The roles are as follows:

Members of the Planning Committee of the local council
You commissioned the new plan and want it to go ahead. You are willing to offer the residents compensation for problems caused. Some of this will be in the form of very cheap electricity. The project will also create 50 new jobs in a high-unemployment area.

Residents of the area
You don't like the idea at all. Apart from the noise and smoke from the plant itself, there will be additional lorry traffic. You believe the plant should be built outside the city and away from the residential area.

Members of the local Conservation Society
You like the idea behind the plan, but sympathize with the residents. On the other hand, you are against the idea of putting the plant outside the city, where it would damage the natural beauty of the countryside and affect the habitat of rare butterflies and wild flowers.

Answers to questions in exercise 1 on page 198:

The number of nuclear reactors planned or operating in the rest of the world in 1991: 53

The amount of petroleum used on an average day by a Canadian in 1991: 10.42 kg

UK taxes allocated to solar energy research in 1991: £2 million

Lowest reckoning of the area of tropical forests cut down each working day in 1991: 629 square kilometres

Quantity of oil discharged into the seas each working day by oil tankers in 1991: 4,230 tonnes

Percentage of the world's water which is drinkable: 3%

Number of satellites launched into space: about 3,400

Answers to questionnaire on page 201

1. b) – the cooker/stove is one of the most *energy-hungry* machines in the house. But gas is more efficient than electricity. Ask about energy consumption when you buy them.
2. a) – all these options are useful but a catalytic converter will cut out 90% of emissions that are harmful to human health. However, a catalytic converter does not tackle carbon-dioxide emissions, which contribute to the greenhouse effect. By far the best course is to use your car less.
3. c) – taking too much vitamin C is unlikely to be harmful. Aspirin – one of the most widely used painkillers – can damage the stomach lining, and more cases of food poisoning were caused by beef during 1984 than by any other single meat.
4. a) – major uses of water in the home

Use	Average water water used	% of total consumption
WC flush	10 litres	32%
baths and showers	80 litres 30 litres	17%
washing machines	100 litres	
dishwashers	50 litres	12%

5. c) – some non-CFC aerosols still damage the ozone layer. And the manufacture of aerosols consumes considerable resources. Refillable pump-action containers are preferable.
6. c) – relying on bottled water encourages a *wasteful* trade, and there is no way of checking that bottled water is clean. Rain is often too polluted to drink. Boiling tap water does nothing to remove harmful traces of pesticides. But a dual water supply would mean that less good water would be used for wasteful purposes.
7. b) – incinerators sound like a good option but they release highly *toxic* gases. Composting is good, but the waste has to be sorted manually into biodegradable and *non-biodegradable* material. At least recycling saves on raw materials.
8. c) – gas appliances are usually more *energy-efficient* and cheaper to run, and gas also produces less pollution than oil or coal. There is no totally green energy source. If we want to help the environment, we must be *sparing* with energy and campaign for greater investment in *renewable* energy sources, like wind, waves and solar power.

FOCUS WORDS

affect	ecological	lunar	repair
allocate	ecologically	mar	result
biodegradable	edible	neglect	ruin
cause	environment	non-	satellite
congest	environmental	biodegradable	scrap
congestion	fell	nuclear reactor	sewage
control	garbage	oil tanker	solar
create	harm	pollute	sparing
creation	harmful	provide	spoil
creative	harness	purify	stellar
damaging	improve	purification	trash
debris	improvement	reckoning	tropical forest
destroy	industrialized	recycle	unthinkable
destruction	inedible	recyclable	untouchable
discharge	junk	reduce	waste
disposable	launch	refuse (n)	wasteful
drinkable	litter	renewable	

FOCUS PHRASES

acid rain	environment-	greenhouse effect
energy-efficient	friendly	ozone-friendly
energy-hungry	food shortage	ozone layer
energy-intensive	fuel-efficient	population
	global warming	explosion

WORD CHECK

Refer to Focus Words and Focus Phrases only.

1 How many different endings for nouns are represented in the list?
2 Put all the adjectives in the list under the following headings:

Generally positive   Generally negative   Generally neutral

3 Write advertisements for two imaginary products. Use at least four of the Focus Phrases.
4 Which words do you find hardest to pronounce? Why? Which do you find most interesting? Why?

PART A | DEVELOPING YOUR VOCABULARY

UNIT 1
USING DICTIONARIES: DEFINITIONS

Note: It is desirable to have available in the classroom at least two dictionaries like the Longman Dictionary of Contemporary English.

Ex 1

explanatory	4	furniture	6	admittance	1
sticky	10	pineapple	8	expletive	5
island	7	together	12	explain	3
admitted	2	teaspoon	11	scorpion	9

Ex 2 Open exercise

Ex 3

jumper	5	nestle	9
sportsmanlike	15	sports	13
place	10	jumpsuit	7
elemental	1	negative	8
sportsmanship	16	jumping-off place	6
elementary particle	2	rampage	11
sports car	14	elementary school	3
elements	4	ramrod	12

Ex 4

quiet   steer   rich   read

Ex 5

a drag b warmth c whinge d thongs
e break(up) with f shuffle

Ex 6

a two people: both called Bruce or Bru
b partly open question, but:
fat stomach (pot belly) and slow moving (shuffles)

Ex 7

bright: entry 4   mate: entry 4

Ex 8

a they're all nouns
b i) car, bus, lorry, tank, jeep, van, juggernaut, ambulance . . .
ii) fool, idiot, child, Australian, American...
iii) beers, women, friends, companions...
iv) noisily, lazily, slowly, angrily...

Ex 9

1 a 2 i 3 f 4 d 5 b 6 h 7 g 8 c 9 e
10 f 11 b

Ex 10 Open exercise

UNIT 2
USING DICTIONARIES: TECHNICAL INFORMATION

Ex 1

At least two dictionaries like the *Longman Dictionary of Contemporary English* are necessary for this exercise. Students need to refer to them to play the game

Ex 2

a 9 b 3 c 4 d 8 e 5 f 6 g 10,6 h 1 i 7 (10)
j 10 k 9,6 l 9 m 6,9,5 n 1

Ex 3

1 a 2 b 3 d 4 c

Ex 4

a prettiness b responsible c (correct) d foetus
e (correct) f completely g correct (both 'sterilize' and 'sterilise' are possible in British English) h movement

Ex 5

a import b topical c topicality d export
e progress f progression g prohibition
h professionalism

Ex 6

1 b 2 f 3 c 4 a 5 d 6 e

Ex 7

a 'collapse' can't take an object. You need a verb like 'demolish'.
b When followed by a preposition, 'harmful' is usually followed by 'to'.
c 'information' is uncountable – no s
d In this phrase 'for' comes before the object.
e 'Graduate' takes the prepostion 'from'.
f 'Grease' must have an object, like 'suspension'.
g Any noun ending in -'ness' is likely to be uncountable (exception: illnesses)
h 'Different' is usually followed by the preposition 'from' (some people use 'to')
i Like d: 'around' should come before the object.
j 'the key' should come immediately after the verb 'gave'.

Ex 8

(suggested answers)
a She picked up the hammer/picked the hammer up.
b He was looking after the children/his elderly uncle
c Look it up in the dictionary/look up 'serendipity' in the dictionary.
d When are you going to give up smoking/give it up?
e She ran away with her best friend's fiancé.
f Try this jacket on/on this jacket. I think it'll suit you.
g He really made a fool of himself last night. He'll never live it down.
h I have my reputation for good taste to live up to.

UNIT 3
UNDERSTANDING AND REMEMBERING NEW WORDS

Ex 1
a White ('...we few whites...') and male ('...My wife and I...') – fourth paragraph.
b Firstly he felt it was a miracle that no whites at the funeral were threatened with violence or hurt. Secondly, blacks in South Africa seem less prone to racism than whites.

Ex 2, 3 Open exercises

Ex 4
anger
a (suggested answer) It dramatically portrays the mood of the crowd to contrast it with the 'two miracles'.
b (suggested answer) He is angry and ashamed of the attitude of whites in South Africa at that time

Ex 5

State of mind	Behaviour
fear	viciousness
anger	callousness
apprehension	cruelty
	exploitation
	murder

Ex 6
a 'whip up' and 'touch off' are phrasal verbs.
b i) a figurative use of 'whip': compare 'whip up the horses' when they were used to pull coaches.
   ii) Yes, different from 'touch'.
   iii) Yes, different from 'take'.
   iv) No, except that it is hard to literally 'look at' this kind of record unless it is written down.

Ex 7
a believing that one's own race is best, and that racial differences between people are what influences character, abilities etc
b usually people who are not white, and particularly those whose skin is naturally black.
c Extreme: Ku Klux Klan lynchings in the southern USA earlier this century.
   Mild: Children making fun of a schoolmate because of skin colour or other racial features (including accent).
d Open question (but this is taking anti-racism to extremes. Even if the origins of 'blackmail' were racial, almost nobody using the word makes a racial association).

Ex 8
a In alphabetical order. You could also group them according to related meanings.
b She has used translations and a definition in English. You could use drawings in the case of 'hammock' and 'hut'.

c She has put in the part of speech (n, adv). You could mention whether the word is countable, what position the adverb comes in, etc.

Ex 9 Open exercise
Note: this is an opportunity for the teacher to mention her/his own preferences – and to point out that different individuals may need different methods of recording things.

Ex 10 Open exercise

UNIT 4
WORD FORMATION AND COMPOUND WORDS

Ex 1
a postwar, stepmother   b darkness,
c unfriendly, realignment   d fishtank, makeshift, laptop

Ex 2

Two words		One word with a prefix	One word with a suffix
rosewood	coalmining	semi-detached	kitchenette
walking-stick	chambermaid	great-grandmother	childhood
granny flat	landowner	stepbrother	spider-like
workshop	saucepan		endless
bedroom	fourteen-hour	mid-nineties	girlhood
teapot	faint-hearted	wide-eyed	
second-eldest	hair-raising		

Ex 3
a useful, usefully, disuse, useable, useless
b careful, careless, carefully, carelessly, caring, uncaring, cared
c safe, safety, unsafe, safely, unsafely
d touch, touchable, untouchable, touching
e responsible, irresponsible, responsibility, responsibly, irresponsibly, irresponsibility
f reason, reasonable, reasonably, unreasonably

Ex 4
a granny flat, cowshed
b second eldest, fourth fastest
c walking-stick, knitting needle
d coalmining, rice-growing
e hair-raising, blood-curdling
f chambermaid, shop assistant
g fourteen-hour, ten-week
h workshop, playroom
i wide-eyed, redfaced

Ex 5, 6, 7 Open exercises

Ex 8
a ashtray   b housework   c blood-test   d daydreaming
e darkroom   f paperback

Ex 9
a hardworking   **b** prejudiced   **c** handmade
d home made   **e** cost-cutting

Ex 10, 11 Open exercises

Ex 12 (possible answers)
object + verb   bear-baiting, nail-biting
adverb + verb   sleepwalking, hang-gliding
purpose + noun   hunting horn, assembly line
two nouns   homework, wristwatch

UNIT 5 BRIDGING VOCABULARY GAPS

Ex 1 (suggested answers)
a a place where you can leave your cat
b a person who collects bees/looks after people's feet
c an instrument for finding your way/tuning other instruments
d A shop where you can buy needles, pins and thread
e A utensil for mixing eggs

Ex 2, 3, 4 Open exercises

Ex 5

Sarah: . . . There I was merrily driving along this country lane when suddenly a tractor pulled out in front of me. I swerved, and . . .
Isabella: You what?
Sarah: Swerved . . . you know, I pulled the steering wheel over to one side to avoid this twit. . . .
Isabella: Is a 'twit' a kind of tractor?
Sarah   (laughing): No, of course not – a 'twit' is an idiot, a stupid person.
Isabella: Oh right . . . Did you hit him?
Sarah: No. I just missed the back of the spreader...that's a machine for spreading manure . . .
Isabella: 'Manure'?
Sarah: . . . natural fertiliser – animal droppings, but I ran into a ditch, which is a sort of channel used for draining. The car somersaulted . . .
Isabella: I'm sorry, could you explain what that means?
Sarah: Sorry . . . the car turned over . . .
Isabella: Oh my God, did it really?
Sarah: Yes, and I ended up driving through the hedge..
Isabella: The edge? The edge of what?
Sarah: No, the hedge – the line of bushes between the roads and the fields. Where was I?
Isabella: Driving through the 'hedge' – is that the correct pronunciation?
Sarah: Fine . . . and I found myself in the middle of the field he'd just spread with manure.
Isabella: Oh no (laughing) You mean, you fell out of the car? Were you hurt?
Sarah: No I was in the car, in the middle of the field. Of course the car was a write-off.
Isabella: Write-off . . . does that mean the car was destroyed, that you couldn't drive it any more?
Sarah: Yes, a complete write-off.

Ex 6
The pictures that form part of the story are: b, d, g, h and i

Ex 7

Ways of asking for help with vocabulary	
informal:	you what? 'manure'? The edge? The edge of what? Is twit a kind of tractor? You mean you fell out of the car?
more formal:	Does that mean the car was destroyed ..... I'm sorry, could you explain what that means I'm afraid I don't understand what X means Would you mind explaining what an X is?

Ways of giving help with vocabulary	
informal:	you know I pulled the steering wheel.. a 'twit' is an idiot.... natural fertiliser, animal droppings No, the hedge Sorry, the car turned over
more formal:	that's a machine for spreading manure ..which is a sort of channel used for draining I'm so sorry. X is a word which means.... It's a bit difficult to explain but it means....

Ex 8 Open exercise

UNIT 6 USING WORDS CREATIVELY AND INVENTING NEW WORDS

Ex 1 (suggested answers)
a freezing, icy, chilling, shiver, blue with cold etc
b boiling, humid, sticky, sweating, sunburnt etc

Ex 2, 3
Open exercises

Ex 4
the air – a 'viscous overcoat'
the surface of the street – gum
the sky – faded dungarees
the buildings – orthodox Jews

Ex 5
a bleached, saffron, slash   **b** viscous, gum
c strut, flaunt, bitch   **d** rhinestone, dungarees
e dizzying, shimmer

Ex 6, 7 Open exercises

Ex 8
a 6   **b** 3   **c** 2   **d** 4   **e** 1   **f** 5

Ex 9
a Open exercise
b i) bookfairies = people who buy and sell books at antiquarian or secondhand book sales.

ii) mockumentary = a television or radio programme made in the style of a documentary, and purporting to be factual, but containing fictitious elements.

iii) flip-flopped = to change to an opposite point of view: to do a U-turn

iv) rurbania = land on the edge of cities, containing a mixture of town and country

Ex 10, 11 Open exercises

PART *B*

HUMAN BEINGS AND THE WORLD WE LIVE IN

UNIT 1 FAMILIES

Ex 1 Open exercise

Ex 2

(suggested answer) the bridegroom was disastrously drunk and so he was replaced with a suitably sober bachelor. The writer's attitude is slightly superior. We know this from sentences such as "we can assume, his horoscope, too" and "one can only guess at the feelings of the bride"

Ex 3

a bride **b** bridegroom **c** counterparts **d** sacked **e** prospects **f** fitted the bill

Ex 4 Open exercise

Ex 5

a i) 'wedding' means the actual ceremony only; 'marriage' can refer to the ceremony, but it also refers to the (permanent) state of being married.

ii) 'bride' and 'bridegroom' refer to the woman and the man just before, during and just after the wedding; 'wife' and 'husband' refer to their (permanent) married roles.

iii) 'to marry' simply describes the action; 'to get married' describes the event; 'to be married' describes the (permanent) state.

iv) 'batchelor' means unmarried male, 'single' means someone (male or female) who is not currently married, 'unmarried' means someone who has never got married (e.g. 'umarried mother'), 'unattached' means someone who does not have a partner of any kind.

b 'bridesmaid' means the girl who escorts the bride at the wedding.
'best man' is the male who escorts the bridegroom at the wedding.
'reception' means the party given immediately after the wedding.
'honeymoon' is the holiday the newlyweds go on immediately after the wedding.

c wedding dress, wedding present, wedding guest

d orphan

Ex 6 (suggested explanations)

a the priest who was to have been the bridegroom was embarrassed when his bride did not turn up at the wedding.

b At the last moment the bride married the best man instead of the intended bridgegroom.

c 'For richer or poorer' are words used in the wedding ceremony; here they cause comment because the bridegroom is a millionaire.

d At a wedding a bridesmaid (not the bride) went off with the bridegroom in the car that had been hired to transport the bride and bridegroom.

e A newly-married couple on their honeymoon have been denounced by a man who says he is actually the husband of the woman involved.

f at the wedding of an undertaker coffins were used as tables.

Ex 7 Open exercise

Ex 8

widow(F)
bachelor(M)
spinster (F)
lover (FM)
fiancée (F)
spouse (FM)
mistress (F)
fiancé (M)
divorcee (FM)
widower (M)

a fiancée
b divorcees
c widow, widower
d spouse
e mistress
f spinster

Ex 9 Open exercise

Ex 10

Open exercise: note that different people may see these relations in very different ways.

Ex 11

1 father, mother: the verbs mean to look after someone's interests and wellbeing like a father or a mother does.

2 fatherless, motherless, childless

3 a brother-in-law can be your wife/husband's brother (or the man married to your wife/husband's sister). It can also be the man married to your sister. A half-brother is someone who shares one parent with you, but not both. The same is true of step-brother. Foster brother is someone who has been accepted into the family although he is not related by blood.

4 **a** sister-in-law, step-sister, half-sister, foster-sister
b mother-in-law, step-mother
c cousin-in-law
d father-in-law, step-father
e son-in-law, stepson
f uncle-in-law
g step-parent, foster-parents
h step-children, foster children
i daughter-in-law, step-daughter
j step-grandchild

5 orphan

Ex 12, 13 Open exercises

UNIT 2 RELATIONSHIPS

Ex 1 Open exercise

Ex 2

like	I'm fond of, we fell madly in love, adores.
dislike	I can't stand, hate, despises, detest, loathe

Ex 3
1 i   2 d   3 j   4 a   5 b   6 c   7 h   8 g   9 f   10 e

Ex 4

verbs	adjectives	nouns
to flirt	flirtatious	flirt
to become acquainted	acquainted	acquaintance
to row	rowing	row
to be attracted to	attractive	attraction
to love	loving/loveable	love
to seduce	seductive	seduction
to live together	xxxxxxx	xxxxxxx
to be close to	close	closeness
to fancy	fanciable	xxxxxxx
to be infatuated with	infatuated (with)	infatuation
to be fond of	fond	fondness
xxxxxxx	shy	shyness
to quarrel	quarrelsome	quarrel
to respect	respectful	respect
xxxxxxx	affectionate	affection
xxxxxxx	jealous	jealousy

Ex 5
a Martin and I met at a party and immediately fell for each other.
b I saw you chatting up that pretty waitress at Bilbo's restaurant on Friday night.
c How do you get on with Bill? Very well.
d How's Mary? I don't know. She and I have broken up.
e Darling I can't bear you to be angry with me. Can we make it up? Why don't we let bygones be bygones?

Ex 6
The order of pictures is a, f, g, h, c, d, b, e

Ex 7
From the moment I first set eyes on you (e)
Love at first sight (e)
Crazy about him (a)
Lovesick (a)
Old flame (d)
Make a fresh start (b)
Let bygones be bygones (b)

Ex 8
a partner   b ally   c acquaintance   d enemy   e companion
f lover   g comrade   h friend   i colleague   j accomplice

Ex 9
friendship, companionship, acquaintanceship, partnership, comradeship

Ex 10 Open exercise

Ex 11
a flotsam is pieces of wood, plastic etc that is washed up (tossed up) onto a beach. The use of the word here suggests the wreckage of an earlier passion.
b chastity means being sexually pure. It is required of women before marriage in many societies; it is required of priests in many religions. The use of the word here suggests that the relationship between the two people is completely non-sexual – an almost enforced purity because of the coolness of their relationship.
c thread is the line of cotton, wool etc used in sewing or weaving. Winding the thread in for this couple would bring them too close, perhaps; or perhaps the thread would snap!

Ex 12, 13, 14 Open exercises

UNIT 3 COMMUNICATION AND LANGUAGE

Ex 1
a pictures a, f   b a, c, e, h   c a, b, c, d, e, f   d a, c, f, e

Ex 2 Open exercise

Ex 3
Diane seems to have a fairly stereotypical relationship with her parents: she is determined to lead her own life, but her parents still want her to be an obedient child.

Ex 4
FATHER: (interrupting) I forbid you to speak about it again!
DIANE: I'm over fifteen, and anyway a friend has offered to do it for me.
FATHER: Until you're eighteen you will have to abide by my rules. Now go and apologize to your mother.
DIANE: I'm going to be my own person. You're just a dictator!

Ex 5

Good relationship	bad relationship	neutral relationship
apologized	argued	suggested
agreed	screamed	pointed out
	shouted insults	mentioned
	forbidden	insisted
	ordered	stressed
	accused	asked
	pleaded	explained
		persuade
		emphasized

Ex 6
a to + infinitive   persuade, forbid, order, ask, agree
b that + clause   insist, imply, argue, scream, stress, suggest, point out, mention, explain, agree
c both to + that   ask, agree

Ex 7

argument, suggestion, insistence, scream, persuasion, mention, implication, apology, emphasis, stress, explanation, order, accusation, agreement

Ex 8 Open exercise

Ex 9

cordless phone (c)
cardphone (g)
mobile phone (i)
answering machine (h)
entryphone (d)

satellite TV dish (b)
facsimile (fax) machine (e)
telex machine (f)
radio-pager (a)

Ex 10

a With a cardphone you can make a phone call using a special card instead of money.
b With an answering machine people who phone you can leave messages for you when you aren't at home.
c With a fax machine you can send/receive documents instantaneously through the telephone network.
d With a radio-pager in your pocket, people can page you and ask you to contact them soon.
e With a satellite TV dish you can receive programmes that are transmitted through space from another country.
f With a mobile phone you can talk to people from your car, the train etc.
g Using a telex machine/fax machine you can send short messages to someone on the other side of the world instantaneously.
h With a cordless phone you can make a phone call without moving from wherever you happen to be: the garden, the bathroom or your comfortable chair.

Ex 11

make a phonecall
use a phonecard, a fax machine
contact a person
phone a person
get/receive a message/phonecall/telex/fax
send a message/telex/fax
page a person
leave a message

Ex 12 Open exercise

Ex 13

a *to talk at cross purposes* means that two people are talking about different subjects even though they are trying to talk about the same thing!
b *to get your wires crossed* means to have understood different things – to have misunderstood each other
c *to take it all back* means to withdraw what you said
d *to get the wrong end of the stick* means to completely misunderstand something
e *didn't make any sense* meant that I couldn't understand it at all
f *to eat your words* means to (be forced to) withdraw what you said
g *to give someone a piece of your mind* means to tell them

exactly what you think (usually hostile to the listener)
h *to not be able to make head or tail of it* means to not understand a thing

---

UNIT 4
SPEAKING AND WRITING

Ex 1, 2
Open exercises

Ex 3 (suggested answers)
a In Britain, if you leave a conversation without waiting for an appropriate moment, people think you are very rude.
b There may be an embarassed silence if people don't cooperate to make a conversation finish sucessfully.
c If you look at your watch sometime before you need to leave, you will help to begin the ending of a conversation.
d When talking to strangers in England, you will be unlikely to give offence if you talk about things like pets, children and the weather.
e If you ask an English person you don't know about their religious or political beliefs, they may think that you are being rather impolite.

Ex 4 Open exercise

Ex 5
1 told **2** told **3** speak **4** said **5** speak **6** tell
7 said **8** tell **9** telling **10** talk

Ex 6
a tell **b** say **c** speak **d** talk **e** tell

Ex 7
a gossip **b** interrogation **c** lecture **d** chat
e heart-to-heart **f** debate **g** conversation
h argument

Ex 8
b They were interrogating her about her movements on the night of the 13th May.
c Yesterday morning he lectured them on the second law of Thermodynamics.
d He chatted about their holiday in Wales.
e They had a heart-to-heart about Mary's problems.
f They debated the arguments in favour of the resolution.
g They conversed about the difference between a high salary and the quality of life.
h They argued furiously about the damage to his car.

Ex 9

	chatter	whisper	shout	mutter	babble	mumble	moan
loudly			✓				
normally	✓						
in a low voice		✓		✓			
with no voice	✓						
just breathing							
slowly/in-distinctly						✓	
too quickly					✓		

in a cheerful way	✓
in a complaining way	✓
while crying	✓

b chatter, babble

Ex 10

a shouted **b** whispered **c** muttered **d** babbled **e** moaned

Ex 11 Open exercise

Ex 12

a
1 a memo
2 (business) letter
3 poem
4 note
5 invoice
6 agenda
7 will
8 diary

Ex 13

	Purpose	Who writes it?	Who reads it?
essay	written to explain a point of view or tell a story	students, academics, literary people	teachers academics, literary people
diary	record events of anybody the writer's life		the diarist, later generations in the case of famous diarists
novel	to tell a fictional story well	novelist	people who buy the novel - the public
catalogue	to list things that are available	cataloguer	buyers, visitors to museums/ art galleries etc
biography	to tell the story	biographer	anybody of someone's life
curriculum vitae	to list your education and work record	someone applying for a job	The interviewer
invoice/bill	to ask for payment	invoicer/clerk	the person who owes money
receipt	to confirm that money has been paid	the person who has been paid	the person who has paid
poem	to explore and communicate feelings and emotions	poet	anybody – people who who like poetry
love letter	to tell someone that you love them	someone in love	the person who is loved
directory	to list names and addresses	a directory writer	people who want to find out phone numbers etc

Ex 14

a reading, novel **b** look it up, directory
c received, summons **d** paid, invoice **e** scribbled, note
f write down **g** preparing, agenda

Ex 15 (possible answers)

```
To:       Managing director
From:     Jane Wilson
Subject:  Smoking in the common room
```

Jim Wilson has been to see me. He claims to suffer ill-health from the others smoking (he has been off sick).

I explained that others enjoyed smoking. He suggests dividing the common-room in half. I would welcome your input on this.

```
                    30 Palmeira Drive,
                    Hove,
                    Sussex
```
Dear Union organiser,
   I am writing to you about smoking in the workplace
   I have recently been off work and I have been advised by my doctor that this is due to the effect of passive smoking. I am myself a non-smoker but many of my colleagues at work smoke, especially in the common-room where we all meet.
   I have spoken to the Director of the Laboratory, but she has told me that the interests of the smokers are more important than mine. I suggested a compromise of making half the common room a no-smoking area but I don't think this is likely to be accepted.
   I would be grateful for your advice as my union official. I think I have strong rights which are being abused by the company I work for.
   I look forward to hearing from you.
       Yours sincerely,

       Jim Read

Ex 16 Open exercise

UNIT 5 THE MEDIA

Ex 1, 2 Open exercises

Ex 3

TV & radio	Newspapers & magazines (The press)	both
broadcast live programme	publish article headline column	edit record(v) censor advertise report

Ex 4

a broadcaster, Broadcasting **b** advertisements
c reported **d** live, record **e** censorship **f** editor
g columnist

Ex 5

Top diagram = 2
Middle diagram = 1
Bottom diagram = 3
a satellite **b** transmitter **c** satellite dish aerial
d transmitter **e** signals **f** aerial **g** fibre-optic cables

Ex 6, 7 Open exercises

Ex 8

soap opera (b)
quiz game (d)
documentary (f)
news (a)
chat show (c)
sitcom (situation comedy) (e)

Ex 9

Ex 9

a the news, documentaries   **b** the news
c chat shows, quiz shows   **d** soap operas (films)
e discussion programmes

Ex 10

	newspaper	magazine	section	supplement
daily	✓			
evening	✓			
Sunday	✓	✓		✓
fashion		✓	✓	✓
local	✓		✓	
business		✓	✓	
tabloid	✓			

Ex 11

Item		Writer	
report	editorial	reporter	editor/leader writer
column	review	columnist	reviewer
forecast	horoscope	forecaster	astrologer
letters page	crossword	readers	compiler

A *report* is a news story.
A *column* is a regular feature in which (usually regular) journalists write about issues that concern them.
A *forecast* tells you what the weather (or the economy) is going to be like.
A *letters page* publishes letters from readers, usually in reply to something that was in the paper.
An *editorial* is written by the editor or a special writer (a leader writer) and gives the newspaper's opinion about current issues.
A *review* gives the reviewer's opinion of a play, film, ballet, concert or book.
A *horoscope* tells you about your future as governed by the stars.
A *crossword* is a puzzle where you fit words into a special grid.

Ex 12

a forecaster   **b** reviewer   **c** reporter   **d** editor
e reader   **f** astrologer

Ex 13

a forecast   **b** review   **c** report   **d** editorial
e letters page   **f** horoscope

Ex 14

obituaries	recount the life of people who have just died
small ads	offer things for sale or rent, often in restricted language
share prices	give you information about the price of shares on the stock exchange
announcements	announce births, deaths, engagements, weddings etc
results service	tell you who has won and lost at sporting events
strip cartoons	are humorous continuing features with illustrated characters.
pin-ups	are photographs of attractive people, frequently women
Programme listings	tell you what's on radio & TV

Ex 15, 16   Open exercises

Ex 17

a A photographer from a newspaper called the Chronicle has forced his way into the private life of somebody (by sneaking into their house, talking to their friends and making public details of their private life which are not 'in the public interest')
b A paper has agreed to pay £25,000 to the wife of someone who is a conviced murderer.
c The Prime Minister thinks that most of the 'popular' newspapers are too right-wing.
d The editor of the 'Clarion' whose newspaper wrote things about an industrialist is being taken to court by the industrialist who wants the paper to pay for telling lies about him or her.
e A singer says that what a paper said about him or her (what the newspaper suggests he or she did or is) has completely wrecked his or her life.

UNIT 6 POLITICS

Ex 1   Open exercise

Ex 2

a 2   **b** 4   **c** 6   **d** 5   **e** 1   **f** 7   **g** 3

Ex 3

(Suggested answers only)

Ex 4 a

Noun (concept)	Noun (person)	Adjective
democracy	democrat	democratic
totalitarianism	totalitarian	totalitarian
monarchy	monarch	monarchic
dictatorship	dictator	dictatorial
oligarchy	oligarch	oligarchic
tyranny	tyrant	tyranical
anarchy	anarchist	anarchic
capitalism	capitalist	capitalist
communism	communist	communist
conservatism	conservative	conservative
fascism	fascist	fascist
liberalism	liberal	liberal
nationalism	nationalist	nationalist
socialism	socialist	socialist
social democracy	social democrat	social democratic

b i) democratic
ii) extremism, moderation
iii) totalitarian
iv) radical, conservative
v) socialism, monarch

Ex 5 Open exercise

Ex 6
a broad-minded, not strict
b disorder ; everyone does what they please
c an estimate that is cautious
d domineering, wanting people to do what she wanted
e unreasonably harsh and strict
f an imaginative and bold solution
g unwilling to consider anyone else's suggestions

Ex 7
a Open exercise
b i) they may disagree with what their party is doing
ii) they may have made a serious mistake, or they may be blamed for someone else's (eg the Prime Minister's) mistake
iii) they may get ill, or into financial or family difficulties
iv) they may be asked to resign by the leader of their party

Ex 8
stand for: parliament, election
stand as : a candidate
nominated by: (parliament), your local party, a constituency
represent: (parliament), your local party, a constituency
resign from: parliament, your local party

Ex 9
a Open exercise
b 1 nominated **2** selected as a candidate **3** election
7 stand for **9** councillor **10** represent **15** cabinet
16 opposition

Ex 10, 11 Open exercises

Ex 12
a vote against it **b** a vote of confidence **c** you abstain
d there's a tied vote

Ex 13

	victory	defeat	majority
sensational	✓	✓	✓
landslide	✓		
crushing	✓	✓	
humiliating	✓		
slim		✓	
small		✓	
unassailable	✓		
large	✓		
overwhelming	✓	✓	✓

Ex 14
a) unassailable **b)** crushing, landslide, (an) overwhelming
c) voted against **d)** tied vote **e)** casting vote
f) no confidence **g)** humiliating

b Open exercise

Ex 15 (suggested answers)
a the Government was able to win an important vote because it had a majority in Parliament.
b a minister who had perhaps had to resign from the Cabinet lost his/her seat at a parliamentary election.
c A senior member of the opposition with special responsibility tells the media that he/she believes his/her party is sacrificing one of its key policies.
d the largest party in a local council were surprised by the success of an opposition councillor in a local election.
e The Government have denied that the country is becoming a police state under their rule
f a very successful politician has become a senior minister only five years after entering politics at local level.

UNIT 7
PEACE, WAR AN
INTERNATIONAL RELATIONS

Ex 1
ambassador: embassy, (official residence), United Nations (UN)
consul: consulate
diplomat: consulate, embassy, UN
emperor: official residence, palace
foreign minister: ministry, palace, parliament, UN
foreign secretary: ministry, palace, parliament, UN
secretary of state: ministry, palace, parliament, UN
secretary general: UN
head of state: official residence, palace, parliament, UN
king: official residence, palace
president: official residence, palace, parliament
prime minister: official residence, parliament, UN
queen: official residence, palace

Ex 2 Open exercise

Ex 3
a ambassador **b** border **c** foreign minister
d Prime Minister **e** President **f** palace **g** country's
h region

Ex 4
a unilateral **b** trilateral,three-way **c** multilateral
uniform, unisex; bicycle, binational, bifocal; tricycle, triangle

Ex 5 , 6 Open exercises

Ex 7
a aid **b** allegations of torture **c** hostages
d political prisoners **e** exports **f** human rights
g economic sanctions **h** imports **i** trade imbalance

Ex 8
a importing **b** political prisoners **c** economic sanctions
d export **e** foreign aid **f** human rights

Ex 9

talks *break down*
invade a country
declare a ceasefire, war
break off diplomatic relations, talks
sign a treaty
restore diplomatic relations
agree to a ceasefire, talks
a 'break down' can't take an object
b Open exercise

Ex 10 (suggested answers)

a it is likely that the two countries will begin imposing taxes on imports from the other, or stop exporting important commodities to the other
b Emeria is saying that the Darda government has tortured people or taken political prisoners etc.
c the Ambassador of Emeria walked out of the UN during a session in protest at what was being said
d the level of tension is rising because people are anxious about an invasion.
e a guerilla army wants part of Emeria to be independent.
f there are no inidications that the war is coming to an end.

Ex 11

1 autonomy . . . independence **5** a revolution . . . a coup
2 a rebellion . . . a revolution **6** a battle . . . a war
3 a protest . . . a demonstration **7** a civil war . . . a
4 a rebellion . . . a riot   guerrilla war

Ex 12 (suggested answers)

rebel 4   revolutionary 2   terrorist 5
guerrilla 3   freedom fighter 1

Ex 13 Open exercise

Ex 14

a resolve **b** holds . . . negotiations **c** disputed . . . surrender **d** lifted **e** enter

Ex 15 Open exercise

UNIT 8
CRIME, THE LAW AND THE POLICE

Ex 1

a 6 per cent
b the very young
c USA, Canada, Holland, Germany, Britain, Finland, Switzerland, Northern Ireland

Ex 2 Open exercise

Ex 3

	Crimes Against People	Crimes involving things or property
a	murder rape sexual assault assault causing grievous bodily harm mugging homicide	robbery burglary car theft
b	blackmail child abuse kidnap pickpocketing	arson embezzlement fraud shoplifting stealing

Ex 4 Open exercise

Ex 5

a

	the bank	a house	a warehouse	a watch	an old lady	a car	the bank manager
steal				✓		✓	
rob	✓	✓	✓		✓	✓	✓
break into	✓	✓	✓				
burgle		✓	✓				
mug					✓		✓

b break into, mug

Ex 6

a embezzling **b** rapist, raped **c** abusers
d blackmailer **e** robbery **f** mugger
g murderers, are murdered **h** thief **i** assault **j** arsonist

Ex 7

a witnesses **b** held, arrested **c** brutal **d** hunt
e breathalysed **f** petty crime **g** suspect **h** leads
i booked for speeding **j** habitual offender **k** clues
l superintendent, chief inspector, constable

Ex 8

vicious – murder, criminal, crime
brutal – murder, criminal, crime
cold-blooded – murder, crime
common – criminal, crime
habitual – criminal, offender
petty – criminal, crime

Ex 9 Open exercise

Ex 10

a murder **b** murder **c** murder **d** murder **e** robbery
f stole

Ex 11

b 3 plead **4** found **7** probation **8** fined
9 life **11** lose **12** win **13** sentence **14** reduced

Ex 12

a to **b** of **c** with **d** of **e** of **f** to **g** for **h** for **i** of

Ex 13
1 witness   2 judge   3 defending counsel
4 police officer   5 witness box   6 the accused   7 jury

Ex 14
a charging   b witness   c jury...guilty
d verdict ...sentence   e appeal

Ex 15, 16 Open exercises

UNIT 9 EDUCATION

Ex 1
a
A. off   B. at   C. by   D. on   E. outside   F. through
G. out of   H. in   I. in   J. as
b,c Open exercises

Ex 2
a Open exercise
b Waterloo was the place in what is now Belgium where
the final battle of the Napoleonic Wars took place
between the British led by the Duke of Wellington and the
French led by The Emperor,Napoleon Bonaparte.
Napoleon lost and was taken prisoner and exiled to the
island of Elba.
c Open exercise

Ex 3
a Pre-school Education: kindergarten, playgroup, nursery
school, teacher, playground
Primary Education: preparatory school, reception class,
pupil, playground, teacher, head teacher, deputy head,
(headmaster, headmistress),classroom
Secondary Education: high school, (college),
comprehensive, public school, sixth form, master,
mistress, teacher, tutor, head teacher, headmaster,
headmistress, deputy head, pupil, playground,
classroom.
Further Education: college, evening classes, technical
college, lecturer, tutor, student, classroom, lecture theatre
Higher Education: polytechnic, university, lecturer,
professor, student, graduate, postgradate, doctorate,
lecture theatre
Adult Education: (same as further education)
b public school, preparatory school

Ex 4
a Bachelor of Science   b Bachelor of Education
c Master of Science   d Doctor of Medicine
e Bachelor of Arts   f Master of Arts
g Master of Philosophy   h Doctor of Philosophy

Ex 5 , 6 Open exercises

Ex 7
a
Behaviour Problems	Learning Problems
Tom	Samantha
Sarah	Jemma
Dulal	Jeffrey
Bill	Sasha
Penny and Jasmin	Stella
	Mary
	Dulal? (Maybe learning problems are causing
	Bill? behaviour problems)

b (suggested answers)
Samantha: needs a lot of time to learn new concepts and
skills
Tom: interrupts the class a lot because he wants
attention
Jemma: can't read or write yet
Sarah: is distracted and doesn't concentrate
Jeffrey: has difficulty with numbers (arithmetic etc)
Sasha: is unusually intelligent and needs to go faster
than the average child
Dulal: can't concentrate (like Sarah)
Stella: tries hard to do the work but can't seem to learn
Bill: finds it hard to remember anything
Mary: gets confused about the order of letters and
sounds, so finds it hard to read and write
Peny and interrupt the class a lot (like Tom) and don't do
Jasmin: what the teacher asks.

Ex 8
(suggested answers)

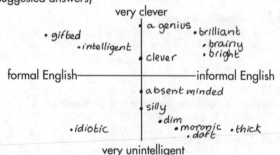

b cleverness, brightness, intelligence, braininess, brilliance,
(giftedness), (thickness), silliness, idiocy, stupidity,
daftness, dimness, (a moron), absent-mindedness

Ex 9
The original meaning of 'gift' is 'a present' offered to
someone willingly, eg for birthdays, Christmas etc.

Ex 10 Open exercise

Ex 11
a, b
cram for: a test, an exam
get: a degree, a distinction

get into: a school, a university
get a place at: a school, a university
expel from: a school
exclude from: an exam, a school
send down from: a university
take: a test, an exam, a degree
pass: a test, an exam, a degree
fail: a test, an exam, a degree
resit: a test, an exam

Ex 12
a failed **b** got into **c** sent down from
d passed/got a distinction

Ex 13
a university **b** exam **c** test **d** school
e school **f** testing
Many nouns can be used as adjectives without change in
their form.

Ex 14 Open exercise

Ex 15
The first passage doesn't say whether school is good or
bad, but it implies that learning probably happens more
easily outside school.
The song says that school and teachers are bad for
children.

UNIT 10 RELIGION

Ex 1
a belief: the feeling that something is true
Christian: believing in the teachings of Jesus Christ
creed: a system of beliefs
Hindus: people who believe in Hinduism, the main
  religion of India
holy: connected with God and religion
Islam: the Muslim religion established by the prophet
  Mohammed
Muslims: people who believe in Islam
mosque: a Muslim place of worship
temple: a building or place of worship, especially for
  Hindus and Buddhists.
b mosque – creed – Christian – Islam – Hindus – belief –
holy – Muslims

Ex 2
a in a mosque you don't take off your shoes to please other
  people who might be there but because it is a holy place
b, c Open exercises

Ex 3
a 1 synagogue 2 monastery 3 chapel 4 mosque
  5 temple 6 cathedral 7 church 8 shrine
b Christianity: cathedral, church, shrine, chapel, monastery
Hinduism: temple, shrine
Islam: shrine, mosque
Judaism: temple, synagogue, shrine
Buddhism: shrine, temple, monastery
Shintoism: temple, shrine, monastery

Ex 4
a Some other religions are:
various branches of Christianity: Greek Orthodox,
Russian Orthodox, Coptic, Catholic, Protestant, Quaker,
Baptist, Methodist etc
branches of Islam: Sunni, Shi'ite etc.
Jehovah's Witnesses, Mormon
Sikhism, Bahai
b reincarnation: Hinduism, Buddhism
resurrection: Christianity
c pope: Christian – catholic
rabbi: Judaism
imam: Islam
priest: Buddhism, Christianity
monk: Buddhism, Christianity, Shintoism
guru: Hinduism, Sikhism
nun: Christian
d Most senior to least senior:
pope – cardinal – archbishop – bishop – vicar – minister
– priest

Ex 5
a sing a hymn
chant a prayer (a hymn)
say a prayer
kneel in prayer
preach a sermon
confess a sin
read from the holy book
b the priest: all of them
the choir: sing a hymn (chant a prayer)
the worshippers: all except preach a sermon and read
from the holy book

Ex 6
Open exercise
a heaven is where you go after living a good Chistian life;
hell is where you go if you have sinned a lot in your life.
b repentance is feeling sorry for your sins; forgiveness is
pardon from God for your sins (if you're sorry for them!)
c a monk is a man who swears to live a life of service to
God. A nun is a woman who does the same.
d a pilgrim is someone who travels some distance to reach
a shrine. A prophet is someone who believes he (or she)
is chosen by God to make known His will.
e an angel is a messenger and servant of God who lives in
heaven; a demon is a servant of the devil who lives in
hell.
f a saint is a person officially recognised after her/his
death as being especially holy; a martyr is someone who
is killed because of his/her religious beliefs.
g secular means not to do with religion; religious means
related to a religion or the church.
h a missionary is someone who goes to convert people to a
given religion, especially if they don't know the religion;
a pilgrim is smeone who travels a distance to go to a
shrine.

Ex 8
a martyr **b** monk **c** pilgrims **d** forgiveness – repentance
e secular **f** demons **g** heaven – hell

Ex 9 Open exercise

Ex 10
heavenly   sinful   devilish   angelic   faithful, faithless
demonic   saintly   prophetic
4 different endings

Ex 11
sinful thoughts
sinful behaviour, devilish behaviour, angelic behaviour
angelic child, devilish child
heavenly day
faithful friend
demonic plot, devilish plot
sinful acts, saintly acts
devilish plan

Ex 12 Open exercise

Ex 13
a 8 **b** 6 **c** 3 **d** 7 **e** 1 **f** 9 **g** 10 **h** 4 **i** 2 **j** 5

Ex 14, 15 Open exercises

UNIT 11
WORK AND EMPLOYMENT

Ex 1 Open exercise

Ex 2
a receptionist **b** traffic warden **c** surgeon **d** butcher
e checkout clerk **f** surveyor **g** TV assembler

Ex 3 Open exercise

Ex 4
a i)   bank clerk, cashier
   ii)   managing director (chairman)
   iii) dustman
   iv)   optician
   v)   lecturer
   vi)   plumber
   vii) conjurer
   viii) labourer
   ix)   roadsweeper
   x)   pilot
   xi)   projectionist
   xii) ticket collector
   xiii) travelling salesman/salesperson/saleswoman/sales
         representative
b Open exercise

Ex 5
Jobs: bank clerk, managing director, dustman, plumber,
conjurer, labourer, roadsweeper, projectionist, ticket
collector, travelling salesman
Professions: optician, lecturer, pilot

A job is what you do to earn your living. A profession is a
job that needs special training/a good education (e.g.
doctor, lawyer etc)

Ex 6
a A profession is a job that needs special training/a good
education (e.g. doctor, lawyer etc); a career is a job or
profession which you mean to follow all your life.
b a job is something you do to earn your living; a vocation
is a job you do because you think you are 'called' to help
others.
c a certificate is the piece of paper you receive which says
that you have achieved something (passed an exam,
gained a level of skill); a qualification is a title which says
that you have achieved something.
d skills are abilities which you can be taught; experience is
what you gain over a period of time in the same job.

Ex 7
get work   find work   have work   look for work

Ex 8

a

Noun		Verb	
application	resignation	apply for	resign
dismissal	rejection	dismiss	reject
increase	reprimand	increase	reprimand
interview	rise	interview	rise
offer	retirement	offer	retire
promotion	shortlist	promote	shortlist

b i)   apply for   vi)   promote
    ii)   reject   vii) reprimand
    iii) shortlist   viii) dismiss
    iv)   interview   ix)   resign
    v)   increase

Ex 9

A1 Curriculum Vitae (CV)	B1 rejection	C1 rise
A2 application	B2 job centre	C2 promotion
A3 shortlist	B3 temporary job	C3 reprimand
A4 job description	B4 part-time job	C4 dismissal
A5 interview	B5 retirement	C5 resignation
A6 offer	B6 pension	C6 redundancy
A7 contract		C7 unemployment benefit (dole)

Ex 10 (possible answer)
Sally applied for a job as a newspaper reporter. She sent in
a letter of application and her CV. She was shortlisted for
the job and invited for an interview. The interview was a
success and she was offered a temporary one-year contract.
Sally was a success and soon got promoted to foreign
editor. But after a terrible argument with her boss she
resigned and now she is a freelance editor.

Ex 11

a It is a good thing that. . ..
b Something is wrong with it; it doesn't function
c I can't understand/discover. . .
d didn't complete the task successfully
e It will be very difficult.
f I have accepted the fact (though unhappily)
g Don't be so critical.
h useless
i go up to my bedroom/go to bed

Ex 12

a on strike **b** sacking **c** shop steward **d** pickets
e dispute **f** return to work **g** lay off **h** ballot

Ex 13, 14 Open exercises

UNIT 12
LEISURE, SPORT AND ENTERTAINMENT

Ex 1, 2 Open exercises

Ex 3

a flower-arranging **b** stamp-collecting **c** oil-painting
d rock-climbing **e** water-skiing **f** model-plane making

Ex 4

A magnifying glass is a glass lens which makes things bigger when you look at them through it. It can be used in stamp-collecting.
A tripod is a 3-legged platform to put cameras etc on and therefore make them stable. It can be used in photography
A needle is a sharp-pointed pin which has thread attached to it. It is used for dress-making and other types of sewing.
A rod is a long stick which has a line attached to it. It is used for fishing.
An easel is the frame you put your canvas on when you want to do a painting.
An album is a book where you stick collections of stamps/photographs etc
A wetsuit is a garment which covers the whole body and is used by surfers, water-skiers etc to keep them warm in cold water.
A loom is a wooden machine used for weaving.
Clay is the earthy substance used in pottery to make plates, cups etc
Wool is the coat taken from sheep. It is used in knitting.
Glue is the sticky substance used to bind two things together. It is used in model-making.
A net is a criss-cross of material used for catching things like butterflies, fish etc

Ex 5

A train-spotter watches different kinds of trains and writes down the numbers of the ones that are seen.
A pot-holer explores caves etc under the ground.
An angler catches fish.
A gambler bets money on cards/horses etc.
A canoeist is someone who spends time in a boat (a canoe). They use a paddle to make it go through the water.

Ex 6, 7 Open exercises

Ex 8

(Difficult to judge, but a possible order might be:)

violin	(5)	flute	(9)
guitar	(6)	clarinet	(8)
double bass	(7)	drums	(1)
trombone	(2)	piano	(4)
saxophone	(3)		

Ex 9

A person who	Noun
plays the piano	pianist
plays the drums	drummer
plays a violin	violinist
plays a trumpet	trumpeter
plays football	footballer
plays tennis	tennis-player
rides a bicycle	cyclist
collects stamps	stamp-collector
skis	skier
jumps from a plane using a parachute	parachutist
makes sculptures	sculptor
takes photographs	photographer
plays chess	chess player

Ex 10

a swimming **b** surfing **c** boxing
d baseball **e** swimming **f** motor-racing

Ex 11

course	golf, horseracing
stadium	football, American football, baseball, athletics, rugby
court	tennis, squash, rackets
pool	swimming, water polo, diving
ring	boxing, wrestling
track	athletics (running, hurdling etc), horse racing, greyhound racing, motor racing

Ex 12

Enthusiasm	Ability
keen	gifted
lover	musical
mad about	no good at it
freak	a natural (✓)
obsessive(✓)	rusty
	novice
	talented
	expert

Ex 13 Open exercise

UNIT 13 ANIMALS, PLANTS AND THEIR HABITATS

Ex 1

cobra (d) fox (c) hedgehog (j) lizard (i) monkey (a)
parrot (h) scorpion (b) shark (f) tiger (k) tortoise (e)
whale (g)

Ex 3
Open exercise

Ex 4
a a shell: turtle, tortoise
  fins: whale, shark, dolphin
  a beak: parrot, peacock,
  prickles: hedgehog
  a tail: donkey, scorpion, crocodile, parrot, peacock,
           tiger, lizard, monkey, wolf, whale, shark,
           dolphin, fox
  teeth: donkey, crocodile, tiger, monkey, turtle, wolf,
           whale, shark, hedgehog, fox, dolphin,
           hedgehog

b The poisonous animals are: scorpion, cobra, spider,

Ex 5

Reptiles	mammals	amphibians	birds	fish	insects
crocodile	donkey	crocodile	parrot	shark	scorpion
lizard	tiger	turtle	peacock		spider
	monkey	tortoise			
	wolf	frog			
	whale				
	hedgehog				
	fox				
	dolphin				

Ex 6, 7 Open exercises

Ex 8

Neutral	Female	Male	Young
dog	bitch	dog	puppy
cat	cat	tomcat	kitten
frog	frog	bullfrog	tadpole
duck	duck	drake	duckling
horse	mare	stallion	foal
chicken	hen	cock	chick
fox	vixen	dog	fox cub
cattle	cow	bull	calf
deer	doe	stag	xxxx
sheep	ewe	ram	lamb

Animal		Noise	
pig	dog	grunt	bark
horse	cock	whinny	crow
lion	bird	roar	sing
cat	dog/coyote	purr	howl

Ex 9

Animal		Way of moving	
horse	tiger/cat	gallop	pounce
spider/scorpion	fish	crawl	dart
snake	eagle/vulture	slither	hover
dog		bound	

Animals		Home	
birds, insects	dog	nest	kennel
fox/lion	pig	lair	sty
rabbit	lion	burrow	den
horse	bee	stable	hive

Ex 10, 11, 12 Open exercises

Ex 13
According to the writer, man has damaged Mauritius by bringing onto it animals (such as dogs, rats, pigs etc) and plants (such as chinese guava, wild raspberries and privet) which have attacked the local animals and plants.

Ex 14
a plants: vegetation, flora
  animals: beasts, predator, familiars, species, fauna
  disappeared: vanished
  world: globe
b i)   annihilating
  ii)   predator
  iii) voracious
  iv) throng
  v)   a handful of

Ex 15 (suggested answers)
a Before the arrival of man and domesticated animals in Mauritius, the island had a great variety of animal and plant species.
b Great pressure is put on the remaining species of birds and lizards because man has introduced so many domestic animals and birds.
c Imported plants like Chinese Guava also cause difficulty because they strangle native flora and fauna
d Durrell uses words like 'incredibly', 'enormous, and 'unthinking' in order to show his own feelings and also to make a powerful impression on the reader.

Ex 16, 17 Open exercises

Ex 18
a 1 **b** 2 **c** 4 **d** 6 **e** 3 **f** 5

Ex 19
a 1 tropical 2 temperate 3 temperate 4 arid
  5 temperate 6 arid
b Open exercise

Ex 20
Land formation
MOST BARREN ⬅━━━━━➡ LEAST BARREN
        dunes cliffs hills shore fields

Vegetation
FLATTEST ⬅━━━━━━━━━➡ HIGHEST
     undergrowth bush oassis forest/jungle
MOST LUXURIANT ⬅━━━➡ LEAST LUXURIOUS
   jungle forest swamp bush oasis undergrowth

Water
LARGEST ⬅━━━━━━━━━➡ SMALLEST
      ocean swamp oasis stream
SAFEST ⬅━━━━━━━━➡ MOST DANGEROUS
     stream oasis swamp ocean

Ex 21 Open exercise

UNIT 14
TOWNS AND CITIES

Ex 1
(suggested answers)

If we stop breathing for long enough, we die.

I can't bear driving with a fogged-up windscreen when it's raining. I like to be able to see clearly.

I never smacked my children when they were young. I hate the idea of violence.

I groaned when I heard the train had been cancelled, and I heard a lot of other people groan as well.

I was annoyed when I found my new sweater had shrunk and was too small for me to wear.

We were driving into the city, but suddenly we got snarled up in a traffic jam and spent half an hour hardly moving.

The pollution was so bad in the centre of town I was gasping for air.

I like the clank-rattle of the train as it goes over the bridge near my house.

The phone rang and I picked it up, but I couldn't hear what the person was saying because there was a loud crackle on the line.

I left my bicycle outside the shop. When I came back, I found a lorry had run over it: it was really mangled.

Ex 2
a breathe, smack, groan, snarled, gasp, clank-rattle, crackle

b QUIETEST ◄————————————► LOUDEST
breathe gasp crackle groan snarl smack rattle clank

Ex 3, 4 Open exercises

Ex 5 suggested answers

Living in cities	Living in the country
noisy	peaceful
exciting	boring
unhealthy	healthy
convenient	inconvenient
dirty	pure
polluted	unpolluted
etc	etc

Ex 6
SMALLEST/LEAST IMPORTANT

settlement – a small, usually remote group of houses

hamlet – a small village

village – a group of houses, with a place of worship, shops etc

town – a large area with houses and other buildings where people live and work

city – a very large town

county – a large area including several towns and villages

metropolis – a large city covering a very large area

capital – the place in a country where the seat of government is; usually a large city

province – a main subdivision of a country or state

region – an area of a country which may contain more than one county or province

state – a partly idependent political unit within a country or federation

country – an independent nation

LARGEST/MOST IMPORTANT

Ex 7
district – geographical area

quarter – an area with a distinctive identity

shanty town – a poor area without propoerly built houses

ghetto – an area where one racial or religious group live together

slum – an area with very poor quality and dirty housing

Ex 8
housing: precinct, estate, development
office: block, development
block: block of flats
apartment: block
shopping: precinct, mall, centre
building: site, development
housing: development
industrial: area, estate, site, development
residential: area, site, estate, block, development
commercial: area, site, development, centre

Ex 9 Open exercise

Ex 10
a of or like the countryside. . .
b typical of the country. . .
c of a town or city
d an outer area of a town. . .
e of, for or in the suburbs. . .
f outer areas or limits

Ex 11
a outskirts **b** urban **c** suburb
d rustic **e** suburban **f** rural

Ex 12 Open exercise

Ex 13
1 village green **2** cottage **3** windmill
4 church steeple **5** pub **6** schoolhouse **7** shop

Ex 14
a probably the writer, or the hero of the story
probably in a city a long way from his home
it's about homesickness
b pub, church, shop, school
c open exercise

Ex 15
a empty of people and activity
b visiting another place
c make a big effort involving a lot of resources
d evening out e.g. in a restaurant or club, for example to mark some occasion
e celebrate, probably with alcoholic drink, dancing etc

f living in very unsatisfactory circumstances
g a small company with only a few workers and no heavy machinery

Ex 16, 17 Open exercises

UNIT 15 STORES, SHOPS AND SERVICES

Ex 1 Open exercise

Ex 2
a,b,c Open exercises
d people who sell things: stallholders
places where things are sold: market, bakery
food: vegetables, bread, loaf, goat's cheese, aubergines, tomatoes, beans, olives, eggs, rabbits, red peppers, basil, peaches, lettuce, onions, almonds, cake

Ex 3
1 supermarket, delicatessen
2 newsagent
3 hairdresser
4 building society
5 post office
6 greengrocer, supermarket
7 stationer, department store
8 hardware shop
9 florist
10 tobacconist

Ex 4
greengrocer, butcher, fishmonger, baker, tobacconist, chemist, stationer, newsagent, florist, hairdresser

Ex 5

WORKERS	PLACES
shop assistant	tobacconist, chemist, bookshop, stationer, newsagent, florist, hardware shop, toyshop, boutique, department store
manager	any of these establishments (unless they are very small)
counter clerk	bank, building society, post office
cashier	bank, building society, post office, supermarket, department store, garage
checkout person	supermarket
store detective	department store, some bigger shops
customer	any of these establishments except a library
salesperson	department store or bigger shop
street trader	market or the street
mechanic	garage
(head) waiter	restaurant (café, hotel etc)
security man/woman	large shop, bank, office

Ex 6 Open exercise

Ex 7
shop

Ex 8
a shop floor **b** shop around **c** talk shop
d window shopping **e** all over the shop **f** shoplifting
g set up shop with **h** closed shop **i** shop soiled

Ex 9 Open exercise

Ex 10
a lend = give temporarily,
borrow = take temporarily with permission
b bargain = something that is cheaper than it ought to be
discount = a reduction to the original price
c a loan = an amount of money borrowed, usually with interest
hire purchase = a way of paying for goods over a period of time in regular amounts, eg every month
d in credit = with money in the bank
overdraft = money owed to the bank because more has been spent than is in the account
e withdraw = take money out (eg of the bank)
deposit = put money in (eg the bank)
f a cheque book = a book of cheques that can be made out to pay for things with
a paying in book = a book of forms to use when depositing money
g save = keep money in the bank, adding more and more
pay back = return money owed to someone else, eg the bank
h credit account = an account to which things can be charged, with payment later
expense account = an account to which things can be charged to be paid for by your employer
i a credit card = a plastic card with a credit account
a cash card = a card that can be used to draw money from a cash machine
j part exchange = use something used (eg a car) in part payment for something new
pawn = deposit something valuable for a period of time in exchange for a cash loan
1 withdraw – deposit
2 expense account – credit account
3 lend – borrow
4 discount – bargain
5 loan – hire purchase
6 save – pay it back
7 pawn – part exchange
8 paying in book – cheque book
9 in credit – overdraft
10 credit card – cash card

Ex 11 Open exercise

Ex 12
a Health service: medical orderly, doctor, surgeon, specialist, nurse, sister, health visitor, hospital porter, administrator
Postal service: postal delivery worker, postman
Social services: social worker, administrator
Sanitation services: dustman, administrator
Police force: police officer, constable, sergeant, detective
Fire service: firefighter
Other emergency services: ambulanceman
Other services: milkman
b Open exercise
c (in the UK) a sugeon or medical specialist probably gets paid the most, and a social worker, dustman or medical orderly the least

Ex 13

a firefighter   **b** social worker   **c** postman   **d** milkman
e police officer   **f** dustmen/refuse collectors   **g** doctor
h ambulance men   **i** nurses

Ex 14

a surgeons   **b** firefighter   **c** ambulance men   **d** dustmen
e police officers   **f** the milkman   **g** the police

Ex 15

Mabel: at the bank, seeing the bank manager and asking
for an overdraft.
Keith: at the garage, talking to a mechanic
Mr Tubbs: at the chemist, buying some cough medicine
Stephen: at the post office, buying some stamps
Tracey: at the supermarket, buying food
Jack and Katie: at the stationers, buying paper etc
Ronald: at the fishmonger's, buying some fish
Anne: at the tobacconist, buying some cigarettes

Ex 16 (suggested answer)

Police officers held back the crowd of sightseers.
Ambulancemen ferried the injured to hospital, where
surgeons fought to save their lives. Nurses tended to the less
seriously injured, most of whom were well enough to receive
visitors, or be allowed home. Health visitors later made sure
that they had made a complete recovery.
After the blaze, Police officers arrested several people who
were stealing from the damaged building.

Ex 17 Open exercise

UNIT 16 THE HOME AND ACCOMMODATION

Ex 1 **a, b** Open exercise

Ex 2

a 1   **b** 5   **c** 8   **d** 2   **e** 7   **f** 4   **g** 9   **h** 3   **i** 6

Ex 3

a studio flat   **b** balcony   **c** bedsitter   **d** ground floor flat
e penthouse flat   **f** second floor flat   **g** maisonette
h basement flat

Ex 4, 5 Open exercises

Ex 6

a inhabit (b)   **b** occupy (e)   **c** settle(a)   **d** lodge (g)
e reside (f)   **f** squat (h)   **g** stay (c)   **h** dwell (d)

Ex 7

a lodged   **b** stay   **c** inhabit   **d** squatted
e settled   **f** occupied

Ex 8

a guests   **b** hospitality   **c** hosts   **d** agency   **e** let   **f** landlady
g rent   **h** landlord   **i** rent   **j** evict   **k** contract/agreement
l tenant   **m** contract   **n** deposit   **o** rent

Ex 9

a lodger   **b** residence   **c** occupier   **d** lodging
e squatters   **f** settlement   **g** inhabitants   **h** settlers

Ex 10, 11 Open exercises

Ex 12

size: spacious, good-sized, well-proportioned, double-fronted
distance: prime, close, secluded, convenient, handy
age: pre-war, period, mature,
quality: fair, superb, impressive, luxury, charming, purpose-built, open-plan

Ex 13 (possible answers)

good-natured, open-ended, well-meaning, well-written,
purpose-designed, double-breasted

Ex 14 Open exercise

Ex 15

a organise himself
b We went an uneccessarily long and complicated route to get there.
c made everyone laugh a lot
d he eats a fantastic amount – he nearly clears the house!
e free drinks (in a pub, for example, or in a restaurant)

Ex 16

a Home is where the heart is
b I wish I were homeward bound (from a Paul Simon song)
c Keep the home fires burning (from a war song, sung by soldiers thinking of their homes)
d There's no place like home
e Absence makes the heart grow fonder
f Home sweet home

UNIT 17 FURNISHING AND DECORATING THE HOME

Ex 1 Open exercise

Ex 2

sideboard **f** (dining room)   dresser **a** (kitchen)
chest of drawers **e** (bedroom)   bunk-bed **b** (bedroom)
dressing table **c** (bedroom)   hat-stand **d** (hall)
stool **g** (kitchen, playroom)   divan bed **h** (sitting room)

Ex 3

a an armchair is made of soft material and has arms; an upright chair has a straight back, sometimes has arms, and is usually made of wood.
b a king-size bed is the biggest kind of double bed; a double bed sleeps two people; a sofa-bed can fold up to become an ordinary sofa.
c a coffee table is low and placed near sofas, chairs etc for putting cups on; a dining table is where main meals are eaten; a bedside table is put next to the bed for books, lights etc; a desk is where people work/write letters.
d a fitted cupboard is a wardrobe that has been built into the wall; a wardrobe is a cupboard for hanging clothes.

e a bookcase is a piece of furniture with more than one shelf designed to take books; a bookshelf is one plank/level for storing books; a mantelpiece is the level surface above a fire.

f a refrigerator keep things (like butter and milk) cool; a freezer freezes foods for long-term storage; an icebox is an airtight container to take bottles and food on journeys, picnics etc

g a washbasin is for washing hands, brushing teeth etc in the bathroom; a sink is for washing plates etc, often in the kitchen

h a washing machine washes clothes; a dishwasher washes plates, glasses and cutlery

i a cooker is a unit with an oven, rings and a grill; an oven is the enclosed space for cooking; a toaster is for toasting bread.

j a cushion is a piece of filled material for extra comfort on sofas, chairs etc; a pillow is to put your head on in bed.

k a sheet is the cotton, linen or silk material which covers the matress and the sleeper on a bed; a blanket goes on top of the sheet and is designed for warmth; a duvet is a quilt which can be used (with a cover) instead of sheets and blankets.

Ex 4

	chair	table	bed	bedroom
double			✓	✓
single			✓	✓
dining		✓		
breakfast		✓		
folding	✓			

Ex 5

(possible answers)

a Mary hung her dress in the wardrobe

b On her bedside table there were three books, her spectacles and a glass of water

c After the party the sink was full of dirty dishes and glasses

d Before the meal George took the silver knives and forks out of the sideboard

e Although the sofa was hard it was quite comfortable because there were some soft cushions on it.

f Mary sat at her dressing table in order to put on her make-up and brush her hair

g There was a wide mantelpiece above the fire. On it there were some small porcelain statues

h David went into the bathroom and washed his hands in the sink

Ex 6

a The items are: a sofa, a telephone, a table, a table lamp.

b Open exercise

Ex 7 Open exercise

Ex 8 (suggested answers)

Advantages	Disadvantages
not so expensive	takes a lot of time
don't have to rely on other people	easy to get it wrong
fun	dangerous
sense of achievement	no one to complain to
can do it when you want	

Ex 9

bright/gloomy well-maintained/neglected
out-dated/modern ugly/attractive

Ex 10

a gloomy **b** well-maintained **c** neglected, attractive
d bright **e** out-dated

Ex 11 Open exercise

Ex 12

1 e **2** d **3** b **4** i **5** h **6** g **7** c **8** a **9** f

Preparing	decorating
bucket	step-ladder
sponge	roller
step-ladder	paint
scissors	paintbrush
sandpaper	wallpaper

Ex 13 a, b Open exercise

UNIT 18 HOUSEWORK

Ex 1 Open exercise

Ex 2

Some of the problems mentioned are: have to live in & provide services; on call 24 hrs a day; regularly work for 50-100 hrs a week; no payment; often expected to work on holiday; likely to die of cancer; insomnia, dizzinness, headaches, nightmares are very common; lack of job security through divorce; obliged to share a bed with your employer

Ex 3

Paragraph 2 On call – instantly available
Paragraph 3 utensils – devices
Paragraph 4 household – the people who live in the house
Paragraph 5 nightmares – bad dreams
              anxiety – nervousness about the present and future

Ex 4

a washing up **b** ironing **c** washing **d** shopping
e cooking **f** vacuum cleaning **g** window cleaning
h dusting **i** polishing **j** bed making

Ex 5 Open exercise

Ex 6

	cleaning the floor	washing up	washing a sweater	ironing a blouse	making dinner
verbs	mop sweep scrub	dry up wipe drain scour	rinse soak wring drain	rinse fold press	scorch stir beat chop
nouns	sponge broom brush bucket cloth detergent dustpan	sponge detergent bowl tea towel	bowl detergent	ironing board	chopping board

Ex 7
a scorched **b** bucket, mop **c** soak, bowl, scrub
d dry, up, drain **e** fold **f** beat, bowl, chop

Ex 8 Open exercise

Ex 9
cooker (4) dishwasher (3) blender (8)
sewing machine (11) washing machine (–) iron (5)
beater (10) vacuum cleaner (7) microwave oven (2)
coffee machine (6) toaster (9) fridge (–) freezer (1)

Ex 10 Open exercise

Ex 11
a all washed up means finished, his career is at an end
b she made her own decisions and she'll have to live with the consequences
c iron out means sort out, resolve
d wash your dirty linen in public means to discuss your private life and affairs in front of everybody
e cooked up an excuse means to invent, to think up an excuse
f polish up means to improve
g dusted off means to look at something again, to re-introduce something

Ex 12 Open exercise

UNIT 19 PREPARING AND EATING FOOD

Ex 1, 2 Open exercises

Ex 3
a
i) voracious   v) hinted
ii) ladled   vi) assiduously
iii) devoured   vii) starvation
iv) sucking   viii) splashes
b
i) The boys were given a little more food when there was a public holiday or some other public event.
ii) The boys cleaned their bowls with their spoons because they wanted to eat every last scrap of food

iii) After they had got hungrier and hungrier for three months, one of the boys threatened to eat one of his companions.
iv) Oliver was selected to ask for more by drawing lots

Ex 4 (suggested answers)
NOT HUNGRY ◄─────────────► VERY HUNGRY
stuffed full up   off his/her food   peckish   could eat a horse
voracious ravenous starving
NOT THIRSTY ◄─────────────► VERY THIRSTY
dry   dying for a drink   parched

Ex 5 (suggested answers)
a voracious ravenous starving
b i) parched
ii) peckish, dying for a drink
iii) starving, dying for a drink

Ex 6

Noun	verb	adjective to describe food
salt	to salt	salty
sweets	to sweeten	sweet
fat	to fatten	fatty
taste	to taste	tasty
filling	to fill	filling
appeal	to appeal (to)	appealing
spice	to spice	spicey

Ex 7 **a** Open exercise

b

usually positive	usually negative
delicious	salty
appetising	fatty
sweet	sickly
tasty	tasteless
appealing	revolting
spicey	

Ex 8 Open exercise

Ex 9
a bake **b** roast **c** grill **d** fry **e** boil **f** simmer **g** steam

Ex 10
a saucepan, boil **b** frying pan, fried
c baking tin, baked **d** saucepan, simmer **e** roast
f steam, steamer **g** boiled, kettle

Ex 11
The chefs are: cooking a fish in a large pan, boiling some pasta in a large saucepan and putting some pies in the oven. They're going to: pour more butter over the fish, pour the boiling water out of the saucepan and put butter on the hot pasta and leave the pies in the oven until they are done.

Ex 12

mix or move around	stir, beat, whisk
cut into pieces	carve, slice, chop,
Put in liquid	soak, marinate, dip
Make into powder or small pieces	grind, crush, grate

Ex 13 (suggest answer)

For a mushroom omelette you will need eggs, mushrooms, salt and pepper, oil and milk. First, slice the mushrooms thinly. Break the eggs into a bowl, add a little milk and beat. Add oil to a saucepan and put in the egg mixture. Cook for a few minutes until set. Add the mushrooms. When thoroughly cooked turn onto a plate and tuck in!

Ex 14 Open exercise

Ex 15

Miles (**d**)   Lord Belsize (**e**)   Lady Belsize (**a**)
George (**b**)   Jemima (**c**)

Ex 16, 17

	with a lot of appetite	without appetite	neutral
solid food	tucked in stuffing attacking polished off licked his lips overeating gobbled bolt devour gorge gnaw	picked at fasting	nibbled munching chewed crunch bite swallow
Liquid or near-liquid	downing slurping guzzle drained his glass gulp	sipping	swallow

Ex 18 (suggested answers)

a devour, gorge, gnaw   **b** pick at   **c** guzzled   **d** slurp
e slurp, drain   **f** stuffing, tucking in   **g** gnaw   **h** attacking

Ex 19

a gas-guzzler is a car which uses a lot of petrol
b biting cold means cold that really gets under your skin and 'bites' you
c chewing over means considering
d hard to swallow means difficult to accept/agree with
e gulped means to breathe in and swallow because of nervousness or excitement
f gnawing pain means the kind of pain that goes on and on being irritating

Ex 20

(1) breakfast	toast, cornflakes, orange juice, coffee, tea etc
(2) elevenses	coffee, tea and biscuits
(3) luncheon	(main meal) meat & a pudding, juice, beer or wine [note: 'luncheon' is a formal way of saying lunch]
(4) tea	tea & biscuits/cake
(5) dinner	(main meal) soup; meat, fish or poultry, pudding, cheese, wine, port/brandy
(6) a nightcap	brandy/whisky etc or a hot drink

Ex 21 Open exercise

UNIT 20
PRIVATE TRANSPORT

Ex 1, 2, 3, 4 Open exercises

Ex 5

Cars **a** 9 **b** 7 **c** 6 **d** 15 **e** 8 **f** 2 **g** 4 **h** 3
i 1 **j** 10 **k** 5 **l** 13 **m** 14 **n** 12 **o** 11
Bicycles **a** 5 **b** 4 **c** 10 **d** 11 **e** 3 **f** 2 **g** 1
h 12 **i** 6 **j** 9 **k** 8

Ex 6 Open exercise

Ex 7

	wing	bumper	headlight	windscreen	wheel
dented	✓	✓			
shattered			✓	✓	
buckled	✓	✓		✓	
broken			✓	✓	✓
faulty			✓		✓
smashed	✓		✓	✓	

Ex 8

1 The bicycle has a broken chain and a buckled wheel.
2 The windscreen on the van has been smashed, broken, shattered.
3 The cable on the bicycle has broken and the mudguard is twisted.
4 Someone has broken/smashed the back light and dented the boot and the bumper.

Ex 9

a glove compartment   **b** petrol gauge   **c** handbrake
d accelerator   **e** mirror   **f** speedometer   **g** steering wheel
h clutch   **i** gear shift   **j** brake   **k** horn   **l** seat belt

a) It's about someone who is speeding to get somewhere very urgently. She is chased by the police, and (probably) has an accident because a deer crosses the road in front of her.
b) Open exercise

Ex 10

a stop – pull up (C), pull over (C)
start – draw away
move – cycle (B), drive (C), pedal (B)
go fast – speed
go faster – speed up, accelerate
go slower – slow down, decelerate
pass – overtake
lose control – spin (C), skid, swerve
b i) pull over means to go to the side of the road and stop.
pull up means to stop anywhere.
ii) spin means to turn round out of control
skid means that the wheels slide, usually on a wet surface or on ice;
swerve means to change direction violently, usually to avoid something in front of you.

Ex 11 Open exercise

Ex 12
a 3 **b** 1 **c** 2

Ex 13

	driver	driving	vehicle	disregard	attitude	behaviour
speeding	✓		✓			
reckless	✓	✓		✓	✓	✓
careless	✓	✓	✓	✓	✓	✓
dangerous	✓	✓	✓		✓	✓
drunken	✓	✓				✓

Ex 14 Open exercise

Ex 15
a a driver who drove his car through a shop window said he/she had lost control of the car.
b there was a crash involving several vehicles, but no-one in a family riding in one of the cars was hurt.
c a man arrested for killing a hitchhiker (or killing a driver he was hitchhiking with) said it wasn't him.
d because police are trying to catch drivers who are speeding in a certain area, drivers are driving more slowly.
e an attractive woman was arrested for driving while inder the influence of alcohol.

Ex 16 Open exercise

UNIT 21
RAIL, AIR AND SEA TRAVEL

Ex 1 Open exercise

Ex 2
a stairs on a bus **b** a lifebelt – sea travel
c headset – aeroplane **d** tunnel – underground, metro, rail **e** ticket punch – train **f** boarding card – air

Ex 3
a – iii **b** – i **c** - ii
a a plane **b** bus **c** ship
b Open exercise

Ex 4, 5

bus	plane	ship	train	tube/subway
aisle	aisle	aisle		aisle
		tail		
		wings		
luggage rack	luggage rack	luggage rack		
headlights	headlights			
driver			driver	driver
		deck		
		bow		
		stern		
front	front		front	front
back	back		back	back
	nose			
		funnel		
	cockpit			
	cab		cab	cab
	cabin	cabin		
	propeller	propeller		
	rudder	rudder		
	fuselage			
		hull		
body	body			
		undercarriage		
engine	engine	engine		engine
			locomotive	
			carriage	carriage
coach			coach	coach
	take off			
	land	cast off		
		moor		
	move away	move away		
leave	leave	leave	leave	leave
arrive	arrive	arrive	arrive	arrive
steer	steer	steer		
	pilot(n)	pilot(n)		
	fly			
drive			drive	drive
skid		skid		
swerve	swerve			
		capsize		
	pilot(v)	pilot(v)		
		helmsman		
	crew	crew	crew	crew
	cabin crew			
	copilot			
	navigator	navigator		
	captain	captain		
	steward	steward	steward	
	stewardess			
	flight attendant			
			guard	guard
ticket collector			ticket collector	ticket collector
conductor		conductor		
	check-in clerk			

a steering and controlling: driver, captain, pilot, helmsman, navigator
checking tickets: check-in clerk, conductor, ticket collector, guard
serving passengers: steward, stewardess, cabin crew, flight attendant
team (including the above): crew
b Open exercise

Ex 7

a confirm, take   **b** round trip, standing room, first class
c check in, standby   **d** book, reserve   **e** standby, first class

Ex 8

a **1** verb **2** noun **3** verb **4** verb **5** adverb **6** noun
7 adjective **8** adjective **9** noun
b **1** booked **2** round trip **3** reserved **4** check in
5 first class **6** confirmed **7** standby **8** taken
9 standing room
c i) one-way   ii) round trip
d i) single   ii) round trip   iii) return

Ex 9 Open exercise

Ex 10

a

infinitive	past participle	noun
delay	delayed	delay
reserve	reserved	reservation
confirm	confirmed	confirmation
cancel	cancelled	cancellation

b over-

Ex 11

a confirmation   **b** delay   **c** reservation
d cancelled – cancellation   **e** delay   **f** reserve
g cancellation

Ex 12

1 a check-in counter   **b** immigration   **c** departure lounge
d gate 25
2 a immigration   **b** customs hall   **c** arrivals
3 a ticket office   **b** left luggage   **c** platform six

Ex 13 Open exercise

Ex 14

a (train)station   **b** station   **c** station, airport
d airport   **e** airport   **f** tube station

Ex 15, 16 Open exercises

UNIT 22 STREETS, ROADS AND TRAFFIC

Ex 1

a being hit hard and injured (or killed) by a moving
vehicle, especially a car, lorry etc, when you are walking
across or in a road.
b being hit by something when riding a bicycle or
motorcycle (or horse etc)
c being hit by something or someone while you are
walking, so that you fall down (but you may not be hurt).
d walking in the part of the road normally reserved for
traffic.

Ex 2

1 First find a safe place.
2 Stand on the pavement . . .
3 Look all round for traffic . . .
4 If traffic is coming . . .
5 When there is no traffic . . .
6 Keep looking and
listening . . .   -

Ex 3

The instructions are for children or young people.
They are quite well written because they are simple and
clear.

Ex 4

For the use of vehicles only	For the use of pedestrians only	For both vehicles and pedestrians
crossroads	pavement	road
roundabout	kerb	traffic lights
flyover	island	one-way street
junction	pedestrian crossing	cul de sac
	footbridge	

Ex 5

1 a path . . . an alley   **2** a subway. . .an underpass
3 a road . . . a way   **4** a street . . . an avenue
5 a main road . . . a side street   **6** a road . . . a street
7 a road . . . a path

Ex 6 Open exercise

Ex 7

1 d **2** a **3** f **4** b **5** g **6** c **7** e **8** h
slightly formal: g, h

Ex 8 Open exercise

Ex 9 Open exercise

1 clockwise **2** carriageway **3** tailback **4** roadworks
5 alternative routes **6** resurfacing **7** contraflow
8 lane **9** slip road

Ex 10

a Open exercise
b (suggested answer) A1184, B1393, A121
c (suggested answer) From Harlow, take the A1184 to the
motorway roundabout. Turn right towards Epping
(B1393). Continue through Epping, and at Copthall
Green take the second left (A121) for Debden Green. Go
straight on for about a mile, then turn left. This road will
take you to the centre of Chigwell.

Ex 11 Open exercise

Ex 12

1 a
2 c (a bypass goes past or round only one side of a
town/city)
3 c   **4** a   **5** a

Ex 13, 14 Open exercises

UNIT 23
SCIENCE AND TECHNOLOGY

Ex 1
a astronomy   **b** electronics   **c** physics   **d** ecology
e robotics

Ex 2
a solar energy   **b** breathing   **c** launching satelites
d VHF radio   **e** brakes on a car (or truck)

Ex 3

Nouns	Verbs	Nouns	Adjectives
inhalation	inhale	gravity	gravitational
transmission	transmit	frequency	frequent
conversion	convert	cell	cellular
absorption	absorb	fluid	fluid
pressure	pressure	height	high
compression	compress		
application	apply		

Ex 4   Open exercise

Ex 5
a aviation   **b** communication   **c** physics   **d** chemistry
e electronics   **f** mechanical engineering

Ex 6   Open exercise

Ex 7
wing (a)   valve (f)   test tube (d)   screen (e)
radio-activity (c)   wire (b)   piston (f)   channel (e)
radium (c)   charge (e)   lift (a)   bacteria (d)   cure (c, d)
exhaust (f)   altitude (a)   receiver (b)   transistor (e)
energy (c, f)

Ex 8
tele- ; at or over a long distance (telephone, telescope etc)
aero-; concerning the air or aircraft (aeroplane,
       aerodynamics etc)
photo-; concerning light and/or photography
       (photosensitive, photograph etc)
micro-; very small (microcomputer, microlight aircraft etc)
mono; one, single (monoplane, monolingual, monoped etc)
bi-; two of something (biplane, bilingual, biped etc)
auto-; by oneself, itself (autobiography, automatic etc)
hydro-; concerning or using water (hydrolectric,
       hydrocarbon etc)

Ex 9   Open exercise

Ex 10
The collocations are:

to split the atom	to achieve a breakthrough
to fuse atoms	to extract a mineral
to extract/generate energy	to become reality

Ex 11
a Open exercise
b science fiction (imaginary stories about the future)
harnessing (controlling, making use of)
reserach (investigation)
conventional (normal, traditional)
unstable (volatile, not safe)
fuse together (melt/join together)
comissioned (ordered and put into action)
c (suggested answer)
The key difference between nuclear fission and nuclear
fusion is that fission involves splitting atoms apart, while
fusion happens after atoms have been heated to an
extremely high temperature and have violently struck
each other and come together – or fused. Both nuclear
fission and nuclear fusion create enormous amounts of
energy, but the problem with conventional nuclear
reactors is that they use unstable atoms, creating
dangerous elements and enormous heat. Nuclear fusion
has another advantage. It isn't difficult to find the
elements required for it.
In the recent experiment it was only possible to create
energy for a few seconds. This is mainly because there
are considerable technological problems in producing
heat of 200 million degrees. However, scientists hope to
be able to commission the first fusion reactor by the year
2020. If they suceed, the human race will be on the way
to having unlimited cheap power.

Ex 12   (suggested answers)
a Stars like the sun are powered by nuclear fusion
b Because tritium was added to deuterium in the fusion
experiment a major breakthrough was achieved and
more energy was generated.
c Although bombs involving fusion power have been built,
there are not yet any fusion reactors
d The main source of deuterium is water, but tritium has to
be made in a reactor.
e Very small amounts of these chemicals can provide an
individual's energy needs for life.

Ex 13
1 Solids; gold, ice
   Liquids; sulphuric acid, mercury
   Gases; oxygen
2 Elements; gold, oxygen, mercury
   Compounds; sulphuric acid, ice (water)
   metals; gold
3 Melted: ice
   Liquefied; gold, oxygen
4 A molecule
5 A nucleus is the central part of an atom (and of almost all
   living cells)
6 There are 9 planets in the solar system: Mercury, Venus,
   Earth, Mars, Jupiter, Saturn, Uranus, Neptune & Pluto
7 H_2O; Carbon dioxide
8 The heating of the atmosphere because of a rise in
   carbon dioxide and other emissions

Ex 14   Open exercise

Ex 15
a planet **b** atom **c** formula **d** element **e** nucleus

---

UNIT 24
THE ENVIRONMENT AND
THE FUTURE

Ex 1 Open exercises

Ex 2
a dispose of: discharged (used) cut down: felled
budgetted for: allocated calculation: reckoning
b relating to the moon: lunar. relating to the stars: stellar
c can be eaten: edible
can't be touched:
  untouchable
can't be thought about: unthinkable
can't be eaten: inedible
can be disposed of: disposable
d a boat, a publicity campaign

Ex 3
create – destroy save – waste care for – neglect
improve – damage purify – pollute

Ex 4

Verb	Noun	Adjective
waste	waste	wasteful
damage	damage	damaging
improve	improvement	xxxxx
neglect	neglect	neglectful
destroy	destruction	destructive
pollute	pollution	xxxxx
create	creation	creative
purify	purification	purifying
congest	congestion	congested

Nouns: -ment and -ion Adjectives: -ing, -ful, -ive, -ed

Ex 5
a pollutes, reduce **b** reduce, emissions
c destruction, affect **d** damage, repaired
e harness, harmful **f** improve, congestion

Ex 6 Open exercise

Ex 7 (see page 204)

Ex 8
ecologically safer: something which doesn't harm the
  environment as much as other things
fuel-efficient: uses less fuel than something which uses
  a lot – where the design has made low
  fuel consumption a priority
ozone-friendly: something which doesn't damage the
  ozone layer (the shield in the ionosphere
  which protects the earth from ultra-violet
  radiation)

environment- something which does not damage the
friendly: environment
wasteful: using something uneccessarily
non- material which does not decay naturally,
biodegradable: through interaction with natural chemicals
  etc. Plastic is a non-biodegradable
  material.
energy-efficient: something which doesn't use too much
  energy – where the design has made low
  energy consumption a priority
sparing: not using very much
renewable: something that can be used again

Good	Bad
ecologically safer	wasteful
fuel-efficient	non-biodegradable
ozone-friendly	
environment-friendly	
energy-efficient	
sparing	
renewable	

Ex 9
ozone layer air pollution
global warming greenhouse effect
rain forests acid rain
food shortages population explosion

Ex 10
a Air pollution makes life in our cities unhealthy
b Food shortages affect people in several countries in
  Subsaharan Africa
c Acid rain causes many fish in the lakes of northern
  Europe to die
d Global warming results from the accumulation of carbon
  dioxide and other man-made gases in the atmosphere,
  which absorb and reflect more of the sun's heat than is
  normal.
e The rain forests play an important role in the climate
  patterns of the whole world
f The ozone layer protects us from the adverse effects of
  ultra-violet radiation

Ex 11
WEAKEST ◄─────────────────► STRONGEST
    mar harm damage spoil ruin destroy
i) damage ii) mar iii) damage iv) destroy
v) harm vi) spoil vii) ruin viii) ruin

Ex 12
a trash **b** refuse **c** debris **d** junk **e** litter
f garbage **g** sewage **h** garbage **i** scrap
The two words used in American English are garbage and
trash

Ex 13 Open exercise